Where to Eat

IN NORTHERN IRELAND

Restaurants, Coffee Shops, Pubs & Hotels – *plus* 'A Taste of Ulster'

Northern Ireland
Tourist Board

Published by the Northern Ireland Tourist Board
59 North St, Belfast BT1 1NB. ☎ (01232) 231221. Fax 240960.

ISBN 1 86193 041 0

Nineteenth edition

Drawings: Helen Averley
Front cover photograph: Jill Jennings

Printed by W & G Baird Ltd., Antrim.   6m/12/98

Contents

Acknowledgments

The editors are grateful for all the help they have received in compiling the main listings for this, the nineteenth edition of *Where to Eat in Northern Ireland.*

Information provided by organisations and individuals outside the Tourist Board has enabled us to maintain the wide coverage which makes this small book uniquely useful.

The response from local authorities was most helpful, particularly with regard to cafés and unlicensed restaurants. All twenty-six councils supplied us with information on the eating-out situation in their area. This local knowledge ensures that we continue to provide a useful service to visitors and, we hope, gives some welcome publicity to small and out-of-the-way places.

Thanks are also due to the Healthy Eating Circle for keeping us up to date with details of their members.

Some places that deserve to be included in the book may not have come to our attention. In this case we would be glad to hear of them for the next edition. Please write to *Where to Eat in Northern Ireland,* Northern Ireland Tourist Board, St Anne's Court, 59 North St, Belfast BT1 1NB.

How to use the guide

This handy paperback will fit neatly into a pocket or the glove compartment of your car. The 1,800 eating places listed here range from the smallest coffee shop and fish & chip café to the smart places that get into food guides.

Everyone is familiar with that uneasy feeling when, driving through some newly discovered countryside, enjoying the sights and sounds, you are wondering all the same where to stop for a bite to eat. Might there be a coffee shop in the next village? Dare you press on?

To resolve this dilemma we have listed places by town and village within each county. Some villages have only one eating place – perhaps a hotel or maybe just a café serving hot pies and pizzas. The important thing is to know what is available in the area and this book should help you find them.

The canny traveller will plan ahead and a telephone call before setting out is advisable. The more popular restaurants tend to get booked up towards the end of the week and it is best to make a reservation.

Entries are grouped by town and village in each county. There is a map at the back of the book and an index to towns and villages. The Belfast section is divided into five areas, shown on the sketch map on page 32.

City Centre – BT1 postcode area.
Golden Mile – BT2, Great Victoria St.
University and Malone – BT7 & 9, around Queen's University and Lisburn Rd.
East of the River – BT4-6, 8 & 16, from the Lagan to the eastern suburbs.
North and West of the River – BT10-15 & 17, from the Lagan to the city limits.

Restaurants are divided into three price bands based on the average cost for one person of a three-course meal – a starter, main course of meat or fish, plus two vegetables and a pudding. A 10 per cent service is included but not wine or coffee.

£	£8 to £12
££	£12 to £20
£££	over £20
M	followed by £, ££, or £££ refers to average cost of lunch
E	followed by £, ££, or £££ refers to average cost of an evening meal

When no symbol is used, a three-course meal or equivalent will cost less than £8. In general, midday meals cost less than evening meals. E££ means that an evening meal is £8-£12 but you can still get lunch for under £8 in the same place. Some restaurants offer special early evening menus which are good value.

Dishes are mentioned as an indication and are subject to frequent change.

If you are dissatisfied in any way, tell the waiter or ask for the manager – always more effective than writing after you get home. Your comments will help them to improve the service.

Restaurants participating in the Healthy Eating Circle are indicated by ⊘. They provide healthy food choices and set aside non-smoking areas. For further information contact the Health Promotion Agency. ☎ (01232) 311611.

You will find that hotels are good places for meals and snacks throughout the day. For many visitors afternoon tea offers a welcome break from sightseeing. Served from around three o'clock it consists of a pot of tea, sandwiches, and cakes or scones.

High tea starts at about five o'clock and is usually over by seven. Some overseas visitors are quite defeated by the notion of high tea. A typical high tea consists of sausages, or a lamb cutlet, with a plate of cakes and scones. Home-baked ham and salad may be served, and since Ulster is the country of good bread, it is not unusual to have several varieties of bread on the table.

Licensed restaurants in Northern Ireland can serve a complete range of drinks including all kinds of spirits. All licensed establishments are indicated by a wine glass ♈ . Those places which we know from experience welcome customers bringing in a bottle of wine are indicated by ♦.

Pubs in Northern Ireland are open seven days a week. They are open all day from Monday to Saturday 1130-2300, with half-an-hour 'drinking up' time, so that you can savour that last pint. On Sunday most open at lunchtime and in the evening (1230-1430 and 1900-2200) although some publicans continue to observe the traditional Sabbath and remain closed.

More pubs provide food all day and this is why we have given the full licensing hours in many cases. Even so, experience has shown that the widest choice is served around lunchtime and, in some pubs, in the early evening. Many pubs will make you a pot of tea at any time during the day.

Some telephone numbers listed here may change in the course of the year. If you cannot get through dial 100 and ask the operator for help.

Special mentions in restaurant guides

These restaurants are recommended in the latest available editions of the following guides to good eating – Michelin *Great Britain & Ireland*, Egon Ronay *Ireland,* the *Good Food Guide,* the two Bridgestone guides *100 Best Restaurants in Ireland* and *Irish Food Guide,* and the AA *Best Restaurants* guide. Some establishments are also members of 'A Taste of Ulster' (see page 13). Members of Les Routiers organisation are included for the first time. All these restaurants are shown in green in the main listings, preceded by ★

Belfast

Antica Roma Bridgestone, Egon Ronay: p 49.

Ashoka Bridgestone: p 49.

La Belle Epoque Bridgestone, Good Food Guide, Michelin: p 45.

Bengal Brasserie Bridgestone, Egon Ronay: p 49.

Bonnie's Museum Café Bridgestone: p 49.

Cargoes Bridgestone: p 50.

Chez Delbart Bridgestone: p 50.

Deane's Bridgestone, Egon Ronay, Good Food Guide, Michelin star, AA rosettes (3): p 35.

Equinox Café Bridgestone: p 35.

Friar's Bush Bridgestone: p 53.

Long's Fish Restaurant Bridgestone: p 66.

Maloney's Bridgestone: p 54.

Manor House Bridgestone, Egon Ronay, Michelin: p 54.

Mizuna Bridgestone, Egon Ronay, Michelin, Taste of Ulster member: p 55.

Nick's Warehouse Bridgestone, Egon Ronay, Good Food Guide, Michelin, Taste of Ulster member: p 39.

Opus One Bridgestone: p 55.

Roscoff Bridgestone, Egon Ronay, Good Food Guide, Michelin star, Taste of Ulster member: p 47.

Roscoff Café Bridgestone: p 41.

Speranza Bridgestone, Egon Ronay: p 47.

Stormont, Les Routiers: p 62.

Strand Bridgestone, Good Food Guide: p 57.

Sun Kee Bridgestone: p 57.

Villa Italia Bridgestone, Egon Ronay: p 58.

Welcome Bridgestone, Egon Ronay: p 58.

Special mentions in restaurant guides

County Antrim

Bushmills Inn, Bushmills Bridgestone, Taste of Ulster member: p 80.
Chimney Corner Hotel, Newtownabbey Les Routiers: p 89.
Dunadry Inn, Dunadry Les Routiers: p 86.
Galgorm Manor, Ballymena Egon Ronay, AA rosette, Taste of Ulster member: p 76.
Ginger Tree, Newtownabbey Bridgestone, Good Food Guide, Michelin: p 98.
Jourdan's, Kells Bridgestone: p 91.
Londonderry Arms Hotel, Carnlough Egon Ronay, Taste of Ulster member: p 81.
Ramore, Portrush Bridgestone, Egon Ronay, Good Food Guide, Michelin: p 101.
Sweeney's, Portballintrae Egon Ronay, Taste of Ulster member: p 99.
Tullyglass House Hotel, Ballymena Les Routiers: p 78.
Wind-Rose Wine Bar, Carrickfergus Egon Ronay: p 84.

County Down

Bay Tree, Holywood Bridgestone, Egon Ronay, Taste of Ulster member: p 133.
Buck's Head Inn, Dundrum Bridgestone, Egon Ronay, Les Routiers, Taste of Ulster member: p 130.
Clandeboye Lodge Hotel, Bangor AA rosettes (2): p 121.
Dufferin Arms, Killyleagh Les Routiers: p 137.
Culloden Hotel, Cultra AA rosette, Taste of Ulster member: p 127.
Glassdrumman Lodge, Annalong Egon Ronay, AA rosettes (2): p 117.
Grange, Waringstown Bridgestone: p 151.
Hillside Bar, Hillsborough Bridgestone, Egon Ronay, Michelin, Taste of Ulster member: p 131.
Kilmorey Arms Hotel, Kilkeel Les Routiers: p 135.
Marine Court Hotel, Bangor Les Routiers: p 123.
Ming Court, Newtownards Les Routiers: p 146.
Plough Inn, Hillsborough Bridgestone, Egon Ronay, Les Routiers: p 133.
Ritchies, Hillsborough Les Routiers: p 133.
Portaferry Hotel, Portaferry Bridgestone, Egon Ronay, AA rosettes (2), Taste of Ulster member: p 148.
Rayanne House, Holywood AA rosettes (2), Taste of Ulster member: p 134.

Special mentions in restaurant guides

Shanks Restaurant, Bangor Bridgestone, Egon Ronay, Good Food Guide, Michelin star, AA rosettes (3), Taste of Ulster member: p 123.
The Tides Reach, Killinchy Les Routiers: p 137.
Sullivans, Holywood Bridgestone, Egon Ronay, Michelin: p 134.
Villa Toscana, Bangor Bridgestone, Egon Ronay: p 124.
Yellow Door, Gilford Bridgestone, Michelin, Taste of Ulster member: p 130.

County Fermanagh

Blake's of the Hollow, Enniskillen Egon Ronay: p 157.
Cedars, Lisnarick Bridgestone: p 165.
Franco's, Enniskillen Bridgestone: p 159.
Hollander, Irvinestown Bridgestone, Egon Ronay, Taste of Ulster member: p 163.
Lusty Beg Island, Kesh Egon Ronay: p 163.
Melvin House & Bar, Enniskillen Bridgestone: p 159.
Oscar's Restaurant, Enniskillen Les Routiers: p 160.
Tullyhona Farm Guest House, Florencecourt Bridgestone, Taste of Ulster member: p 161.
Sheelin, Bellanaleck Egon Ronay, Michelin: p 155.

County Londonderry

Ardtara, Maghera Egon Ronay, AA rosettes (2), Taste of Ulster member: p 181.
Beech Hill Country House Hotel, Londonderry Bridgestone, Egon Ronay, Good Food Guide, Taste of Ulster member: p 175.
Brown Trout, Aghadowey Egon Ronay: p 167.
Radisson Roe Park, Limavady Egon Ronay, AA rosette: p 173.
Salmon Leap, Coleraine Egon Ronay, Taste of Ulster member: p 170.
Trompets, Magherafelt, Bridgestone: p 183.

County Tyrone

Mellon Country Inn, Omagh Les Routiers: p 196.
Inn on the Park, Dungannon Les Routiers: p 191.

A Taste of Ulster

A Taste of Ulster's distinctive symbol is your guarantee of a menu featuring the best of Ulster produce. You will find traditional and modern dishes created from the finest local ingredients wherever you see the special hexagonal plaque on display.

Listed in this special section are restaurants, pubs and coffee shops which have attained Taste of Ulster membership (applied for under a voluntary registration scheme). These are shown in green preceded by ★ in the main listings. Many have also received special mentions in well known guide books (see page 10) and we have indicated these in the entry. Major credit cards are accepted unless indicated otherwise.

Bittles Bar (p 33)
City centre bar offering classic Belfast pub grub with fresh soups, breads and stews. Champ – a dish of creamed potatoes and scallions (spring onions) – served with sausage is a local favourite. Interesting collection of local art. No credit cards.

Café Society (p 34)
Imaginative dishes, all cooked to order, are served in the first-floor restaurant overlooking the City Hall gardens. The licensed bistro downstairs offers light creative food. Exciting wine list. Resident pianist, and live jazz at five on Friday afternoons.

Copperfields (p 35)
A traditional bar and restaurant in the heart of Belfast offering fresh food at reasonable prices. Head chef Arthur Corry creates daily specials featuring the best local produce, and food is served in both the bar downstairs and restaurant upstairs. Plump sofas and cosy booths make for an interesting and popular meeting place.

Dukes Hotel (p 51)
A bright hotel in a tree-lined avenue close to Queen's University and the Botanic Gardens. Modern style cooking is complemented by traditional local produce. Extensive wine list. Bar snacks.

Eastender (p 60)
This luxurious lounge bar and restaurant has a striking decor of shipping memorabilia, antique mirrors and a hundred drawings of famous east Belfast characters. Baked ham with black velvet sauce is popular at lunchtime.

The Elk, Dundonald (p 60)
The Elk is a recent Community Pub of the Year regional winner. The decor of ornate Irish pub mirrors and Dunville whiskey memorabilia offers a relaxed atmosphere for lunch or a pleasant evening meal. Try the Irish hot pot in the self-service restaurant.

Belfast continued

Fillers Coffee Shop (p 60)

A bright, modern self-service restaurant featuring traditional home baking. The emphasis is on healthy eating and vegetarian alternatives are available. Open until tea-time on Friday evenings. No credit cards.

Mad Hatter (p 54)

Traditional coffee shop offering home cooking at its best in pleasant surroundings, with seating in the tea garden in summer. Extensive breakfast, lunch and afternoon tea menus are served.

Mizuna (p 55)

A cross cultural, eclectic smash of texture and taste issues from chef/patron Paul Clarke's kitchen. Classic techniques and innovation enhance the local game, seafood and organic produce. Well balanced wine list. Bridgestone, Egon Ronay.

Morning Star (p 39)

Historic pub in one of Belfast's 18th-century 'entries'. Specialities include seafood, home-reared meat and poultry and the freshest Ulster vegetables. Food is served in both the public bar and the upstairs restaurant and lounge. Regular gourmet evenings.

Nick's Warehouse (p 39)

Nick's city centre restaurant and wine bar is on two floors of a converted warehouse near St Anne's Cathedral. Fresh, international dishes are strong on flavour and executed with flair and confidence by chef/patron Nick Price. Bridgestone, Egon Ronay, Good Food Guide, Michelin.

Roscoff (p 47)

Bright, uncluttered restaurant with a dynamic style. Paul Rankin complements classical French training with healthy Californian ideas. Creative use of organic vegetables and local seafood. Extensive wine list. Between City Hall and Queen's University. Bridgestone, Egon Ronay, Good Food Guide, Michelin star.

Belfast continued

Skandia, Howard St (p 41)

This unlicensed restaurant is convenient for family dining with special menus for children. Extensive hours makes it an ideal choice for any meal from breakfast to a late supper after the theatre.

Stormont Hotel (p 62)

The Stormont overlooks the landscaped grounds of the former Northern Ireland parliament. In McMaster's restaurant, head chef Stephen Isaac offers fine local produce and daily specials. Less formal fare in the brasserie.

White's Tavern (p 42)

Historic 17th-century tavern is in Winecellar Entry, an old trading alley where the *Mercury* newspaper was founded in the 1850s. It enjoys an established reputation for fine home cooking.

Brown Jug, Ballymoney (p 79)
Pleasant coffee shop with a good selection of home-cooked dishes in attractive surroundings. Convenient parking. No credit cards.

Bushmills Inn, Bushmills (p 80)
Restored coaching inn with peat fires. Dishes feature the produce for which the locality is justly famous, wild salmon and Bushmills whiskey. In summer and at weekends, the Victorian-style bar is also open for full meals and snacks. Michelin, Bridgestone.

Coco's, Lisburn (p 94)
Beside the Irish Linen Centre, Coco's has easy access for wheelchairs and buggies. The interior is cosy wth the aromas of freshly brewed coffee and newly baked bread.

Falstaffs, Ballyclare (p 74)
The coffee is always freshly brewed in this friendly town centre coffee shop. Wheaten bread, tasty soups, stew and special frys, with sandwiches and rolls from the salad counter, are all prepared daily.

Galgorm Manor, Ballymena (p 76)
Local fish and game in season are a prominent feature on the menu at this four-star hotel, converted from a fine gentleman's estate and featuring a dining room with chandeliers and Arcadian murals. Head chef Charles O'Neill and his team are particularly strong on local chargrilled and roasted meat. Egon Ronay, 2 AA rosettes.

Landscape Centre Coffee Shop, Dunadry (p 86)
Views from Donegore Hill encourage an appetite to match menu favourites such as home-made apple pie and vegetarian dishes. A welcoming open fire in winter.

Laurel Inn, Temple, Lisburn (p 95)
Popular inn on the A24 eight miles south of Belfast. The chef features fresh seafood and seasonal game on the menus, and fresh herbs are used extensively. Wide choice of quality wines.

County Antrim continued

Londonderry Arms Hotel, Carnlough (p 81)
Charming coaching inn in a small fishing village on the Antrim coast road 14 miles north of Larne. A reputation for good home-cooked food, simply and freshly prepared – beef, lamb, bread, and smoked salmon from nearby Glenarm. Egon Ronay.

Lynden Heights, Ballygalley (p 75)
From its spectacular coastal location, this family-run restaurant overlooks the Glens of Antrim. Fine sauces and fresh vegetables enhance the local duck, pheasant and salmon, and there is an extensive wine list.

Mattie's Meetinghouse, Larne (p 75)
On the B148, 1 mile inland from the Antrim Coast, this old traditional pub offers chef's freshly prepared dishes using local produce and choice pub food.

McGeown's, Glenavy (p 89)
The chef's imaginative menus are accompanied by a warm traditional welcome in this quaint public house dating from the 17th century. James Gorman uses local produce with a touch of haute cuisine.

Magherabuoy House Hotel, Portrush (p 100)
The hotel is set in a popular seaside resort on this splendid coast. Fine views from the restaurant and good value bistro food.

Marine Hotel, Ballycastle (p 73)
On the seafront at Ballycastle, the hotel offers the best of local produce in its restaurant and bar, and afternoon teas are a speciality.

National Trust Tea Room, Giant's Causeway (p 88)
Tea room and restaurant inside the visitor centre at the world famous Giant's Causeway. A daily choice of home-cooked fare is always on offer, including a range of delicious soups and traditional breads, scones and cakes. Good coffee.

A Taste of Ulster

County Antrim continued

Quality Hotel, Carrickfergus (p 84)
Traditional eating house, convenient for visitors to this historic town. Only the freshest and finest of local produce is used. Carvery on Sundays.

Sweeney's Wine Bar, Portballintrae (p 99)
This converted 17th-century stable block retains much of its original character. A diverse, delicious menu, and fine views of the north Antrim coast from the conservatory. No credit cards. Egon Ronay.

The Tea Shop, Ballymoney (p 80)
Wholesome food in bright and airy surroundings, table service with a smile. The emphasis is on locally sourced quality produce, freshly prepared on the premises. This is a totally smoke-free environment.

Templeton Hotel, Templepatrick (p 103)
A hotel with interesting architectural features near the international airport. Local produce is used in the preparation of a wide range of dishes, from a sandwich in the bar to a three-course dinner in the restaurant. One mile from M2, Templepatrick exit.

Top of the Town, Antrim (p 71)
Friendly staff and home cooking by chef June Davison is the hallmark of this charming old pub with its beamed ceilings. The lunch menu includes soups and a selection of daily special dishes. Beer garden.

Wysner's, Ballycastle (p 73)
Carrick-a-rede salmon and Bushmills malt cheesecake prepared by head chef Jackie Wysner, are among dishes with a local resonance at this sophisticated, good-value family-run restaurant. A French-style café downstairs offers an extensive daytime menu.

A Taste of Ulster

County Armagh

Archway, Armagh (p 105)
In an old Victorian archway near the historic Mall, this pretty coffee house reflects the owner's interest in local history and crafts. The home cooking features the best fresh ingredients and the apple pies are made with local Bramleys. No credit cards.

De Averell House, Armagh (p 105)
The restaurant, in the basement of a magnificent Georgian house - No3 Seven Houses – welcomes non-residents to experience a range of local and international dishes.

El Porto Café, Portadown (p 113)
A busy European-style café with music and atmosphere in the heart of Portadown. Enjoy freshly baked baguettes with tasty fillings, home-made soup and sweet and savoury baking.

Navan Centre, Armagh (p 106)
Up to three tempting hot meals, one vegetarian, and a variety of snacks are served in the friendly smoke-free coffee shop, seven days a week. Another enjoyable memory to take away from this splendid interpretive centre at Ulster's most historic site.

Old Thatch, Markethill (p 112)
Modelled on a traditional thatched cottage, this unusual coffee shop in Alexander's busy department store has a fine range of home-made savoury dishes, cakes and scones – perfect for morning coffee or afternoon tea. Try the bakes and speciality freezer jam to take away.

Seagoe Hotel, Portadown (p 114)
This establishment has been recently refurbished to high levels of comfort and hospitality. The Avanti Resaurant is ideal for fine dining or Sunday lunch. The bar is good for snacks.

A Taste of Ulster

County Down

Balloo House, Killinchy (p 137)
Atmospheric old coaching house with bar, lounge and restaurant.
Enjoy the real log fires in the winter and airy french windows in
summer, with food prepared by the award-winning chef.

Bay Tree, Holywood (p 133)
This little pottery shop and coffee house is warm and welcoming. On
summer days, doors open on to a pretty terrace. Sue Farmer's famous
cinnamon scones feature all day, with bakes and stews at lunchtime.
Bridgestone, Egon Ronay.

Brass Monkey, Newry (p 143)
Town centre bar opposite the courthouse with a country farmhouse
atmosphere, stone floors and a spiral staircase. The fish comes from
Kilkeel and meat and poultry is County Down-bred. Try the Ulster
'Monkey' Fry.

Buck's Head, Dundrum (p 130)
Characterful country pub on the main road from Belfast to the
Mournes. Wood panelling, an open fire and a pretty view to the patio
and garden from the dining room. Bridgestone, Egon Ronay.

Burrendale Hotel, Newcastle (p 139)
In a magnificent setting at the foot of the Mourne mountains, a team
of top chefs create delicate flavours, with an insistence on fresh
ingredients. Families love the high tea menu.

Caroline's Parlour, Saintfield (p 149)
Inside an 18th century coaching house, Caroline's Parlour serves
delicious home-made lunches, soups, breads and scones. Al fresco
dining in summer.

Castle Espie Coffee Room, Comber (p 126)
Set in a nature reserve with views of Strangford Lough, home of
Ireland's largest collection of ducks, geese and swans – a splendid
backdrop for the fine food.

County Down *continued*

The Croft, Moira (p 138)
In old, converted cottages, you enter through a craft shop. The menu features scones, tray-bakes and home-made lunches. Wide choice of speicalist coffees.

Cuan, Strangford (p 150)
Open fires, creamy Guinness, and the warmest welcome are assured at this picturesque village restaurant. Simple food is superbly prepared by head chef Colin Shanks. Bar snacks all day and a range of evening menus. Comprehensive wine list.

Culloden Hotel, Cultra (p 127)
Chef Paul McKnight offers a wide range of dishes in the Mitre restaurant which looks on to a sweep of landscaped gardens below. This characterful gothic mansion – Northern Ireland's first five-star hotel – is seven miles from Belfast on the Bangor road. AA rosette.

Dufferin Arms, Killyleagh (p 137)
A traditional Irish coaching inn with a cellar bar/restaurant, serving the best of Ulster produce – from smoked salmon to lamb, beef, and fresh vegetables. Relaxed atmosphere, music and weekend brunch.

Finnegan's, Kircubbin (p 137)
Enjoy excellent meals at competitive prices at this centrally located establishment on the Ards peninsula. The service is efficient and the atmosphere friendly.

The Food Exchange, Banbridge (p 120)
Inside the Tourist Information Centre on the main A1 Belfast-Dublin Road. Freshly baked scones, wheaten bread, delicious savoury dishes and quality desserts are all freshly prepared on the premises.

Gilberry Fayre, Gilford (p 130)
This former schoolhouse has a distinctive pine interior. Local food is freshly prepared in the kitchen. Despite its emphasis on healthy eating, the coffee shop has a mouth-watering array of sweets! Disabled visitors welcome. No credit cards.

A Taste of Ulster

County Down *continued*

Grace Neill's, Donaghadee (p 128)
Donaghadee's oldest tavern dating back to 1611, Grace Neill's is Ireland's oldest pub according to the *Guinness Book of Records.* The the dish of the day often features locally caught fish.

Halls Mill Inn, Gilford (p 130)
Spacious restaurant, with conservatory and oak-panelled bar, on the main Banbridge-Gilford road. Chefs are local, though internationally trained, and they favour local produce – market-fresh vegetables, Mourne hams, Kilkeel mussels, and County Down ostrich.

Hampton's Coffee Shop, Hillsborough (p 131)
Coffee shop inside furnishings/interiors store. Tea and coffee are prepared from filtered water for a fuller flavour and the scones are always good. A smoke-free zone.

Harry's Bar (Gowdy's), Banbridge (p 119)
Traditional old pub serving 14 different draft ales and all home-made food – Ulster gammon with eggs is especially popular. Salad bar and a wide range of desserts. Try Bailey's cheesecake and Irish coffee trifle.

Heatherlea Tea Rooms, Bangor (p 122)
This pleasant coffee shop at the rear of a home bakery is popular with shoppers. Good home-baked breads, cakes and scones, and a wide range of freshly prepared savoury dishes. No credit cards.

Hillside, Hillsborough (p 131)
Imaginative dishes with a touch of nouvelle cuisine in the Victorian-style first-floor restaurant. The friendly downstairs pub serves Hillside pâté with hot cumberland sauce and toasted wheaten bread. There is a walled herb garden at the back. Bridgestone, Egon Ronay, Michelin.

Interno, Newtownards (p 146)
The simple menu in this elegant coffee lounge emphasises fresh quality local produce, fish and prawns from Portavogie and home-made cakes and pastries.

County Down *continued*

Knott's Cake & Coffee Shop, Newtownards (p 146)
In a large Victorian building with high ceilings, this airy coffee shop offers a wide range of breads and cakes as well as hot pies, stews and casseroles. A popular lunchtime spot. No credit cards.

Lisbarnett House, Killinchy (p 137)
Cosy traditional atmosphere in this family-run former post house for horse-drawn vehicles at Lisbane, on the main Comber-Killinchy road. Fresh local produce is well prepared and presented.

Lobster Pot, Strangford (p 150)
Recently refurbished, the restaurant retains its old-fashioned charm. Head chef Fergus King uses only the finest produce. Renowned for its seafood, especially Lobster!

Maple Leaf Cottage Tea Room, Newcastle (p 140)
Authentic turn-of-the-century cottage tea room 120 yards from the entrance to Tollymore Forest Park. Cakes are home-produced, and local jams, crafts and plants are for sale. Access-friendly.

Old Inn, Crawfordsburn (p 127)
The hotel, situated in the quiet village of Crawfordsburn, is one of Ireland's oldest hostelries, with records dating back to 1614. The chef always purchases local food to ensure dining simplicity at its best.

Old School House, Comber (p 126)
Stylish restaurant close to Strangford Lough. Avril Brown's cooking has traditional roots, but she also experiments with new combinations of seasonal produce. On A22, three miles south-east of Comber.

Olde Priory Inn, Holywood (p 134)
A long established County Down bar and restaurant, known for its excellent food and entertainment. Head chef David McCausland offers unusual and delicious fare at lunchtime, with a memorable evening menu. The very best Ulster produce is used in daily specials.

County Down *continued*

Portaferry Hotel, Portaferry (p 148)
This country hotel has an idyllic outlook across Strangford Lough, and Chef makes the very most of the plentiful supplies of fish and shellfish in the area. Bar food. Bridgestone, Egon Ronay, 2 AA rosettes.

Primrose Bar, Ballynahinch (p 118)
A former blacksmith shop with character. Discerning eaters come from a distance for owner Helen Gordon's open prawn sandwiches and wheaten bread, baked on the premises.

Rayanne House, Holywood (p 134)
The licensed restaurant of this award-winning country house is open for dinner to non-residents. The proprietors , Raymond and Anne McClelland and their family, extend a very personal, warm Irish welcome to diners. 2 AA rosettes.

Red Fox Coffee Shop, Hillsborough (p 133)
Popular coffee shop with views of the parish church and grounds. Owner Mo Mullan offers nutritious home-made food. Craft shop across the courtyard.

Ritchies, Hillsborough (p 133)
A friendly atmosphere combines with an adventurous menu using local produce that includes dishes such as local Crispy Duckling on a caramelised spiced jus.

Roma's, Newtownards (p 147)
Stone walls and an art deco theme in the three bars and upstairs restaurant. Daily blackboard specials complement a full lunch menu downstairs. A la carte menu in the restaurant.

Rosemary Jane Tea Room, Crossgar (p 127)
An intimate atmosphere, with lots of easy chairs. Rosemary McKillen's menu includes vegetarian dishes and an imaginative choice of soups, salads and desserts. No credit cards.

County Down *continued*

Royal Hotel, Bangor (p 123)
Friendly hotel overlooking the marina, with a reputation for good food
and a pleasant atmosphere. Award-winning chef Alex Taylor offers
French-style modern cuisine using the best County Down produce.

Seaforde Inn, Seaforde (p 150)
Traditional country bar at the gateway to the Mournes. Delicious
local ingredients create memorable dishes such as steak & Guinness
pie with herbed puff pastry and Dundrum mussels in tomato sauce.

Shanks Restaurant, Bangor (p 123)
Proprietor Robin Millar uses the freshest Clandeboye estate produce to
create dishes such as venison with caramelised apples and local
scallops with smoked chilli and basil risotto. A smart Conran-
designed interior and keen, friendly service. Must book. Bridgestone,
Egon Ronay, Good Food Guide, Michelin star, 3 AA rosettes.

Tourist Trophy Lounge, Comber (p 126)
An ideal pit stop for good food, the TT Lounge is situated on the route
of the famous Tourist Trophy car races of the twenties and thirties.
A long-standing family business with a loyal local following.

Wheatear Coffee Lounge, Bangor (p 124)
A bright and busy self-service coffee shop which offers a very wide
range of high quality savouries and sweets. No credit cards.

Drumshane Hotel, Lisnarick (p 165)
In the village of Lisnarick in the heart of the Ulster lakeland. The vanishing art of cooking at table has been revived by the remarkable Noel Smith, formerly of Dublin's Burlington Hotel.

The Hollander, Irvinestown (p 163)
Interesting decor with mahogany bar and souvenirs from Holland. Head chef Stephen Holland produces some superb dishes such as salmon en croûte and beef Wellington. Bridgestone, Egon Ronay.

The Killyhevlin, Enniskillen (p 159)
On the shores of beautiful Lough Erne. Lunch-time diners can enjoy a buffet of hot and cold dishes. The evening a la carte menu is exensive.

Le Bistro, Enniskillen (p 159)
Friendly, family-run bistro in the Erneside shopping centre. The Johnstons use only the best local produce and all food is freshly prepared each day. A good place to take a break from shopping.

Manor House Country Hotel, Killadeas (p 165)
Victorian manor on the shore of Lower Lough Erne. Fish from the lakes is imaginatively prepared by French chef Jean-Yves Annino. The menu also features local game, poultry, lamb and beef.

Mulligan's, Enniskillen (p 159)
Almost everything served in this popular family-run bar and restaurant is home-produced in Mulligan's kitchens, from patés and soups to Irish stew with Bushmills whiskey and a wide selection of Ulster meat and seafood dishes.

Tullyhona Guesthouse, Florencecourt (p 161)
The restaurant in this guesthouse near Florence Court is open to non-residents for breakfast and light meals. The menu features home-produced meats and vegetables. Bridgestone.

Ardtara Country House, Maghera (p 181)
This Victorian manor offers gracious old-style service amid an
impressive array of antiques. Head chef Patrick McLarnon's menus
include hand picked berries, wild boar, rabbit, and salmon wrapped
in dulse. 2 AA rosettes.

Badgers, Londonderry (p 174)
A lively bar with ambience in the old part of the city. A trio of chefs –
Paul, Bernadette and Dermot – prepare a wide range of dishes using
the freshest local ingredients. A la carte dining in the evening.

Beech Hill Country House Hotel, Londonderry (p 175)
The 18th-century mansion exudes an old-world elegance. Local
produce in a classical style is the keynote of chef James Nicholas's
adventurous menu. His vegetarian dishes and desserts are outstanding.
Bridgestone, Egon Ronay, Good Food Guide.

Brown's Bar & Brasserie, Londonderry (p 175)
A lively modern European-style brasserie and bar where the diverse
menu features the best local produce, organically grown wherever
possible.

Brown Trout Golf & Country Inn, Aghadowey (p 167)
Co-proprietor Jane O'Hara leads the kitchen team. The upstairs
restaurant is non-smoking but many customers eat around the open
peat fire or on the patio.

Decks Bar & Restaurant, Eglinton (p 171)
A mellow, elegant brasserie with original turn-of-the-century pine
panelling. The chef uses the best local produce and fresh fish from the
bustling seaport of Greencastle, across the Foyle estuary.

Ditty's Home Bakery & Coffee Shop, Magherafelt (p 182)
This small coffee shop is inside a well known home bakery. A good
range of breads and confectionery with a choice of three or four hot
dishes every day. No credit cards.

County Londonderry *continued*

Fiolta's Bistro, Magherafelt (p 182)
Proprietor Mary Scullion offers a wide range of dishes at this spacious bistro. The menu is based around the best available local produce with a different special dish every day and, a recent development, eight-course gourmet meals.

Faerie Thorn, Tobermore (p 184)
Try the speciality salad bar and home-made steak and Guinness pie at this traditional Irish pub. There are two pleasant gardens. Pub of the Year 1997.

Little Tea Shop, Coleraine (p 169)
Decorated in a cosy style, this non-smoking establishment has easy access for wheelchair users. Afternoon cream tea is popular. The lunch menu features simple, well prepared family dishes.

Mary's Bar, Magherafelt (p 182)
Roast pheasant, wild Ulster salmon and home-made pies are among the dishes that attract customers from a wide area. There is an upstairs carvery and food is also served by staff in a lounge downstairs.

The Metro, Londonderry (p 178)
Charming little pub in the shadow of the city walls. Lots of alcoves create a cosy atmosphere. Everything from soup and sandwiches to a hearty beef-and-Guinness stew. No credit cards.

Morelli's, Portstewart (p 184)
This bright and cheerful seafront café offers a clear view to the sea. As well as hot dishes, Morelli's is a long established ice cream parlour with an amazing array of exotic ices. No credit cards.

Reggie's Seafood Restaurant, Londonderry (p 179)
Cosy restaurant based on a traditional chip shop design, conveniently situated just outside the city centre. A range of delicious sauces complements the locally caught fish.

Salmon Leap, Coleraine (p 170)

On a picturesque stretch of the Bann at Coleraine, the Salmon Leap is the place to go for superlative salmon. There is an extensive wine list in the Still Water gourmet restaurant, with food served in the Poacher's Hide bistro. Display of works by local artists. Egon Ronay.

The Sandwich Co, Londonderry (p 179)

Two busy sandwich bars with a great selection of hot and cold sandwiches and cakes. The Strand Road venue is a favourite for live bluegrass and folk music on Saturdays. The city centre bar, on the Diamond, has a musical theme.

Trompets, Magherafelt (p 183)

The menus of chef/proprietor Noel McMeel reflect an eclectic style, using local suppliers and enhancing natural flavours. Enjoy the rich chocolate cake, with Cashel Blue chese and a glass of Elysium Black Muscat!

Waterfoot Hotel, Londonderry (p 181)

With its distinctive circular design, the hotel offers good views of the River Foyle and the Donegal mountains. Chef Kevin McGowan uses fresh Foyle fish and the best local vegetables. Bar snacks.

A Taste of Ulster

County Tyrone

Cent Percent, Ballygawley (p 185)
Chef/Proprietors Mary Tunney and Luc Deville create fine quality seasonal dishes prepared and served with flair. Good wine list.

The Courtyard, Cookstown (p 188)
Ploughs, cartwheels and a farmyard pump create a rustic feel in this attractive coffee shop which serves home-made food. No credit cards.

Greenmount Lodge, Omagh (p 196)
The Lodge is renowned for the Ulster beef and lamb reared on its own farm, and chef Louie Reid is well known for her delicious desserts. Open to non-residents at weekends for dinner. No credit cards.

Mellon Country Inn, Omagh (p 196)
Opposite the Ulster-American Folk Park. The food is traditional with French influences. Extensive restaurant menu and a quick lunchtime buffet service in the bar.

Number 15 Coffee Shop & Restaurant, Dungannon (p 192)
A pleasant haven above Murray Richardson's bookshop serving morning coffee, snacks all day and afternoon tea with scones, gâteaux and pastries. Fresh soups, pies, and salads.

Rosamund's Coffee Shop, Augher (p 185)
In one of the old Clogher Valley Railway station houses. The cooking is simple and good and dishes feature the excellent Clogher Valley cheese, made nearby. Local crafts and linen on sale. No credit cards.

Suitor Gallery, Ballygawley (p 185)
Charming tea room and craftshop in a converted barn. The soups, wheaten bread, sandwiches and cakes are prepared by owner/cook/artist Beryl Suitor and her daughter Penny.

Tullylagan Country House, Cookstown (p 190)
Rural country house and restaurant, halfway between Dungannon and Tyrone. The restaurant has a warm, relaxed atmosphere and serves high quality dishes made with the finest local produce.

Viscounts, Dungannon (p 192)
Good food, efficient service and a medieval theme in this former Victorian church hall, now a fully licensed restaurant. Easy parking.

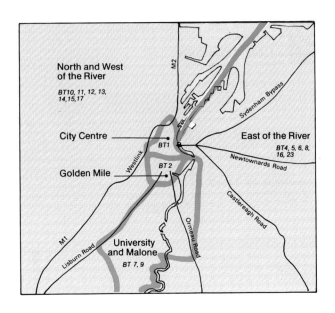

Belfast postal districts
Use this sketch map,
based on postal districts,
to locate restaurants in
the Belfast area.

City Centre *(BT1)* *(STD 01232)*

Aero ♀
44 Bedford St. ☎ 244844.
1200-1430 Mon-Fri, 1730-
2230 Mon-Sat. Trio of salmon
with mosaic of green
vegetables and a crocus cream.

Alambra
114 North St, BT1. ☎ 240682.
0930-1730 Mon-Sat. Fast food.

Alto's ♀
6 Fountain St, BT1. ☎ 323087.
1000-1700 Mon-Tues, until
1800 Wed, 1000-1800 &
1900-2230 Thur-Sat. Italian.

Antrim Coffee House
Masonic Hall, 15 Rosemary St,
BT1. ☎ 329594. 1000-1500
Mon-Sat. Morning coffee,
home-made soups, gammon,
cheesecake, vegetarian dishes.

Arizona ♀
10 Gresham St, BT1.
☎ 323590. 1130-1500 Mon-
Thur, until 1700 Fri-Sat.
Grills, steaks, fish.

Arthur's Place
49a Upper Arthur St, BT1.
☎ 242284. 0800-1700 Mon-
Sat. Pies, sandwiches.

'Backstage' at the Garrick ♀
11 Montgomery St, BT1.
☎ 333875. 1200-1800 Mon-
Fri, until 2300 Sat. Sauté of
duck with balsamic lentils &
wild mushrooms.

Belfast Superbowl
4 Clarence St West. ☎ 331466.
1200-late Mon-Sat, 1200-late
Sun. Fast food.

Benny's
10 Short St, BT1. ☎ 743128.
0800-1600 Mon-Fri, until
1300 Sat. Ulster fry, grills,
sandwiches.

Bewley's
Donegall Arcade, BT1.
☎ 234955. 0800-1730 Mon-
Sat, until 2030 Thur. Breakfast.
Traditional hot dishes, soups,
sandwiches, salads.

BHS Patio Restaurant
BHS, 24 Castle Place, BT1.
☎ 243068. 0930-1645 Mon-
Wed, 0900-1645 Thur-Sat.
Coffee shop and restaurant in
department store.

★ BITTLES ♀
70 Upper Church Lane, BT1.
☎ 311088. 1130-1500 Mon-
Sat. Irish stew, champ.

Blackthorn ♀
3 Skipper St, BT1. ☎ 331087.
1200-1430 Mon-Sat. Roast
beef, fish, salads.

Blinkers
1 Bridge St, BT1. ☎ 243330.
1000-2245 Mon-Sat. Grills,
set lunch.

Blooms
46 Upper Arthur St, BT1.
☎ 313500. 0730-1530 Mon-
Fri. Home baking.

Bocadillo's
2 Little Victoria St. ☎ 581212.
0845-1530 Mon-Fri.
Baguettes, sandwiches, salads.

Bodega ⚲
4 Callender St, BT1.
☎ 243177. 1130-1600 Mon-
Wed, until 2100 Thur, 1700
Fri-Sat. Cajun chicken, stir fry,
pub grub. E£.

Bonne Bouche
19 Fountain St, BT1.
☎ 241454. 0730-1730 Mon-
Sat, until 2100 Thur. Ulster fry,
set lunch.

Boots ⊘
35 Donegall Place, BT1.
☎ 242332. 0900-1730 Mon-
Sat, until 2015 Thur. Cakes,
lasagne, baked potatoes. Self-
service restaurant in store.

Burger King
Cleaver House, Donegall
Place, BT1. ☎ 245314. 0800-
2300 Mon-Thur, until 2400 Fri
& Sat, 1000-2300 Sun.
Fast food.

Café de Ville
58 Wellington Place, BT1.
☎ 234303. 0800-1800 Mon-
Fri, 1100-1530 Sat. Sandwich
bar & restaurant.

Café Espresso
1 Wellington St, BT1. ☎ 314141.
0800-1730 Mon-Sat. Salads,
baguettes, sandwiches, cakes.

Café K
51 Royal Avenue. ☎ 235443.
Salads, soups, pasta, gourmet
sandwiches, French toasted
panini, tray-bakes. Daily specials.
Café in Kookai fashion store.

Café Poirot ⚲
51 Fountain St, BT1. ☎ 323130.
0745-1715 Mon-Fri, until 1930
Thur & 1730 Sat. Salads,
baguettes, sandwiches.

Café Renoir
5 Queen St, BT1. ☎ 325592.
0945-1700 Mon-Sat. Salads,
baguettes, sandwiches, cakes.

★ CAFÉ SOCIETY ⚲
3 Donegall Square East, BT1.
☎ 439525. 0800 till late Mon-
Sat. Fresh pasta, savoury tart,
vegetarian, pan fried chicken
with balsamic tomatoes.
Extensive wine list.

Caffé Casa ⊘
12 College St, BT1. ☎ 319900.
0900-1800 Mon-Sat. Roast
aubergine with roast pepper
panini. Specialist coffee house.

Campbell's
11 Donegall Square West, BT1.
☎ 322658. 0730-1700 Mon-Sat.
Café in cake shop.

Capstan Bar & Lounge ⚲
10 Ann St, BT1. ☎ 329148.
1130-1500 Mon-Sat. Pub grub.

Carlton 🍷
4a Donegall Square West,
BT1. ☎ 326861. 1200-2130
Mon-Sat. Home-made savoury
pies, steaks, stir fry.

Castle Court Centre
12 Royal Avenue, BT1.
☎ 235122. Coffee shops &
restaurant. 0930-1730 Mon-
Sat, until 2100 Thur (coffee
shops). Muffins, sandwiches,
baguettes.

Chalet d'Or
23 High St, BT1. ☎ 245688.
1000-1800 Mon-Sat, until
2000 Thur. Grills, snacks,
set lunch.

Clarence 🍷
18 Donegall Square East, BT1.
☎ 238862. 1230-1430 Mon-
Fri. Bar lunch: pâté, salads,
sandwiches. A la carte: salmon
& monkfish with ginger sauce,
champagne sorbet. ££.

★ **COPPERFIELDS** 🍷
9 Fountain St, BT1. ☎ 247367.
1130-2000 Mon-Wed, until
2100 Thur, 2000 Fri-Sat. Irish
stew, Mexican dishes.

Crow's Nest 🍷
2 Skipper St, BT1. ☎ 325491.
1200-1500 Mon-Sat. Pub grub.

★ **DEANE'S** 🍷
38 Howard St, BT1. ☎ 560000.
Brasserie 1200-1500 & 1700-
2300 Mon-Sat. Restaurant
1215-1400 Tues-Fri, 1900-2130
Tues-Sat. Peppered duck, roast
salmon, Vietnamese noodles
and spiced onions. £££.

Deer's Head 🍷
1 Garfield St. BT1. ☎ 239163.
1200-1900 Mon-Sat. Soup,
baked potatoes, club
sandwiches, lasagne.

Delaney's 🍷
19 Lombard St, BT1.
☎ 231572. 0900-1700 Mon-
Sat, until 2100 Thur. Breakfast,
lasagne, home-baked pies,
self-service. A la carte £.

Dr B's Kitchen ☕
9 Bridge St, BT1. ☎ 321213.
0930-1400 Mon-Fri. Baked
Irish ham, pork in cider sauce,
sirloin of beef in pepper
sauce.

★ **DUKE OF YORK** 🍷
3 Commercial Court.
☎ 241062. 1200-1430 Mon-
Sat. Steaks, vegetarian
lasagne, rolls. Live music.

Eighteen Steps 🍷
17 Ann St, BT1. ☎ 326247.
1130-1700 Mon-Sat. Open
sandwiches, pies, steaks.

★ **EQUINOX**
32 Howard St, BT1.
☎ 230089. 0930-1645 Mon-
Sat. Pasta, sandwiches, salads,
croissants, milkshakes.
Café in shop.

Fibber Magee's 🍷
Keylands Place, BT1.
☎ 247447. 1200-1430 Mon-
Sat. Pan-fried chicken, baked
potatoes, sandwiches.

Forte's
92 Castle St, BT1. ☎ 327189.
0915-1745 Mon-Sat. Soup,
sandwiches, salads.

Fountain Tavern ⚲
16 Fountain St, BT1. ☎ 242049.
1130-1900 Mon-Sat, until 2100
Thur. Steak casserole, quiche,
baked potatoes.

Frames Too ⚲
2-14 Little Donegall St, BT1.
☎ 244855. 1200-1430 Mon-Sat,
1700-2200 Thur-Sat. Lamb, loin
of pork, Mexican chicken. E£.

Front Page ⚲
106 Donegall St, BT1.
☎ 324924. 1200-2100 Mon-Sat.
Soups, steak & Guinness pie,
bar snacks. Live music.

Fusha Chinese Tea House
20 Church Lane, BT1.
☎ 326275.1000-1700 Mon-Sat,
until 1900 Thur. Chinese teas &
Chinese food.

Garrick ⚲
29 Chichester St, BT1.
☎ 333875. 1200-1800 Mon-Sat.
Home-made soup, stew, apple
pie.

Golden Bloom
9 Wellington St, BT1.
☎ 240281. 0745-1730 Mon-Sat.
Ulster fry, pies, sandwiches.

Hardy's
12 Fountain Lane, BT1.
☎ 236308. 0800-1700 Mon-Sat,
until 1900 Thur. Beef &
Guinness pie, lasagne,
pancakes, home-made scones.

Hedley's Coffee Shop
103 Royal Avenue, BT1.
☎ 237077. 0930-1700 Mon-Sat.
Cottage pie, casseroles.
In china shop.

Hercules Lounge Bar ⚲
61 Castle St, BT1. ☎ 324587.
1200-1500 Mon-Wed, until
1800 Thur-Sat. Pub grub.

Holiday Inn Garden Court ⚲
15 Brunswick St, BT2
☎ 333555. Last orders 2230,
2130 Sun. Breakfast. Buffet
lunch: gammon with Guinness
gravy. A la carte. E££.

Kelly's Cellars ⚲
32 Bank St, BT1. ☎ 324835.
1130-1430 Mon-Fri, until 1630
Sat. Pub grub, oysters, grills.
Live traditional music.

Kentucky Fried Chicken
33 Ann St, BT1. ☎ 232585.
1100-1800 Mon-Wed, until
2100 Thur, 1900 Fri-Sat.
Fast food.

Kentucky Fried Chicken
39 Royal Avenue, BT1.
☎ 234188. 1100-1800 Mon-
Wed, until 2100 Thur, 1900 Fri-
Sat. Fast food.

Kentucky Fried Chicken
7 Wellington Place, BT1.
☎ 325146. 1100-2300 Mon-
Thur, until 2330 Fri-Sat.
Fast food.

Kitchen Bar ⚲
16 Victoria Square, BT1.
☎ 324901. 1200-1500 Mon-
Wed & Fri, until 1800 Thur &
Sat. Ulster fry, soup, Irish stew,
champ. Real ale.

Krusty Korner
76 Lower North St, BT1.
☎ 232047. 0900-1700 Mon-Sat.
Sandwiches, coffee.

Laganside Coffee Stop
Laganside Bus Centre, Donegall
Quay, BT1. ☎ 231588. 0800-
1930 Mon-Sat, 1030-1730 Sun.
Snacks, all day breakfast,
sandwiches.

Le Café
38 Hill St, BT1. ☎ 311660.
0930-1430 Mon-Fri. Chicken
curry, pies, cakes.

Library Bar ⚲
2-14 Little Donegall St, BT1.
☎ 244855. 1200-1430 Mon-Sat.
Moussaka, beef casserole, plaice.

Linen Hall Library
17 Donegall Square North, BT1.
☎ 321707. 1000-1600 Mon-Fri,
until 1400 Sat. Soup,
sandwiches, scones. Café in
reading room.

Little Knife & Fork
29 North St, BT1. ☎ 439619.
0900-1800 Mon-Sat, until 2200
Thur. Grills.

Littlewoods Green Room
5 Ann St, BT1. ☎ 241537.
0900-1715 Mon-Sat, until 2100
Thur. Grills, set lunch.
Restaurant in store.

Magennis's Bar ⚲
83 May St, BT1. ☎ 230295.
1130-2300 Mon-Sat. Soup &
baguettes, bangers & mash,
Mother's Lasagne.

Maysfield Leisure Centre
49 East Bridge St, BT1.
☎ 41633. 1000-2200 Mon-Fri,
until 1600 Sat, 1100-1700
Sun. Fish, chicken, lasagne.

McDonald's
2 Donegall Place, BT1.
☎ 311600. 0700-2000 Mon-
Sat, until 2200 Thur, 1100-
1800 Sun. Fast food.

McHugh's Bar ⚲
29-31 Queen's Square.
☎ 247830. 1200-1500 &
1700-2300 Mon-Sun.
Singapore noodles, grilled
salmon, Barbary duck, wok
dishes. Downstairs: Pub food.
Oldest surviving building in
Belfast.

McPaper
20 Callender St, BT1.
☎ 327632. 0930-1730 Mon-
Sat, until 2000 Thur. Scones,
pastries, hot chocolate.
In stationery shop.

Mermaid ⚲
5 Wilson's Court, High St,
BT1. ☎ 327829. 1200-1430
Mon-Sat. Pub grub.

Miss American Pie
Ross's Court, William St South,
BT1. ☎ 311055. 0900-1730
Mon-Wed & Fri, until 2100
Thur. Chilli, club sandwiches.

Monico ⚲
17 Lombard St, BT1. ☎ 323211.
1200-1600 Mon-Sat. Pub grub.

★ **MORNING STAR** ⚲
17 Pottinger's Entry, BT1.
☎ 235986. 1130-2100 Mon-
Thur, until 2200 Fri & Sat. Carrot
& stilton soup, seafood, lamb
fillet with ginger & garlic.
Gourmet night last Sat in month.

Muldoon's ⚲
13 Corporation Square, BT1.
☎ 232415. 1200-1500 Mon-Sat.
Pub grub.

Mulligan's Bar ⚲
95 Castle St, BT1. ☎ 232226.
1200-2100 Mon-Sat. Steaks,
grills, scampi. £.

New Yorker Deli & Diner
Fountain Centre, College St.
☎ 439295. 0800-1700 Mon-Fri,
0900-1700 Sat. Breakfast,
lunches.

Next Café
20 Donegall Place, BT1.
☎ 249636. 0930-1700 Mon-Fri,
until 1730 Sat. Coffee shop in
fashion store.

★ **NICK'S WAREHOUSE** ⚲
35 Hill St, BT1. ☎ 439690.
1200-1500 Mon-Fri, 1800-2300
Tues-Sat. Duck with apple,
halibut with langoustine &
sweet peppers. £££.

O'Neill's ⚲
Joy's Entry, BT1. ☎ 326711.
1200-1800 Mon-Sat, until 2100
Thur. Fish, pasta, grills, salads,
home-made sweets.

Paddy's Bar ⚲
96 Ann St, BT1. ☎ 327162.
1200-1500 Mon-Fri, until
1800 Sat, 1430 Sun. Wine
bar. Theme days. Mexican
specialities.

Pancake House
Haymarket, off Royal Avenue,
BT1. ☎ 240141. 0800-1730
Mon-Sat, until 2100 Thur.
Savoury & sweet pancakes.

Parliament Bar ⚲
2 Dunbar St, BT1. ☎ 234520.
1200-1500 Mon-Sat. Pub grub,
grills.

Patio Restaurant ⌾
BHS, 24 Castle Place, BT1.
☎ 243068. 0930-1645
Mon-Wed, 0900-1645 Thur-
Sat. Coffee shop and restaurant
in department store.

Pat's Bar ⚲
19 Prince's Dock St, BT1.
☎ 744524. 1200-1430 Mon-
Fri. Pub grub. In summer
1600-1900 Mon-Fri, buffet
dinner. Live music.

Poachers
Unit 10, Victoria Centre, BT1.
☎ 332162. 0900-1600 Mon-
Fri. Home baking, sandwiches.

Queen's Bar ⚲
4 Queen's Arcade, BT1.
☎ 321347. 1200-1800 Mon-
Sat, until 2000 Thur. Pub grub.

Romano's
12 Queen St, BT1. ☎ 249484.
0830-1730 Mon-Sat. Set
lunch, grills.

★ ROSCOFF CAFÉ 🍶
21 Fountain St. ☎ 315090.
0730-1730 Mon-Wed & Sat,
until 2100 Thur, 2030 Fri.
Breakfast. Soups, pasta,
croissants, pastries.

Rotterdam 🍺
54 Pilot St, BT1. ☎ 746021.
1200-1500 Mon-Fri. Pub grub.

Rumpole's 🍺
81 Chichester St, BT1.
☎ 232840. 1200-1500 Mon-Sat,
1600-2200 Tues & Thur-Sat.
Crab pâté, seafood pancake,
chicken & ham pie.

Sandwich Scene
18 High St, BT1. ☎ 332240.
1030-1600 Mon-Sat. Fresh
sandwiches.

Shakespeare 🍺
103 Victoria St, BT1. ☎ 328788.
1130-2300 Mon-Sat. Pub grub.

Shenanagan Rooms 🍺
15 Howard St, BT1.
☎ 323313. 1200-1500 Mon-Sat,
1700-2100 Tues-Sat. Mexican,
barbecue ribs, steaks, pancakes.
Live music. E££.

Skandia 🍶
12 Callender St, BT1.
☎ 245385. 0930-1800 Mon-Sat,
until 2100 Thur, 1930 Fri.
Salads, open sandwiches. £.

★ SKANDIA 🍶
50 Howard St, BT1.
☎ 240239. 1100-2300 Mon-Sat.
Grills, salads, open sandwiches,
gâteaux. E£.

Snakkers
63a Prince's Dock St, BT1.
☎ 352387. 0800-1600 Mon-
Fri, until 1400 Sat. Home-
made savoury pies, casseroles,
Ulster fry, roasts.

Strike Four (Belfast) Ltd 🍺
35 Bedford St, BT1. ☎ 238238.
1200-2300 Mon-Thur, until
2400 Fri-Sat, 1230-2200 Sun.
Hamburgers, steaks, salads.
American theme restaurant. E£.

Strikes
19 Bridge St, BT1. ☎ 320945.
0900-1800 Mon-Sat, until
1900 Thur. Soup, grills,
toasties.

Sunflower Café 🍶
90a Castle St, BT1. ☎ 246660.
0900-1800 Mon-Wed, until
2200 Thur & Fri. Peppered
chicken, Irish stew, spaghetti,
vegetarian.

Tedfords 🍺
5 Donegall Quay. ☎ 434000.
1200-1500 Mon-Fri & 1800-
2230 Tues-Sat. Brasserie: Wok
seafood calamari, smoked
salmon bruchetta.

The Mulberry
38 Upper Arthur St, BT1.
☎ 249009. 0730-1700 Mon-
Sat. Salad bar, pizzas.

Tiffins
4 Montgomery St, BT1.
☎ 320906. 0800-1930 Mon-
Fri. Coffee, scones.

Trotters
Lower Garfield St. ☎ 231714.
0800-1600 Mon-Sat. Sit-in
sandwich bar.

Upper Crust
15 Lombard St, BT1.
☎ 323132. 0930-1630 Mon-
Sat. Home-made pies, chicken
& broccoli bake, gateaux.

Vino Parnassus ♨
22 Berry St. ☎ 236549. BT1.
1200-1600 Mon-Wed, until
1900 Thur-Fri, and 1600 Sat.
Lasagne, baked potatoes,
chicken tikka, baguettes and
pitta bread.

Waterfront Hall ♈
Terrace Restaurant, 2 Lanyon
Place, BT1. ☎ 244966.
1000-2100 Mon-Sun.
Breakfast, afternoon tea.
Salmon with parmesan champ.
Brasserie style.

Weavers' Café
44 Montgomery St, BT1.
☎ 404236. 0900-1730 Mon-
Sat. Bakes, quiche, cakes.

Whistle Stop ♈
Central Station, East Bridge St,
BT1. ☎ 238637. 1130-1500
Mon-Sat. Soup, stew, fish &
chips. Self-service.

★ **WHITE'S TAVERN** ♈
Winecellar Entry, High St, BT1.
☎ 243080. 1200-1430 Mon-
Sat. Chicken & broccoli bake,
baked potatoes. Live music
Thursday.

Windsor Dairy
4 College St, BT1. ☎ 327157.
0830-1730 Mon-Sat, until
2100 Thur. Home baking,
Irish stew, coffee.

Woolworth's ⊗
11 High St, BT1. ☎ 322888.
0900-1730 Mon-Sat, until
2100 Thur. Snacks, grills,
salads. Restaurant in store.

Golden Mile *(BT2)* *(STD 01232)*

Acapulco ⚲
Botanic Avenue. ☎ 585100.
1800-2300 Mon-Sun. Mexican.

Archana ⚲
53 Dublin Rd, BT2. ☎ 323713.
1200-1400 Mon-Sat, 1700-
2400 Mon-Sun. Indian. Balti
dishes. E££

Arthur's ⚲
7 Hope St, BT2. ☎ 333311.
1200-1430 Mon-Fri, 1800-
2300 Tues-Sat. Ginger chicken
strips, lemon sole with prawns,
peach ice cream. E££.

Backpacker
Belfast International Youth
Hostel, 22 Donegall Rd, BT12
(off Shaftesbury Square).
☎ 324733. Open 7 days.
Breakfast. Fish & chips.

Beaten Docket ⚲
48 Great Victoria St, BT2.
☎ 242986. 1200-1800 Mon-
Wed, until 2100 Thur-Sat.
Traditional pub grub. E£

Bergman's ⚲
12 Brunswick St, BT2.
☎ 248398. 1130-2100 Mon-
Sat. Pub food. Baked potatoes,
stew, champ, burgers, rice,
salad.

Café Deauville
10 Bedford St, BT2. ☎ 326601.
0800-1600 Mon-Fri. Fresh
sandwiches.

Chicago Pizza Pie Factory ⚲
1 Bankmore Square, Dublin
Rd, BT7. ☎ 233555. 1200-
2300 Mon-Thur, until 0100
Fri- Sat, until 2230 Sun. Pizza,
burgers, salads.

Crescent ⚲
197 Sandy Row, BT2.
☎ 320911. 2100-0130 Mon-
Sat. Pub grub.

Crown Liquor Saloon ⚲
46 Great Victoria St, BT2.
☎ 249476. 1130-1500 Mon-
Sat. Bar lunches, champ,
oysters, stew. Victorian pub in
National Trust care.

Dempsey's Terrace ⚲
45 Dublin Rd, BT2.
☎ 234000. 1200-1430 &
1700-2130 Mon-Sat. Mussels,
stuffed duck. E££.

Dunkin' Donuts
6 Great Victoria St. ☎ 248899.
0800-2200 Mon-Sun.
Breakfast. Doughnuts,
sandwiches, bagels.

Emerald City ⚲
59 Dublin Rd. BT2.
☎ 235072. 1200-1400 &
1700-2330 Mon-Thur, until
0030 Fri & Sat, 1630-2300
Sun. Chinese & European. ££.

Esperanto Café Bar ⃟
89 Dublin Rd, BT2.
☎ 248708. 1700-2300 Mon-
Fri, 1600-2300 Sat, until 2200
Sun. Mediterranean & Asian.
E£££.

Europa Hotel ⃟
Great Victoria St, BT2.
☎ 327000. Last orders in
restaurant 2330. Patisserie
0630-2400 Mon-Sun.
A la carte. M£, E££££.

Fatty Arbuckle's ⃟
60 Great Victoria St. BT2.
☎ 330442. 1100-2230 Mon-
Sat & 1200-2230 Sun. Steaks,
fish, jacket potatoes, salad,
country style ribs. American
diner. ££.

Flannigan's ⃟
19 Amelia St (above Crown
Liquor Saloon), BT2.
☎ 279901. 1200-2100 Mon-
Sat, 1230-2100 Sun. Champ,
ham & cabbage, buffet lunch,
Sunday roast.

Glengall Cafe
Great Northern Mall, Great
Victoria St, BT2. ☎ 239942.
0700-2000 Mon-Sat, from
0900 Sun. Lasagne, quiche,
sweet & sour pork,
sandwiches.

Graffiti Italiano ⃟
50 Dublin Rd, BT2. ☎ 249269.
1800-2300 Mon-Sat, 1700-
2200 Sun. Steamed mussels,
seafood spaghetti. ££

Jenny's
81 Dublin Rd, BT2. ☎ 249282.
0900-1700 Mon-Sat. Lasagne,
quiche.

Katy Daly's & Limelight ⃟
17 Ormeau Avenue, BT2.
☎ 325942. 1200-1430 Mon-
Fri, 1900-2200 Mon-Sat.
Sandwiches, grills, salads.
Live music. E£.

Keating ⃟
103 Great Victoria St.
☎ 594949. 1230-1430 Mon-Fri
& 1730-2300 Mon-Sat. Duck
with balsamic mash,
chargrilled Mediterranean
vegetables with sweet potato,
banana creme brulee.

★ **LA BELLE EPOQUE** ⃟
61 Dublin Rd, BT2. ☎ 323244.
1200-2300 Mon-Fri, from
1800 Sat. Fillet of beef with
seed mustard cream, roast
breast of Barbary duck with
grape sauce. E£££.

Larry's Piano Bar ⃟
36 Bedford St, BT2. ☎ 325061.
1700-0115 Tues-Sat. Pasta,
steaks, fish. A la carte.
Live music. E£££.

Little China ⃟
29 Shaftesbury Square. BT2.
☎ 313338. 1700-2400 Mon-
Sun, closed Tues. Chinese &
European.

Morrison's Spirit Grocers ⚲
21 Bedford St, BT2.
☎ 248458. 1200-1415 Mon-Sat. Oriental spiced chicken, salmon in orange sauce, salads.

Oriental International ⚲
25 Dublin Rd, BT2. ☎ 232485.
1200-1400 Mon-Fri, 1730-2315 Mon-Thur, until 0030 Fri-Sat, 2330 Sun. Peking, Cantonese, European. £££.

Parks Caffe
68 Great Victoria St.
☎ 314903. 0900-1830 Mon-Sat, 1300-1700 Sun. Breakfast. Filled panini, ciabatta, Italian cheese, salamis. Coffee selections.

Pierre Victoire ⚲
85 Dublin Rd, BT2. ☎ 559911.
1200-1500 & 1730-2300
Mon-Sat, 1800-2200 Sun.
Melon & avocado salad, escalope of salmon with orange hollandaise. £££.

Pizza Express ⚲
23 Bedford St, BT2. ☎ 329050.
1130-2300 Mon-Sun. Pizzas, salad bar.

Pizza Hut ⚲
44 Dublin Rd, BT2. ☎ 311222.
1200-2400 Mon-Sat, until
2300 Sun. Pizzas, salad bar.

Planet Harvey's ⚲
95 Great Victoria St. BT2.
☎ 233433, Tues-Thur & Sun,
until 2400 Fri-Sat. Tacos, ribs,
deep-pan pizza. E£.

Ponte Vecchio ▲
73 Great Victoria Street,
☎ 242402. 1700-2330 Mon-
Sat, until 2200 Sun. Pizzas,
pasta. E££.

Revelations Internet Café
27 Shaftesbury Square, BT2.
☎ 320337. 1000-2200 Mon-
Fri, until 2000 Sat, 1200-2200
Sun. Sandwiches, hot snacks.

Robinson's ⚲
38 Great Victoria St, BT2. ☎
247447. 1230-1430 & 1700-
1930 Mon-Sat. Four themed
bars.

★ ROSCOFF ⚲
Lesley House, Shaftesbury
Square, BT2. ☎ 331532. 1215-
1415 Mon-Fri, 1830-2230
Mon-Sat. Venison with salsify
& wild mushrooms, monkfish
with soy glaze & coriander
cream. M££. E£££.

Sinbad's Rib & Steak House ⚲
13 Amelia St, BT2. ☎ 325667.
1200-1500 & 1800-late Mon-
Sun. Steaks, ribs, chicken, stir
fry. E££.

★ SPERANZA ⚲
16 Shaftesbury Square, BT2.
☎ 230213. 1730-2330 Mon-
Sat, until 2230 Sun. Italian.
Pizzas, pasta. £.

Spires
Church House, Fisherwick
Place, BT2. ☎ 312881. 0900-
1730 Mon-Sat, until 2000
Thur. Ulster fry, chicken,
scampi.

Starlite Café
60 Great Victoria St, BT2.
1100-2400 Sun-Wed, until
1400 Thur-Sat. Fast food.

Summer Palace ⚲
126 Great Victoria St, BT2.
☎ 235828. 1800-0100 Mon-
Sat, until 2200 Sun. Chinese.
E££.

The Square ⚲
89 Dublin Rd. BT2. ☎ 239933.
1200-1500 & 1730-2230
Mon-Sat. Morning coffee,
lunch, dinner. Duck with
mandarin & cointreau sauce,
duo chocolate mousse.

Tokyo Joe's Warehouse ⚲
9 Bruce St, BT2. 1800-2300
Wed-Sat. Pizzas, pasta.

Vico's Refettorio ⚲
10 Brunswick St, BT2.
☎ 321447. 1230-1430 Mon-
Sat, 1900-2200 Sun. Pasta,
steaks. Italian. ££.

ANTICA ROMA

RESTAURANT

NOW OPEN FOR LUNCH

67/69 Botanic Avenue, Belfast BT7 1JL
☎ (01232) 311121 Fax (01232) 310787

Ashoka

Now under new management

• *Award-winning Restaurant* •

FULLY LICENSED • Parties & Banquets

• *a la carte menu also available* • *booking advisable* • *extensive wine list* •

Opening hours: Mon-Sat 5.30- 11.30pm, Sun 5.30-10.30pm

★ *Free bottle of wine for parties of 4 or more* ★

• **New tea room opening early 1999** •

363/365 Lisburn Road, Belfast. Tel: (01232) 660362 - Fax: (01232) 660228

University and Malone (BT7 & 9) (STD 01232)

Acapulco ♀
75 Botanic Avenue, BT7.
☎ 319422. 0800-2200 Mon-Fri, until 2230 Sat, 0900-1500 Sun. Breakfast. Thai stir fry, roast pimento. ££.

All That Jazz ♠
241 Lisburn Rd, BT9
☎669191. 0930-2400 Mon-Sat. Crispy duck, pigeon casserole, creme brulée. Live entertainment weekends. ££££

★ **ANTICA ROMA** ♀
67 Botanic Avenue, BT7.
☎ 311121. 1200-1430 Mon-Fri, 1830-2300 Mon-Sat. Seafood salad, veal escalope with cheese & ham filling. £££.

Ashbrooke Cottage
35 Botanic Avenue, BT7.
☎ 245321. 0745-1700 Mon-Sat. Scones, toast, quiche, lasagne.

★ **ASHOKA** ♀
363 Lisburn Rd, BT9.
☎ 660362. 1730-2330 Mon-Sat, 1730-2230 Sun. Indian & European. £££.

Attic ♠
54 Stranmillis Rd, BT9.
☎ 661074. 1100-1500 & 1700-2230 Mon-Sun. Steaks, chicken, fish. £££.

Beatrice Kennedy's ♀
44 University Rd, BT7.
☎ 202290. 1700-2230 Mon-Sun. Game terrine, potato salad & pesto.

★ **BENGAL BRASSERIE** ♀
339 Ormeau Rd, BT7.
☎ 647516. 1200-1400 & 1730-2315 Mon-Sat, until 2215 Sun. Indian, European. £££.

Bishops
32 Bradbury Place, BT7.
☎ 311827. 1100-0300 Mon-Sun. Gourmet fish & chips.

Bluebells
50 Botanic Avenue, BT7.
☎ 322662. 0800-2230 Mon-Sat, 1000-1800 Sun. Quiche, salads, cakes.

Bob Cratchit's ♀
Russell Court, 38 Lisburn Rd, BT9. ☎ 332526. 1200-1430 Mon-Tues, until 1830 Wed-Sat. Lasagne, club sandwich. £.

★ **BONNIE'S MUSEUM CAFÉ**
11a Stranmillis Rd. ☎ 664914. 0900-2300 Mon-Thur, until 0130 Fri-Sun. Fisherman's pie, paté, soup, baguettes.

Bookfinders
47 University Rd, BT7.
☎ 328269. 1000-1730 Mon-Sat. Soup, toasties, pasta with courgettes. In bookshop.

Botanic Inn ♀
23 Malone Rd, BT9.
☎ 660460. 1200-1500 Mon-Sat, 1230-1430 Sun. Grills, pub grub. Tapas menu 1600-2300 Mon-Sat.

Café Bongo ♀
42 Malone Rd, BT7.
☎ 663667. 1700-2300 Mon-Sun. Thai green chicken curry, vegetarian dippers. E£.

Café Clementine ♦
245 Lisburn Rd, BT9.
☎ 382211. 0930-1630 Mon, until 2230 Tues-Sat, 1000-1530 & 1830-2100 Sun. Brioche with chicken livers, blue cheese soufflé. E££.

Café Montmartre
102 Stranmillis Rd, BT9.
☎ 668032. 1100-2300 Mon-Sat. Fish & chips, grills.

Café Vincents ♦
78 Botanic Avenue, BT7.
☎ 242020. 0900-2300 Mon-Thur & Sun, until 2400 Fri-Sat. Grills, pasta. E££.

★ CARGOES
613 Lisburn Rd, BT9.
☎ 665451. 0900-1700 Mon-Sat. Mediterranean salads, prawn paté, cinnamon scones. Café in delicatessen.

Chelsea ♀
346 Lisburn Rd, BT9. ☎ 665136. 1200-1800 Mon-Wed, until 2000 Thur-Sat. Pizza, salads.

★ CHEZ DELBART ♀
10 Bradbury Place, BT7.
☎ 238020. 1700-2400 Tues-Sat, until 2130 Sun. Mixed kebabs, savoury & sweet pancakes. E££.

Cloisters
Queen's University,
1 Elmwood Avenue, BT9.
☎ 324803. 0900-2100 Mon-
Sat. Refectory in student's
union building. Must book.

Conversations ⊙
141 Stranmillis Rd, BT9.
☎ 664212. 0900-1700 Mon-
Sat. Prawn salad, chilli,
banoffi, coffee.

Cutter's Wharf ⬚
Lockview Rd, Stranmillis BT9.
☎ 663388. Bar 1200-1430
Mon-Sun. Irish stew, Ulster fry.
Restaurant 1200-2230 Mon-
Fri, 1800-2230 Sat. Apple &
cheese flan, seafood. E££.

Dignity
112 Lisburn Rd, BT9.
☎ 666537. 0900-1700 Mon-
Sat. Coffee, pies, salads.

Dragon City ⬚
82 Botanic Avenue, BT7.
☎ 439590. 1200-2400 Mon-
Sun, closed Wed. Cantonese.
E££.

Dragon Palace ⬚
16 Botanic Avenue, BT7.
☎ 323869. 1200-1400 &
1700-2400 Mon-Thur, until
0100 Fri-Sat. 2400 Sun. Peking
& European. E££.

★ DUKES HOTEL ⬚
65 University St, BT7.
☎ 236666. Last orders 2130.
Glenarm salmon, Bushmills
whiskey beef. E££.

Ebony Coffee Shop 🍶
727 Lisburn Rd, BT9.
☎ 660855. 0900-1700 Mon-
Sat, 1700-2200 Wed-Sat,
0900-1500. Irish breakfast,
croissants, beef goulash,
peppered pork.

Eglantine Inn ⬚
32 Malone Rd, BT9.
☎ 381994. 1200-2000 Mon-
Sat. Pub grub.

Elms ⬚
36 University Rd, BT7.
☎ 322106. 1100-1800 Mon-
Sat. Champ, stew, ribs, chilli.
Live music.

Empire ⬚
42 Botanic Avenue, BT7.
☎ 328110. 1200-2000 Mon-
Sat. Pizza, pasta. Bar in former
variety theatre.

Errigle Inn ⬚
320 Ormeau Rd, BT7.
☎ 641410. 1130-1430 &
1700-2330 Mon-Fri, 1130-
2300 Sat, 1230-2200 Sun. Pub
grub. A la carte. Roof garden.
Live music. E£

Fitzy's ⬚
25 University Rd, BT7.
☎ 247725. 1700-2300 Mon-
Sun. Pasta, steak, vegetarian.
E££.

Four in Hand ⬚
116 Lisburn Rd, BT9.
☎ 665440. 1200-1500 Mon-
Fri. Pub grub.

Beatrice Kennedy

We all deserve those little rewards,
so why not try our seasonal menu at..

Beatrice Kennedy's Quality Dining

We will be pleased to serve you in our comfortable period restaurant,
just what you deserve, an enjoyable evening out.
Open 7 evenings a week,
for reservations ☎ 01232 202290
Kennedy Room available for larger parties and functions

44 University Road, Belfast BT7 1NJ

http://ds.dial.pipex.com/town/park/gcu25 - E-mail: beatricekennedy@dial.pipex.com

---

MANGE TOUS

Café . Bistro
30 University Road, Belfast BT7 1NH

*'...in the heart of the
University area...'*

Open:
Mon-Sat 1100 to 2300
Sunday 1230 to 2200

TEL: (01232) 222722
For Bookings

Open 7 days a week
All major Credit Cards accepted

THE STRAND
**12 STRANMILLIS ROAD
BELFAST BT9 5AA**
☎ **(01232) 682266**
Fax **(01232) 663189**

The original and still the best
OPEN 7 DAYS PER WEEK

**BUSINESSMAN'S LUNCH £4.95
& LITE BITE SPECIAL £7.95**

Served Mon - Sat 1200-1900

EXTENSIVE WINE LIST

BREAKFAST AT THE STRAND
Served Sat 1000-1230 Sun 1000-1230

SUNDAY AT THE STRAND
3 Course Lunch
Children welcome

Full à la carte menu is also available
*Mackintosh Lounge available
for private parties*

** *Egon Ronay recommended 1985 - 1997*

French Village
70 Stranmillis Rd, BT9.
☎ 381671. 0915-1715 Mon-Sat. Lasagne, stew, soup, rolls, sandwiches, coffees.

★ FRIAR'S BUSH 🍷
159 Stranmillis Rd, BT9.
☎ 669824. 1900-2200 Tues-Sat. Terrine of wild venison, pork in cider, turbot. £££.

Gandhi's 🍷
701 Lisburn Rd. BT9.
☎ 683760. 1700-2330 Mon-Sun. Indian & European. E£.

Gigolo's Restaurant 🍷
23 Donegall Pass, BT7.
☎ 246900. 1700-2330 Mon-Sat. Italian. ££.

Good World 🍷
627 Lisburn Rd, BT9.
☎ 666821. 1200-1400 Mon-Sat, 1700-2400 Mon-Thur & Sun, until 0100 Fri-Sat. Chinese & European. E£.

Graffiti
258 Ormeau Rd, BT7.
☎ 693300. 1000-2200 Mon-Sat, 1100-1500 Sun. Breakfast, pasta, steak.

Holiday Inn Express 🍷
106 University St. ☎ 311909.
0700-1000 Mon-Fri, until 2330 Sat & Sun. Breakfast. Supreme of chicken with ginger and mushroom sauce, passion cake, profiteroles with chocolate sauce. E££.

Hong Kong 🍷
361 Ormeau Rd, BT7.
☎ 491621. 1200-1400 Mon-Sat, 1700-2400 Mon-Thur & Sun, until 0100 Fri. Peking, Cantonese & European. E£.

Interno
613 Lisburn Rd, BT9.
☎ 662224. 0800-1630 Mon-Fri, 0900-1800 Sat, until 1500 Sun. Chicken pies, fries, toasties. Paintings for sale.

Isibeal's
699 Lisburn Rd, BT9.
☎ 682726. 1200-2400 Mon-Sat. Fast food.

Jharna Tandoori 🍷
133 Lisburn Rd, BT9.
☎ 381299. 1200-1400 & 1730-2330 Mon-Sat, until 2300 Sun. Indian. E££.

Just Cooking
332 Lisburn Rd. ☎ 682810.
0900-1645 Mon-Sat. Casseroles, home-made soup, wheaten bread.

Kentucky Fried Chicken
1 Bradbury Place, BT7.
☎ 325129. 1000-0230 Mon-Tues, until 0400 Wed-Sat, 0300 Sun. Fast food.

King's Head 🍷
829 Lisburn Rd, BT7 (opposite King's Hall). ☎ 660455. 1200-1430 Mon-Sat. Chilli, lasagne, open sandwiches.

La Salsa ♿
23 University Rd, BT7.
☎ 244588. 1700-2300 Mon-Sat, until 2230 Sun. Mexican.

Lavery's ♿
12 Bradbury Place, BT7.
☎ 327159. 1200-1700 Mon-Fri, until 1500 Sat. Pub grub.

Legends ♿
133 Lisburn Rd, BT9.
☎ 661652. 1730-2400 Mon-Sat, 1700-2300 Sun. Pizza, pasta, steaks.

★ MAD HATTER ◉
2 Eglantine Avenue, BT9.
☎ 681005. 0900-1715 Mon-Sat, 1100-1600 Sun. Quiche, lasagne, gâteaux.

Madison's ♿
59 Botanic Avenue, BT17.
☎ 330040. 0700-2300 Mon-Sun. Breakfast. Confit of duck, sirloin steak, pasta, warm salads. E£.

Maharaja ♿
62 Botanic Avenue, BT7.
☎ 234200. 1200-1400 & 1700-2345 Mon-Sat, 1630- 2300 Sun. Indian & European. E££.

Malone House ♿
Barnett Demesne, BT9.
☎ 681246. 0930-1730 Mon-Sat. Morning coffee, set lunch, afternoon tea. Gourmet menu 1830-2130 Fri & Sat. E££.

Malone Lodge Hotel ♿
60 Eglantine Avenue, BT9.
☎ 382409. 1200-1400 & 1830-2200 Mon-Sat. Steak, fish, chicken.

★ MALONEY'S ♿
33 Malone Rd, BT9.
☎ 682929. 1200-2300 Mon-Sat, until 2200 Sun. Chicken breast stuffed with tiger prawns, seafood pasta. ££.

Mandarin Palace ♿
157 Upper Lisburn Rd.
☎ 622142. 1200-1400 Mon-Fri, 1700-2400 Mon-Sun. Cantonese & European. E£.

Mangetous ♿
30 University Rd, BT7.
☎ 222722. 1100-2300 Mon-Sat, 1230-2200 Sun. Pasta, fish, chicken, vegetarian. ££.

Manhattan ♿
23 Bradbury Place, BT7.
☎ 233131. 1200-2200 Mon-Sat. Clam chowder, cajun chicken. E£.

★ MANOR HOUSE ♿
47 Donegall Pass, BT7.
☎ 238755. 1200-1400 Mon-Fri, 1700-2330 Mon-Sun. Exotic Chinese, Cantonese. E££.

McDonald's
24 Bradbury Place, BT7.
☎ 332400. 1000-0200 Sun-Wed, until 0300 Thur-Sat. Fast food.

McErlean's
353 Ormeau Rd, BT7.
☎ 205037. 0800-1730 Mon-Fri.
Breakfast, snacks. In home
bakery

Metro Brasserie ♀
13 Lower Crescent, BT7.
☎ 323349. 1200-1500 & 1800-
2200 Mon-Sat ex Sat lunch.
Crostini of salmon with
sundried tomato mayonnaise,
Indian mango cheesecake with
fresh coconut sorbet. M££.

★ MIZUNA
99 Botanic Avenue, BT7.
☎ 230063. 1800-2230 Mon-Sat,
until 2100 Sun. Salmon,
chargrilled lamb, cheesecake.
E£££.

Mortar Board
3 Fitzwilliam St, BT9.
☎ 310313. 0900-1700 Mon-Sat,
until 2300 Thur. Salads, quiche,
coffee.

O'Hara's
3 Botanic Avenue, BT7.
☎ 326567. 0830-1730 Mon-Sat.
Coffee shop in bakery.
Sandwiches, pies.

★ OPUS ONE ♀
1 University St, BT7.
☎ 590101. 1200-2300 Mon-
Sun, later opening Sat. Sundried tomato and goat's cheese
ravioli, sea bass, rack of lamb.

Pavilion ♀
296 Ormeau Rd. ☎ 641545.
1200-1430 & 1700-2200 Mon-
Sun. Grills, salads, set lunch. E£.

Planks ♣
479 Lisburn Rd, BT9.
☎ 663211. 0900-1430 Mon-
Sun, 1800-2230 Mon-Sat.
Chicken with sage & onion,
pork with peppered sauce.
E££.

Queen's Espresso
17 Botanic Avenue, BT7.
☎ 325327. 0900-1730 Mon-
Sat. Grills, salads, toasties,
coffee.

Queen's University
Great Hall, Lanyon Building,
University Rd, BT7. ☎ 245133.
1015-1130 & 1200-1400 Mon-
Fri. Lunch. Coffee, afternoon
tea.

Rajput ♀
461 Lisburn Rd, BT9.
☎ 662168. 1200-1400 &
1700-2400 Mon-Sat, until
2300 Sun. Set meals, à la
carte. Indian. E££.

Randals
569 Lisburn Rd, BT9.
☎ 682600. 0900-1600 Mon-
Sat. Lunch, coffee, home
cooking.

Renshaws Hotel ♀
75 University St. BT7.
☎ 333366. Last orders 2230.
A la carte. E£.

Royal Sandwich Bar
152 Lisburn Rd, BT9.
☎ 687515. 0800-1600 Mon-
Sat. Sandwiches, baguettes,
salads.

La Salsa specialises in authentic Mexican cuisine.
Our chef makes frequent trips to Latin America
to source new ideas and ingredients
- we currently use 12 different types of chillies
in our dishes.

These culinary delights are complemented by
a tempting range of cocktails and wine
(frozen margaritas are a speciality!)

La Salsa is designed in traditional Mexican style
to create a true hacienda ambience. Mariachi
music ensures a fantastic Latino experience.

La Salsa is fully licensed and open 7 nights
a week from 1700. Live flamenco guitar
music is a feature every Wednesday downstairs.

LA SALSA MEXICAN RESTAURANT
23 UNIVERSITY RD, BELFAST BT7 1NA
☎ **01232 244588 FAX 01232 278788**

Ruby Tuesday's ☐
157 Stranmillis Rd, BT9.
☎ 667749. 1200-1530 &
1700-2330 Mon-Sat, 1700-
2100 Sun. Steaks, beef,
pastrami salad, seafood. ££.

Ruby Tuesday's ♦
629a Lisburn Rd, BT9.
☎ 661220. 0815-2230 Mon-
Sun. Breakfast. Ulster fry,
pasta, chicken, salads.

Scarlet's Bistro ♦
423 Lisburn Rd. ☎ 683102.
1000-2000 Sun-Tues, until
2200 Wed-Sat. Wild Irish
salmon in filo, hot baguette
wth strips of sirloin & sauteed
onions. £££.

Somewhere Different ♦
393 Ormeau Rd. ☎ 648888.
0800-2300 Mon-Sun.
Breakfast. Fish, steak, baked
potatoes, vegetarian, teas.

Spuds
37 Bradbury Place, BT7.
☎ 331541. 1000-0100 Mon-
Sun. Baked potatoes.

Stables Restaurant
Upper Malone Rd (in Dixon
Park). ☎ 601087. 1000-1730
Mon-Sun. Soups, stew, scones.

★ **STRAND** ☐
12 Stranmillis Rd, BT9.
☎ 682266. 1200-2300 Mon-
Sat, until 2130 Sun. Breakfast
1000-1230 Sat-Sun. Irish lamb
noisettes, stuffed baked
aubergine. ££.

★ **SUN KEE** ♦
38 Donegall Pass, BT7.
☎ 312016. 1700-0100 Sun-
Thur, 1700-2330 Sat. Chinese,
very ethnic. £££.

Taj Mahal ☐
96 Botanic Avenue, BT7.
☎ 313999. 1730-2330 Mon-
Sat, until 2300 Sun. Indian &
European. ££.

Terrace ☐
253 Lisburn Rd, BT9.
☎ 381655. Wine bar bistro
1900-0100 Mon-Sat.
Restaurant 1200-1430 & 1800-
2230 Mon-Sun. Smoked
salmon, brill with prawns &
dill butter, stuffed duck. £££.

The Cello Restaurant ♦
164 Lisburn Rd, BT9.
☎ 667960. 1000-1600 Mon-
Fri. Smoked haddock in a
cucumber boat. Kids menu.

The Fly ☐
5 Lower Crescent, BT7.
☎ 246878. 1200-1430 Mon-
Sat. pub grub.

Three Bears
455 Ormeau Rd, BT7.
☎ 491636. 0900-1630 Mon-
Sat. Shepherd's pie, quiche,
open sandwiches, banoffi pie.
Café above fashion shop.

Ulster Museum
11a Stranmillis Rd, BT9.
☎ 383000. 1000-1630 Mon-
Sat, 1430-1630 Sun. Soups,
chilli, pies, vegetarian, all
home made.

Ventnor's Sandwich Bar
73 Botanic Avenue, BT7.
☎ 241191. 0900-1730 Mon-Fri, until 1600 Sat. Gourmet sandwiches to order.

★ **VILLA ITALIA** ♁

39 University Rd, BT7.
☎ 328356. 1730-2330 Mon-Fri, 1600-2330 Sat, 1600-2230 Sun. Italian. ££.

★ **WELCOME** ♁

22 Stranmillis Rd, BT9.
☎ 381359. 1200-1400 & 1700-2330 Mon-Fri, 1730-2300 Sat, 1730-2230 Sun. Chinese & European. £££.

Wellington Park Hotel ♁
21 Malone Rd, BT9. ☎ 381111.
Last orders 2145. Dressed crab, steaks. £££.

East of the River
(BT4-6, 8, 16 & 23)
(STD 01232)

Alden's ♀
229 Upper Newtownards Rd.
1200-1500 & 1800-2200 Tues-
Thur, until 2300 Fri, 1800-
2300 Sat, 1200-1600 Sun.
Parma ham & melon, fish,
steak. Extensive wine list. £££.

Avenue One ♀
175 Newtownards Rd, BT4.
☎ 455608. 1130-1500, 1700-
2200 Mon-Sat. Pub grub.

Avoniel Leisure Centre
Avoniel Rd, BT5. ☎ 451564.
1030-2200 Mon-Fri, 1000-
1600 Sat & Sun. Chilli,
sandwiches, home baking.

Barnett's at the Mill ♀
231 Belfast Rd, Dundonald.
☎ 480117. Coffee shop: 1000-
1700 Mon-Sun. Restaurant
1700-2130 Tues-Sun. Sauté of
breast of chicken with spicy
yellow pepper puree. Beside
garden centre.

Beechill Inn ♀
Cedarhurst Rd, BT8.
☎ 693193. 1230-1430 &
1700-2000 Mon-Fri, 1230-
2000 Sat. Bistro. £.

Belfast City Airport ♀
Airport Rd, BT3. ☎ 457745.
0600-2000 7 days. All-day
breakfast, snacks.

Belmont ♀
295 Upper Newtownards Rd,
BT4. ☎ 652295. 1230-1430
Mon-Sat. Pub grub.

Bethany
246 Newtownards Rd, BT4.
☎ 54498. 1130-2245 Mon-Fri,
until 1945 Sat. Fish & chips,
coffee, scones, ice cream.

Bunch of Grapes ♀
72 Beersbridge Rd, BT5.
☎ 457332. 1200-1430 &
1100-2130 Mon-Sat. Pub grub.

Capers ♨
313 Upper Newtownards Rd,
BT5. ☎ 655550. 1700-2300
Thur-Sun. Pizzas, salads.

Castle
152 Castlereagh Rd, BT5.
☎ 731461. 1200-1400 &
1600-2245 Mon-Thur, 1200-
2245 Fri-Sat. Grills.

Chatters Coffee House
64 Bloomfield Avenue, BT5.
☎ 731654. 0930-1645 Mon-
Sat. Scones, lunch.

Coffee Pot
340 Newtownards Rd, BT4.
☎ 655415. 0730-1600 Mon-
Fri, until 1330 Wed, 1630 Sat.
Soup, stew, desserts.

Cosy Bar ⚲
44 Omeath St, BT6.
☎ 458178. 1130-2400 Thur-
Sat. Set lunch. Pub grub.

Desano's
344 Newtownards Rd, BT4.
☎ 451608. 1200-2000 Tues &
Thur-Sun in summer, Fri-Sun
only in winter. Ice cream
parlour.

Dundonald Ice Bowl
Dundonald, BT16. ☎ 482611.
1400-2200 Mon-Thur, from
1000 Fri-Sun. Burgers, chips.

Dundonald Old Mill
231 Belfast Rd, Dundonald,
BT16. ☎ 480117. 1000-1700
Mon-Sat, 1100-1700 Sun.
Quiche, lasagne, pastries.
Restored waterwheel, craft
shop.

★ **THE EASTENDER** ⚲
237 Woodstock Rd, BT6.
☎ 732443. 1130-2145 Mon-
Sat. Baked ham with black
velvet sauce, champ, home-
made soup. E£.

Eda Inn ⚲
41 Belmont Rd, BT4.
☎ 658810. 1700-2330 Mon-
Sun. Chinese & European. E££.

★ **ELK INN** ⚲
793 Upper Newtownards Rd,
Dundonald, BT16. ☎ 480004.
1130-2330 Mon-Sat. Irish hot
pot, baked gammon, banoffi
pie. E££.

★ **FILLERS COFFEE SHOP** ⊙
233 Saintfield Rd, BT8.
☎ 701409. 1000-1730 Mon-
Sat, until 1900 Thur & Fri.
Lasagne, salads, apple pie.

★ **FOUR WINDS INN** ⚲
111 Newton Park, Saintfield Rd,
BT8. ☎ 401957. 1200-1430 &
1900-2200 Mon-Sat. Closed
Easter & Christmas. Hot & cold
lunch buffet. A la carte. Open
fires. M£, E£££.

Fusco's
369 Woodstock Rd, BT6.
☎ 288242. 1030-2130 Mon-
Sun. Italian. Ice cream.

Giant Sandwich Company
91a Cregagh Rd, BT6.
☎ 469990. 0930-1630 Mon-
Sat. Breakfast, gourmet
sandwiches.

Gypsy Queen Café ▮
361a Ormeau Rd (entrance in
Deramore Avenue). ☎ 640818.
1000-1500 & 1800-2200 Tues-
Sat, 1100-2000 Sun. Parsnip &
walnut croquettes, moussaka,
mushroom tagliatelle.

Hillmount Nursery Centre
Gardener's Rest. 56 Upper
Braniel Rd, BT5. ☎ 448213.
0900-1700 Mon-Sat, from
1400 Sun. Soups, pies, pasties,
sandwiches.

Holly's
74 Holywood Rd, BT4.
☎ 653345. 0830-1630 Mon-
Wed, until 2200 Thur-Sat.
Chicken & ham pie, steaks.

Hong Kong ☕
King's Rd Shopping Centre,
9 King's Square, BT5.
☎ 792560. 1200-1400 Mon-
Sat, 1700-2400 Mon-Sun.
Chinese & European.

La Mon House Hotel ☕
41 Gransha Rd, BT23.
☎ 448631. Last orders 2200
Mon-Sat, 2100 Sun. Buffet
lunch, carvery Sun. A la carte.
M£, E£££.

Leaf & Berry
516 Upper Newtownards Rd,
BT4. ☎ 471774. 0930-1630
Mon-Fri, 1000-1600 Sat.
Speciality coffees, lunch.

Melting Pot ☕
38 Mountpottinger Rd, BT5.
☎ 454080. 1200-1430 Mon-
Sat. Pub grub.

**Mount Ober Golf
& Ski Club** ☕
24 Ballymaconaghy Rd.
☎ 792100. 1200-2130 Mon-
Sat, 1200-1800 Sun. Grills.
A la carte.

Mr J.D.'s
222 Newtownards Rd, BT4.
☎ 458383. 1130-1900 Mon-
Sat. Fish & chips.

Mr Pickwick's Kitchen
Connswater Shopping Centre,
BT5. ☎ 459965. 0900-1730
Mon-Sat, until 2100 Wed-Fri.
Baked potatoes, Irish stew.

Neighbours Coffee Shop
10 Cregagh Rd, BT6. 1030-
1630 Mon-Sat. Lasagne, home-
made pies, curries.

Old Moat Inn ☕
933 Upper Newtownards Rd,
☎ 480753. 1200-1500 & 1700-
2130 Mon-Sat. 1700-2030
Sun. Steak, burgers.

Park Avenue Hotel ☕
158 Holywood Rd, BT4.
☎ 656520. 1200-2100 Mon-
Sat, until 1930 Sun. Closed
Christmas. Smoked salmon,
grilled halibut, steaks, roasts.
A la carte. E££.

Piggly Wiggly's ♠
Library Court, 3 Eastleigh
Drive, Upper Newtownards
Rd, BT4. ☎ 672114. 0930-
1700 & 1900-2200 Mon-Sat.

Pizza House ☕
991 Upper Newtownards Rd,
BT16. ☎ 482533. 1200-1400 &
1700-2300 Mon-Sun. Pizzas.

Poppins ◠
241 Upper Newtownards Rd,
BT4. ☎ 671893. 0900-1630
Mon-Sat. Pies, quiche, pizza.

Quarry Inn ☕
1095 Upper Newtownards Rd,
BT4. ☎ 480492. 1200-1500 &
1800-2130 Mon-Sat, 1230-
1930 Sun. Carvery, bistro. E££.

Queen's Inn ☕
King's Square, King's Rd, BT5.
☎ 792395. 1200-1500 Mon-
Sat. Set lunch, pub grub.

Rendezvous
443 Newtownards Rd, BT4.
☎ 451100. 0900-1600 Mon-
Sat. Home-baked pies, salads.

Ritchie's
142 Castlereagh Rd, BT5.
☎ 457318. 1200-1400 &
1630-1900 Mon-Sat. Fish &
chips.

Robinson Centre
Montgomery Rd, BT6.
☎ 703948. 1000-2200 Mon-
Fri, 1800 Sat, 1400-1800 Sun.
Pasta, chicken kiev, potato
skins, salads.

Rose Bowl
59 Belmont Rd, BT4.
☎ 652895. 0930-1630 Mon-
Sat. Soup, sandwiches, quiche.

Rosetta ⬙
75 Rosetta Rd, BT6. ☎ 649297.
1230-1430 Mon-Sat, 1900-
2100 Thur-Sat. Pub grub.

Scoffs Coffee House
52 Bloomfield Avenue, BT5.
☎ 450183. 0800-1730 Mon-
Sat. Ulster ham, champ, home-
made scones.

Shanghai ◗
18 Holywood Rd, BT4.
☎ 650400. 1200-1400 Mon-
Sat, 1700-2400 Mon-Sun.
Chinese & European.

Silver Leaf
15 Belmont Rd, BT4.
☎ 471164. 1200-1400 &
1600-2230 Mon-Fri, 1600-
2000 Sat. Fish & chips.

★ **STORMONT HOTEL** ⬙
587 Upper Newtownards Rd,
BT4. ☎ 658621. 1200-2200
Mon-Sun. Brasserie salads,
open sandwiches. A la carte.
E£££.

Stormont Inn ⬙
165 Holywood Rd, BT4.
☎ 654509. 1230-1500 Mon-
Sat. Pub grub.

Sugar 'n' Spice
12c Comber Rd, Dundonald.
☎ 484814. 0830-1700 Mon-
Sat. Soups, pies.

Weaver's Cafe
44 Montgomery Rd, BT6.
☎ 403200. 0930-1700 Mon-
Sat. Quiche, pies, salads,
bakes. In Ulster Weavers'
factory shop.

Wellworths
1009 Upper Newtownards Rd,
BT16. ☎ 481118. 0900-1700
Mon-Sat, until 2100 Wed-Fri.
Grills, snacks. Restaurant in
chainstore.

Willows
273 Woodstock Rd, BT6.
☎ 458210. 0900-1645 Mon-
Sat. Toasties, salad, chips,
coffee.

North and West of the River
(BT10-15 & 17)
(STD 01232)

Alexandra ⚲
1 York Rd, BT15. ☎ 742838.
1230-1430 Thur-Sat, 1900-
2200 Sat. Pub grub.

Andersonstown Leisure Centre
Andersonstown Rd, BT11.
☎ 625211. 1100-2200 Mon-
Fri, until 1600 Sat-Sun. Chilli,
sandwiches.

Arnie's
Balmoral Fruit Market,
Boucher Rd, BT12. ☎ 663282.
0600-1500 Mon-Sat. Champ,
roasted ham shank, Arnie's fry.

Ballysillan Leisure Centre
71 Ballysillan Rd, BT14.
☎ 391040. NGs: 1000-2200
Mon-Fri, until 1600 Sat, 1100-
1700 Sun. Pies, stew,
sandwiches.

Balmoral Hotel ⚲
Blacks Rd, BT10. ☎ 301234.
1130-2300 Mon-Sat, 1230-
2200 Sun. Grill bar, restaurant.
Steaks, fish. A la carte E££.

Bay Leaf
Unit 48, Park Centre, Donegall
Rd, BT12. ☎ 235773. 1000-
1730 Mon-Tues, until 2000
Wed-Fri, 1930 Sat, 1300-1700
Sun. Set lunch, grills, snacks.

Beattie's Supper Saloon
220 Shankill Rd, BT13.
☎ 240273. 1000-1800 Mon-
Sat. Fish & chips.

Beechmount Leisure Centre
281 Falls Rd, BT11. ☎ 328631.
1200-1500 & 1800-2100
Mon-Fri, 1000-1500 Sat-Sun.
Fast food.

**Belfast Castle – Ben Madigan
Restaurant** ⚲
Antrim Rd, BT15. ☎ 776925.
1200-1430 Sunday lunch.
Roast beef, chicken, lamb.
Restaurant overlooks Belfast
and Belfast Lough. £.

Belfast Castle – Cellar ⚲
Antrim Rd, BT15. ☎ 776925.
1100-1430 & 1830-2145 Mon-
Sat. Morning coffee, afternoon
tea, baked chicken, salmon.
Roast guinea fowl, ostrich E££.

Belfast Zoo
Antrim Rd, BT15. ☎ 776277.
Ark: 1000-1730 Mon-Sun,
until 1600 in winter. Plaice,
chicken, sandwiches.
Mountain Tea House: 1030-
1700 Mon-Sun Easter-Aug,
weekends only Sept. Ice
cream, pastries, sandwiches.

Ben Madigan ⚲
192 Cavehill Rd, BT15.
☎ 711904. 1230-1500 Mon-
Sat. Pub grub.

Big Boppers Inn
118 Antrim Rd, BT15.
☎ 752022. 1900-2300 Fri-Sat,
1200-1500 & 2100-0130 Sun.
Fish, beef stroganoff, chicken,
E£.

Blackstaff Bar ⚲
149 Springfield Rd, BT12.
☎ 324355. 1200-1500 &
1700-2000 Mon-Sat. Pub grub.

Burger Bar
119 Andersonstown Rd, BT11.
☎ 611465. 1200-2400 Mon-
Wed & Sun, until 0100 Thur-
Sat. Fast food.

Burger King
Yorkgate, York St, BT15.
☎ 746060. 0900-2400 Mon-
Thur, until 0100 Fri-Sat, 1400-
2300 Sun. Fast food.

Cassidy's Bar ⚲
347 Antrim Rd, BT15.
☎ 745208. 0900-1500 Mon-
Sat, until 2000 Sun.

Circus Bar ⚲
10 Antrim Rd, BT15.
☎ 351610. 1200-1500 Mon-
Sat. Salads, lasagne.

Coffee House
132 Andersonstown Rd, BT11.
☎ 617155. 0830-1730 Mon-
Sat. Quiche, lasagne, pies.

Concepts
100 York St, BT15. ☎ 743873.
1000-1800 Mon-Tues, until
2100 Wed-Fri, 0900-1800 Sat.
Baked potatoes, quiche.

Cosy Grill
81 Upper Lisburn Rd, Finaghy,
BT10. ☎ 613555. 0930-2000
Mon-Sat. Home-made soup,
chicken & broccoli bake. E£.

Country Fayre
294 Limestone Rd, BT15.
☎ 740919. 0900-1630 Mon-
Sat. Ulster fry, grills.

Cultúrlann
216 Falls Rd, BT12.
☎ 245255. 1000-1700 Mon-
Sat. Soup, wheaten bread,
salads. Café in arts centre. Irish
spoken. Menu in Irish.

Devenish Arms ⚲
37 Finaghy Rd North, BT10.
☎ 301479. 1200-1430 Wed-
Fri, 1700-2130 Mon-Sat,
1230-1430 & 1700-2030 Sun.
Soups, steak, lasagne, mixed
grill, scampi, chicken kiev. E£.

Devine's
297 Antrim Rd, BT15.
☎ 747604. 0900-1800 Mon-
Sat. Sandwiches, stew.

Dicey Reilly's ⚲
123 New Lodge Rd, BT15.
☎ 746371. 1200-1530 Mon-
Sun. Champ, stew.

Ed's Bread
6 Shaw's Rd, BT11. ☎ 612077.
0900-1700 Mon-Sat. Irish
stew, pasties, sandwiches

Fatty Arbuckle's ⍾
Yorkgate, York St, BT15. 1100-
2200 Mon-Thur, until 2230
Fri-Sat. 1200-2200 Sun.
Steaks, hamburgers, chilli,
chicken, salads, vegetarian.
American diner. £.

Fernhill Restaurant ⍾
Glencairn Rd, BT13.
☎ 713076/715599. 1000-1500
Mon-Sat, 1900-2200 Fri & Sat,
1200-1700 Sun. Steak, roast
beef, trout. Restaurant in
converted stables, adjacent to
People's Museum. E£.

Fiddler's Inn ⍾
11 Kennedy Way, BT11.
☎ 605094. 1200-1500 &
1900-2200 Mon-Sat, 1200-
1700 Sun. Pub grub.

Fortwilliam Lodge ⍾
2 Fortwilliam Park, BT15.
☎ 370537. 1030-1700 Mon-
Sat. Quiche, coffee, home-
baked bread, cakes.

Francie's ⍾
12 Ardoyne Avenue, BT14.
☎ 742325. 1200-1500 Mon-
Sat, 1800-2330 Wed-Sat,
1230-1400. 1900-2100 Sun.
Pub grub.

Fulton's Fine Furnishings
Boucher Crescent, BT12.
☎ 382168. 0930-1730 Mon-
Sat, until 2100 Thur. Salmon,
chicken & broccoli bake,
home-made scones. Coffee
shop in store.

Gallery
333 Crumlin Rd, BT14.
☎ 745408. 0900-1500 Mon-
Thur, until 1400 Fri. Toasties,
soup.

Glenowen Inn ⍾
108 Glen Rd, BT11.
☎ 613224. 1230-1430 Mon-
Sun, 1800-2230 Mon-Thur
(2330 Fri-Sat), 1900-2200 Sun.
Set meals. E££.

Glenview Arms ⍾
167 Oldpark Rd, BT14.
☎ 745455. 1200-1400 Mon-
Sat. Pub grub.

Golden Bloom
124 Upper Lisburn Rd, BT10.
☎ 798661. 0800-1730 Mon-
Sat. Pizzas, quiche, pies.

Gourmet Foods
648 Antrim Rd, BT15.
☎ 778263. 0800-1900 Mon-
Fri. Moussaka, roast beef,
lamb.

Grove Leisure Centre
York Rd, BT15. ☎ 351599.
0900-2100 Mon-Fri, 1000-
1600 Sat-Sun. Salads, lasagne,
grills.

Grove Tavern ⚲
203 York Rd, BT15. ☎ 771610.
1230-1430 Mon-Sat. Pub grub.

Harry Ramsden's ⚲
Yorkgate, York St, BT15.
☎ 749222. 1130-2230 Mon-
Thur, until 2300 Fri-Sat, 1230-
2230 Sun. Gourmet fish &
chips, desserts.

Heel & Ankle ⚲
346 Shankill Rd, BT13.
☎ 247488. 1200-1430, 1800-
·2100 Thur-Sat, 1300-1800
Sunday lunch. Steaks, salmon.

Julie-Ann's Bistro
49 Park Shopping Centre,
Donegall Rd ☎ 243534. 0900-
1730 Mon-Sat. Fast food.

Laurel Glen Roadhouse ⚲
Dairy Farm Lane, 208
Stewartstown Rd, BT11.
☎ 601737. 1200-1500 Mon-
Fri. Pub grub.

★ LONG'S FISH RESTAURANT
39 Athol St, BT12.
☎ 321848. 1145-1830 Mon-
Fri. Fish & chips.

Maginty's ♀
466 Antrim Rd, BT15.
☎ 779376. 1200-2200 Mon-
Sat, 1200-1630 & 1700-2100
Sun. Peppered steaks, roast
chicken with rosemary, chilli,
salads. M£.

McCabe's Ice Cream Parlour
129 Andersonstown Rd, BT11.
☎ 603303. 1200-2200 Mon-
Fri, from 1000 Sat-Sun. Fudge
cake, ice cream.

McEnaney's ♀
1 Glen Rd, BT11. ☎ 613951.
1130-1430 Mon-Sat. Pub grub.

McErlean's
456 Antrim Rd, BT15.
☎ 370759. 0830-1730 Mon-
Fri, 0900-1700 Sat. Cornish
pasties, curries.

Mile Cafeteria
351 Shankill Rd, BT13.
☎ 223350. 1000-2200 Mon-
Fri, until 1800 Sat. Salads,
pizzas, Ulster fry.

Moby Dick
Dargan Rd, BT3. ☎ 776208.
0800-1530 Mon-Fri. Grills.

Mount Inn ♀
156 North Queen St, BT15.
☎ 741769. 1200-1500 Mon-
Sat.

Muldoon's ♀
13 Corporation Square.
☎ 232415. 1200-1500 Mon-
Fri, until 1630 Sat. Pub grub.

Olympia Leisure Centre
Boucher Rd, BT12. ☎ 233369.
1000-1400 & 1600-2200
Mon-Fri, 1000-1600 Sat,
1200-1800 Sun. Fast food.

Opels Recreation Centre
41 Suffolk Rd, BT11.
☎ 601386. 0900-2100 Mon-
Fri. Fast food.

Paninaro
48D York St, BT15. ☎ 239333.
0700-1445 Mon-Fri.
Sandwiches, snacks, coffee.

Patio
Kennedy Centre, 564 Falls Rd,
BT12. ☎ 628118. 0900-2000
Mon-Fri, until 1730 Sat, 1100-
1730 Sun. Pies, lasagne.

Portside Inn ♀
Dargan Rd. ☎ 370746 1000-
1900 Mon-Fri, 1000-1800 Sat
& 1100-1900 Sun. Breakfast,
sandwiches, steak, fish,
vegetarian. Off Fortwilliam
roundabout.

Red Barn Barbeque
127 Andersonstown Rd, BT11.
☎ 625558. 1200-0030 Mon-
Sun. Fish & chips, pasties.

Rock Bar ♀
491 Falls Rd, BT12. ☎ 323741.
1200-2200 Mon-Sat. Pub grub.

Rocktown Bar ♀
120 Great George's St, BT15.
☎ 242414. 1200-1430 Mon-
Sat. Pub grub.

Rosebank Tavern 🍷
Rosebank Industrial Estate, Flax St, BT14. ☎ 753329. 1200-1430 Mon-Fri, 1700-2100 Fri & Sat. Pub grub, grills.

Shankill Leisure Centre
100 Shankill Rd, BT13. ☎ 241434. 1000-2200 Mon-Fri, until 1600 Sat-Sun. Grills.

Tudor Coffee House
123 Falls Rd, BT12. ☎ 231035. 0800-1700 Mon-Sat. Breakfast. Sandwches, snacks.

Village Tavern 🍷
165 Ligoniel Rd, BT14. ☎ 715328. 1200-1430 Mon-Sat, 1900-2130 Fri & Sat. Pub grub.

Whiterock Leisure Centre
195 Whiterock Rd, BT12. ☎ 233239. 1000-2100 Mon-Fri, until 1700 Sat & Sun. Soup, sandwiches, pies.

Ye Olde Shaftesbury Inn 🍷
739 Antrim Rd, BT15. ☎ 370015. 1200-1600 Mon-Sat, 1700-2100 Mon-Thur, until 2200 Fri & Sat. Pub grub. High tea. Sole paupiettes with shrimp sauce, steak rossini, salads. E£.

AGHALEE
(STD (01846)

Clenaghan's Bar & Restaurant ⟨⟩
48 Soldierstown Rd. ☎ 652952.
1800-2130 Tues-Sat, 1200-1430
& 1800-2030 Sun. Escalopes of
Irish salmon, fine herb chicken,
herb crusted loin of beef.

Gate Inn ⟨⟩
2 Derryola Bridge Rd, Gawley's
Gate. ☎ (01846) 652575. 1830-
2130 Thur-Sat, 1230-1430 &
1900-2100 Sun. Steaks, pasta,
fish. E££.

AHOGHILL
(STD 01266)

Diamond Bar ⟨⟩
17 The Diamond. ☎ 871251.
1200-1400 Mon-Sat. Pub grub.

Fair Hill Tavern ⟨⟩
29 Church St. ☎ 871223. 1130-
1530 Mon-Sat, 1230-1430 Sun.
Pub grub.

ALDERGROVE
(STD 01849)

Aldergrove Airport Hotel ⟨⟩
☎ 422033. 1130-1530 & 1800-
2200 Mon-Sun.
Wild boar paté, red snapper,
black bean & beef chilli. E££.

Food Court ⟨⟩
Belfast International Airport.
☎ 453630. 0630-2200 Mon-
Sun. Hot & cold buffet, salad bar,
snacks, pastries. Self-service.

White Horse Inn ⟨⟩
20 Dungonnell Rd.
☎ 428341.1930-2230 Fri &
Sat,1230-1430 Sun. Steaks,
chicken, duck. E£.

ANTRIM
(STD 01849)

Bailie ⟨⟩
111 Main St. ☎ 273947.
1130-1500 & 1700-2100
Mon-Sun. Pub grub.

Bailiwick Inn ⟨⟩
Market Square. ☎ 428807.
1200-1800 Mon-Wed, until
2000 Thur-Sat. Pub grub.

Barleycorn ⟨⟩
103 Sevenmile Straight.
☎ 463450. 1200-2045 Wed-
Thur, until 2200 Fri-Sat, until
1900 Sun. Steakhouse.

Barney's ⟨⟩
19 Market Square. ☎ 466966.
1200-2130 Mon-Sat. Pub grub.

Boardwalk Café ⟨⟩
12 Market Square. ☎ 428118.
0900-1730 Mon-Wed, until
2100 Thur-Sat, 1400-1730
Sun. Internet café

Casa Antonio ⟨⟩
4 Bridge St. ☎ 468684. 1200-
1400 & 1730-2230 Tues-Fri,
1730-2300 Sat & Sun. Italian.

China Court ☖
69 Church St. ☎ 428513.
1200-1400 & 1700-0030
Mon-Wed, 1200-0030 Thur,
until 0130 Fri & Sat, 1300-
2400 Sun. Chinese &
European. £££.

Cova Inn ☖
19 Bridge St. ☎ 428429. 1200-
1500 Mon-Sat.
Pub lunches.

Deerpark Hotel ☖
71 Dublin Rd. ☎ 462480.
Last orders 2100 Mon-Sat,
2015 Sun. Sunday high tea.
A la carte. ££££.

Den's Deli
30 Fountain St. ☎ 466469.
1400-2200 Mon-Sun.
Café menu.

Dunsilly Inn ☖
20 Dunsilly Rd. ☎ 466129.
1200-1400 Mon-Fri,
1700-2330 Mon-Thur,
until 0030 Fri& Sat.

Furama ☖
68 Church St. ☎ 465585.
1200-1400 Mon-Fri, 1700-
2400 Mon-Sat, 1300-1500
& 1700-2400 Sun. Chinese.

Galleon ☖
Antrim Arcade, 18-24 High St.
☎ 467748. 1200-2000 Mon-
Sat. Chicken parcels, braised
steak, snacks.

Galley
Antrim Arcade, High St.
☎ 468693. 0900-1730 Mon-
Wed & Sat. Fast food.

GG's Stables ☖
10 Castle St. 1200-1430 &
1700-2000 Mon-Sat, 1300-
1900 Sun. Peppered beef,
braised steak, chicken
Maryland. £.

Lough Shore Café
Lough Shore, Sixmilewater.
1200-sunset Mon-Sun. Grills,
snacks, coffee.
Antrim

Lowry's Bakery
23 Church St. ☎ 462185.
0900-1700 Mon-Sun. Soup,
pies, sandwiches, pasteries.

Madden's ☖
51 High St. ☎ 462177. 1130-
1530 Mon-Fri, until 1730 Sat.
Pub grub.

Morwood's ⊘
47 High St. ☎ 463575. 0800-
1730 Mon-Sat. Sandwiches,
home-baked bread, pastries.

Mullins
30b Fountain St. ☎ 461478.
1400-2200 Mon-Sun. Ice-
cream, sandwiches, coffee.

Old School House ☖
106 Ballyrobin Rd,
Muckamore. ☎ 428209. 1200-
1500 & 1700-2200 Mon-Sat,
1200-2030 Sun. Set meals.
Sunday lunch. Spinach-stuffed
chicken fillet with basil £££.

Pepper Pot
Castle Shopping Centre.
☎ 460955. 0900-1700 Mon-
Wed & Sat, until 2100 Thur &
Fri. Set lunch, lasagne, quiche,
soups, stews.

Pogues Tavern ⊻
88 Church St. ☎ 428098.
1200-1400 Mon-Sat.
Live music at weekends.

Railway Bar ⊻
24 Railway St. ☎ 428261.
1230-1430 Mon-Sat. Pub grub.

Ramble Inn ⊻
236 Lisnavenagh Rd.
☎ 428888. 1200-2130 Mon-
Sat, 1230-1430 & 1900-2115
Sun. Sunday lunch, grills.
A la carte. E£.

Riverbank Cafe
Antrim Forum, Lough Rd.
☎ 464131. 1000-2200 Mon-
Fri, until 1800 Sat, 1400-1800
Sun. Fish, lasagne, salads.

Riverside Café
15a Market Square.
☎ 462102. 0900-1730 Mon-
Wed, until 1930 Thur-Sat,
1300-1700 Sun.

Shanogue House ⊻
51 Sevenmile Straight.
☎ 428510. 1200-1430 Mon-
Sun. Lunches, grills.

Sodas & Subs
30 Fountain St. ☎ 466469.
1200-2200 Mon-Sun. Sodas,
sandwiches, American style
filled, toasted rolls (subs).

Steeple Inn ⊻
11 High St. ☎ 428527. 1200-
1500 Fri & Sat. Burgers, fish &
chips, daily specials.

★ TOP OF THE TOWN ⊻

77 Fountain St. ☎ 428146.
1200-1500 Mon-Sat. Fish,
chicken, salads.

BALLINTOY
(STD 012657)

Carrick-a-Rede ⊻
21 Main St. ☎ 62241. 1200-
2100 Mon-Sun in summer.
Carvery, grills.

Fullerton Arms ⊻
22 Main St. ☎ 69613. 1230-
2030 Mon-Sun. Bar steaks,
vegetarian bakes. Restaurant in
summer 1730-2030 Wed-Sun,
in winter Fri & Sat only.
Sunday lunch 1200-1500. E£.

Roark's Kitchen
56 Harbour Rd., Ballintoy
Harbour. ☎ 63632. June-Aug
1100-1900 Mon-Sun, May &
Sept Sat-Sun only. Snacks.

BALLYCASTLE
(STD 012657)

Antrim Arms ⌖
75 Castle St. ☎ 62284. 1230-
1430 & 1730-2030 Mon-Sun.
Bar snacks. Steak, lamb
cutlets, trout, scampi. E££.

Beach House
Bayview Rd. ☎ 62262.
0900-2200 Mon-Sun March-
Oct. Lasagne, pizzas, home-
made pies.

Cellar Pizzeria
The Diamond. ☎ 63037. 1730-
2300 Sun-Thur, until 2330 Fri-
Sat. Pizzas, salads.

Checkers
43 Castle St. 1130-2400 Mon-
Sat, from 1430 Sun. Burgers.

Donnelly's Coffee Shop
28 Ann St. ☎ 63236. 0900-
1800 Mon-Sat, until 1700 Sun.
Soup, pizza, quiche, pies.

Good Season
39 Ann St. ☎ 63124. 1700-
2330 Tues-Sun. Chinese &
European.

Herald's Restaurant
22 Ann St. ☎ 69064. winter:
0800-1700 Mon-Sat & until
1900 summer. Breakfast, fish,
cottage pie, salads, scones,
doughnuts.

Hilsea
28 Quay Hill. ☎ 62385. 1700-
1930 Mon-Sun June-Aug.
Home cooking. Must book.

★ MARINE HOTEL ⌖ ⊙
1 North St. ☎ 62222. Last
orders 2045. Steak, plaice,
scampi, fish platters, salad.

McCarroll's ⌖
7 Ann St. ☎ 62123. 1200-1430
& 1730-2045 Mon-Sun.
Lasagne, curries, sandwiches.

Rope Bridge Tea Room
121a Whitepark Rd. ☎ 62178.
1200-1800 weekends in May,
daily June-Aug. Tea, coffee,
pastries, breads. Beside
Carrick-a-rede rope bridge.

The Strand ⌖
9 North St. ☎ 62349. 1100-
2115 Mon-Sun. Pub grub.

Watertop Farm
188 Cushendall Rd. ☎ 62576.
1030-1730 Mon-Sun July-Aug
only. Coffee, salads, pastries in
tea-room.

★ WYSNER'S ⌖ ⊙
16 Ann St. ☎ 62372. 0800-
1700 Mon-Sat ex Wed, 1900-
2100 Fri & Sat. Speciality
sausages and meats, Ulster fry,
salads. E££.

BALLYCLARE
(STD 01960)

Ashers
56 Main St. ☎ 354744.
0830-1800 Mon-Sat.
Lasagne, stew, sandwiches.
Coffee shop in bakery.

Ballyboe ⚲
2 North End. ☎ 352997.
1130-1430 & 1700-2100 Mon-Sat, 1230-1430 & 1900-2100
Sun. Breakfast. Pub grub.

Barnaby's ⚲
153 Ballyrobert Rd.
☎ 354151. 1200-2100 Mon-Sat, until 1900 Sun.

Beck's
33 Main St. ☎ 342414. 0900-1700 Mon-Sat. Sandwiches,
pastries, pies.

Chimes
4a The Square. ☎ 352166.
0900-1700 Mon-Sat. Pizza,
salads, curries.

Coffee Pot
63 Main St. ☎ 323731. 0900-1730 Mon-Sat. Chicken, fish,
snacks, salads.

★ **FALSTAFFS**

66 Main St. ☎ 352336. 0830-1700 Mon-Sat. Breakfast.
Soups, special frys, bakes,
salads, sandwiches, coffee.

Five Corners ⚲
249 Rashee Rd. ☎ 322657.
1200-1400 & 1730-2030 Tues-Sat, 1900-2030 Sun. Chicken,
steak, pasta. E££.

Gathering Inn ⚲
42 The Square. ☎ 352636.
1700-2400 Sun-Thur, until
0100 Fri & Sat. Chinese &
European. E£.

Golden Dragon ⚲
5 Rashee Rd. ☎ 340013.
1200-1400 Fri & 1700-2400
Tues-Sat, 1730-2330 Sun.
Chinese & European. E£.

Henry's ⚲
81 Main St. ☎ 322239. 1200-2100 Mon-Sat, 1230-1430
Sun. Pub grub.

Sportsman's Inn ⚲
17 Main St. ☎ 322475.
1200-1500 Mon-Sat, 1700-2100 Fri & Sat, 1230-1430
Sun. Pub grub.

Square Bar ⚲
16 Main St. ☎ 323789. 1130-2300 Mon-Sat, 1230-1430 &
1900-2200 Sun. Pub grub.

The Grange ⚲
22 The Square. ☎ 323393.
1200-1430 & 1730-2130
Mon-Sat. Pub grub.

BALLYGALLEY
(STD 01574)

Ballygally Castle Hotel ⚲
274 Coast Rd. ☎ 583212.
Last orders 2100. Set lunch.
A la carte. E££.

Halfway House Hotel ⚲
352 Coast Rd. ☎ 583265. Last
orders 2100 Mon-Sat, 2000
Sun. Bar lunch, set lunch
weekend. A la carte. E££.

Lough's Restaurant ⚥
260 Coast Rd. ☎ 583294.
1130-1900 Mon-Wed, 1130-
2100 Thur-Sat, 1130-2000
Sun. Fish, salads. ££.

★ **LYNDEN HEIGHTS** ⚥
97 Drumnagreagh Rd. ☎
583560. 1700-2130 Wed-Sat,
1200-2000 Sun. Every day in
summer. Baked trout, salmon,
scampi. A la carte ££.

Mattie's Meeting House ⚥
Matties, 120 Brustin Brae Rd.
☎ 583252. Bar: 1200-2000
Mon-Tues, until 1830 Wed-Sat,
& 2000 Sun. Dining room:
1900-2045 Wed-Sat. Glenarm
salmon with spring onion
sauce, hot chicken salad.

Adair Arms Hotel ⚥
1 Ballymoney Rd. ☎ 653674.
Last orders 2200, Sun 2100.
Grill bar, set lunch. Salmon,
steak, lamb, grills. £££.

BALLYMENA
(STD 01266)

Bay Leaf Restaurant
23 Wellington St. ☎ 45148.
0900-1730 Mon-Wed & Sat,
until 2000 Thur & Fri. Steak,
chicken, scampi, plaice.

Boss Hoggs
87 Wakehurst Rd. ☎ 655010.
0900-2230 Mon-Thur, until
2300 Fri-Sat, 1700-2230 Sun.
Fish & chips, chicken,
sandwiches.

Burger King
Fairhill Centre. ☎ 42733.
0900-2300 Mon-Thur, until
2400 Fri-Sat, 1200-2300 Sun.
Fast food.

Café Express
10 Greenvale St. ☎ 631888.
0900-1700 Mon-Sat. Soup,
sandwiches, desserts.

Café Rossmore
Fairhill Centre. ☎ 651436.
0900-1730 Mon-Tues, until
2100 Wed-Fri, 1800 Sat.
Soups, sandwiches, salads.

Camerons
23 Broughshane St. ☎ 48821.
0900-1700 Mon-Sat. Soup,
sandwiches, desserts.

Caspers
19 Mill St. ☎ 49303. 0900-
1800 Mon-Thur & Sat, until
2100 Fri. Grills, desserts.

Classic Cuisine
24 Greenvale St. ☎ 46520.
0900-1700 Mon-Sat. Soups,
pies, salads, tray bakes.

Confucius ⚥
45 Springwell St. ☎ 651638.
1200-1400 Thur & Fri,1700-
2400 Mon-Sat, until 2300 Sun.
Chinese & European. £££.

Conservatory Restaurant
Broadway. ☎ 652151. 0900-
1700 Mon-Sat. Breakfast,
lunch, morning coffee.
Restaurant in McKillen's
Fashion store.

Copperfields
Tower Shopping Centre.
☎ 42801. 0900-1730 Mon-Sat,
until 2100 Thur & Fri. Baked
potatoes, salads, snacks.

Countryman Inn ⌕
120 Grove Rd. ☎ 44814. 1130-
1430 & 1700-2145
Mon-Sat. A la carte.
Wine bar, buffet.

Daisy May Café
25 William St. ☎ 41543. 1000-
1600 Mon-Fri, 1000-1700 Sat.
Fish & chips, sandwiches.

Desperate Dan's
12 Ballymoney St. ☎ 49677.
0900-1730 Mon-Sat.
Sandwiches, grills.

Dillingers ⌕
1 Wakehurst Rd. ☎ 44144.
1200-2230 Mon-Sat. 1230-
1430 & 1700-2200 Sun. Steaks,
chilli, vegetarian dishes.

Double Happiness ⌕
83 Broughshane St. ☎ 45101.
1200-1400 & 1700-2300 Mon-
Sat, until 2300 Sun. Chinese &
European E££.

Fern Room ⊘
80 Church St. ☎ 656169.
0900-1700 Mon-Sat. Home-
made soup, salads, vegetarian.
Self-service in McKillen's
department store.

Fort Royal ⌕
4 Loughmagarry Rd, Crankill.
☎ 685588. 1200-2100 Mon-
Sat, 1230-1430 & 1900-2200
Sun. A la carte, grills. E££.

Galgorm Castle ⌕
Pavilion Bar, Galgorm Rd.
☎ 650220. 1200-1430 &
1700-2100 Mon-Fri, until
2200 Sat, 2100 Sun.
Restaurant at golf club.

★ GALGORM MANOR ⌕
136 Fenaghy Rd. ☎ 881001.
1230-1430 daily & 1900-2130
Mon-Sat, 1800-2030 Sun. Pub
lunch daily ex Sun. Dundrum
oysters with smoked halibut,
Donegal salmon with granary
mustard, steamed chocolate
pudding. M££. E£££.

Gateway Café
52 Henry St. ☎ 47794. 0900-
1700 Mon-Fri, until 1500
Wed, 1800 Sat. Pizzas,
sandwiches, desserts.

George Buttery ⌕
54 Mill St. ☎ 656170. 1130-
1500 Mon-Wed, until 2100
Thurs-Sat, 1230-1430 Sun.
Grills, salads.

Go Sun ⌕
43 Bridge St. ☎ 656774.
1200-1400 Mon-Sat, 1700-
2300 Mon-Thur, until 2400
Fri & Sat. until 2330 Sun.
Chinese & European. ££.

Greenhills ♈
166 Glenravel Rd. ☎ (012667)
58743. 1700-2100 Mon-Sat,
1230-1500 & 1900-2100 Sun.
Steak, gammon, champ.
Roast beef Sunday lunch.

Grouse Inn ♈
2 Springwell St. ☎ 45234.
1100-2130 Mon-Thur, until
2200 Fri & Sat. Grill bar.
A la carte. E££.

Jaunty's ♈
9 Larne St. ☎ 659153. 1200-
2400 Tues-Sat, 1700-2330
Sun. Fish & chips, chicken.

Kentucky Fried Chicken
27 Queen St. ☎ 46355. 1100-
2400 Mon-Wed, until 0100
Thur, 0300 Fri-Sat. Fast food.

Knockeden Lodge ♈
15 Crebilly Rd. ☎ 43334.
1130-1500 Mon-Fri, 1800-
2000 Thur, 1730-2030 Fri &
Sat, 1230-1430 Sun. Pub grub.

Leighinmohr Hotel ♈
Leighinmohr Avenue.
☎ 652313. Last orders 2130
Mon-Sat, 2100 Sun. Trout in
white wine, flambé steaks.
Oyster bar, grill. Buffet lunch
Sun. A la carte. M£, E£££.

Lug o' th' Tub ♈
133 Ballycregagh Rd, Clough.
☎ 685423. 1230-1430 &
1800-2100 Mon-Sat. Pies,
hamburgers.

Manley ♈
State Cinema Arcade,
70a Ballymoney Rd. ☎ 48967.
1200-1400 Tues-Sat, 1730-
2330 Tues-Thur, until 0030
Fri-Sat, 1600-2330 Sun.
Cantonese, Peking &
European. E££.

Old Stone Manor ♈
1 Main St, Clough. ☎ 685569.
1800-2200 Wed-Sat, 1200-
1500 & 1800-2100 Sun.
Venison with cranberries &
game sauce, salmon, fresh
fruit pavlova.

Paragon
77 Church St. ☎ 653699.
0900-1730 Mon-Fri, until
1800 Sat. Set lunch, soup,
salads, desserts.

Pizza Parlour ♦
Springwell St. ☎ 49245.
1700-2300 Sun-Wed, until
2400 Thur-Sat. Pizzas, pasta.

Pound Bar ♈
18 Corkey Rd. ☎ (012656)
41287. 1530-2200 Mon-Sat,
1230-1430 & 1900-2200 Sun.
Pub grub.

Raglan Bar ♈
20 Queen St. ☎ 652203. 1130-
2300 Mon-Sat. Pub snacks.

Red Peaches ♈
88 Lower Mill St. ☎ 651170.
1200-1400 & 1700-2400 Tues-
Sat, 1600-2300 Sun.
Cantonese & European. E££.

Rendezvous
48 Ballymoney St. ☎ 44092.
0900-1730 Mon-Sat.
Grills, curries, toasties.

Restaurant Sorrento
Fairhill Centre. ☎ 632168.
0900-1700 Mon-Sat, until
2100 Wed-Fri. Soups, pastries,
salads, pies.

Skandia ⊙
Tower Shopping Centre.
☎ 46781. 0930-1730 Mon-
Wed, until 2100 Thur & Fri,
1900 Sat. Omelettes, fish,
grills, salads, filled rolls.
High tea menu.

Slemish Bar ⚱
35 William St. ☎ 653212.
1200-1430 Mon-Fri, until
1600 Sat. Pub grub.

Solomon Grundy's ⊙
64 Wellington St. ☎ 659602.
0900-1800 Thur-Fri, until
1900 Sat. Pizza, chilli,
vegetarian.

Spires
26 Broughshane St. ☎ 49029.
0800-1700 Mon-Sat.
Set lunch.

Sugar 'n' Spice
7 Church St. ☎ 46010.
0900-1730 Mon-Sat.
Soup, salads, pies.

The Inn ⚱
36 William St. ☎ 652319.
1200-1430 Mon-Sat. Pub grub.

Towers Tavern ⚱
Unit 9, Ballee Centre.
☎ 48969. 1200-1430 Mon-Sat.
Pub grub.

Tullyglass House Hotel ⚱
178 Galgorm Rd. ☎ 652639.
Last orders 2145, Sun 2045.
A la carte. £££.

Vintage Bar ⚱
9 Galgorm St. ☎ 651255.
1200-1430 Thur-Sat. Grills,
steaks, salads.

Water Margin ⚱
8 Cullybackey Rd. ☎ 48368.
1200-1400 Mon-Sat, 1700-
2400 Mon-Thur & Sun, until
0030 Fri & Sat. Cantonese &
European. £££.

YMCA Café
44 Church St. ☎ 49335. 0900-
1500 Mon-Thur, until 1230
Fri. Stew, lasagne, pizza.

BALLYMONEY
(STD 012656)

Angler's Rest ⚱
139 Vow Rd. ☎ (012665)
40280. 1230-1430 & 1730-
2130 Mon-Sat. Sunday carvery
1230-1430 & 1900-2030.
A la carte. ££.

Anne's Hot Bread Shop
Unit 6, Castle Croft Shopping
Centre. ☎ 62979. 0800-1730
Mon-Sat. Breakfast, fresh
home-baked bread, lunches,
Ulster frys, salads.

Bay Tree
29 Church St. ☎ 66088. 0900-1700 Mon-Sat. Breakfast, salads, soups, home-baked scones, pastries.

Brown Jug
23 Main St. ☎ 64212. 0830-1730 Mon-Sat. Breakfast, pies, salads, home-made bread, cakes, pastries.

Bush Tavern ⚲
15 Market St. ☎ 63167. 1130-2300 Mon-Thur, 1130-0100 Fri & Sat, 1230-2200 Sun. Gammon, steak, plaice, scampi, Ulster fry, salads, toasties, snacks.

Conservatory Restaurant
Riada Centre, 33 Garryduff Rd. ☎ 65792. 0900-2100 Mon-Friday, until 1700 Sat. 1330-1700 Sun. Home made food, children's menu & birthday partie.s. Overlooks Riada Centre swimming pool.

Flash in the Pan
52 Queen St. ☎ 63290. 1130-2400 Mon-Thur & Sun, later Fri-Sat. Fish, chips, chicken kebab on pitta bread, salad bowl.

Gracehill Bell Tower ⚲
141 Ballinlea Rd, Stranocum. ☎ (012657) 51209. 1200-2130 Mon-Sat, 1200-2000 Sun. Check times. Restaurant in golf club.

Hoi Yun ⚲
3 Charles St. ☎ 63419. 1200-1400 Mon-Sat, 1700-2400 Mon-Fri, 1200-0030 Sat, 1700-2330 Sun. Chinese & European. E£.

Kelly's ⚲
21 Church St. ☎ 66565. 1200-2030 Mon-Sun. Steak, Chinese chicken, fish, pasta, toasties, sandwiches, salads.

La Petite Baguette
18 Victoria St. ☎ 62801. 0900-1700 Mon-Sat. Wide variety of fillings and different breads. Home-made soups & savouries.

Leslie Hill Open Farm
Leslie Hill. ☎ 63109. July-Aug 1100-1800 & 1400-1800 Sun. Open weekends and Bank Holidays & Easter-Sept. Sandwiches, home-made scones & biscuits. In craft shop.

Main Plaice
53 Main St. ☎ 63475. 0930-1730 Mon-Wed, later Thur-Sat. Fast food.

Manor Hotel ⚲
69 Main St. ☎ 63208. Last orders 2030 Mon-Fri, 2230 Sat. Set lunch, steak, chicken, lamb. E£.

Megabites
39 Charles St. ☎ 66514. 1130-
2330 Mon-Thur, 1130-1430
Fri & Sat, 1630-2330 Sun.
Fast food.

Raymond's ⚑
2 Market St. ☎ 65834. 0900-
1830 Mon-Wed, 0900-1900
Thur, 0900-2200 Fri, 0900-
2100 Sat, 1000-2200 Sun.
Set lunch, grills.

Riada Leisure Centre
33 Garryduff Rd. ☎ 65792.
0900-2100 Mon-Fri, until
1700 Sat. 1330-1700 Sun.
Soup, chicken, plaice,scampi,
burgers, side salad, tray-bakes.

Riverside Self Serve
2 Ballymena Rd. ☎ 63500.
0600-2400 Mon-Sun.
Breakfast. Champ, chicken,
curry, chips, pasta, shepherds
pie. Deli bar at supermarket/
petrol station.

★ **THE TEA SHOP** ⚘
21 Main St. ☎ 63331. 0930-
1430 Mon, 0900-1700 Tues-
Sat. Open sandwiches, salads,
soup, scones, cakes.

Top of the Town
7 High St. ☎ 65400. 0730-
1700 Mon-Sat. Breakfast, fish,
chicken, lasagne, salads.

BROUGHSHANE
(STD 01266)

Pantry
3 Jubilee Mews, Main St.
☎ 862366. 0900-1700 Mon-
Sat. Breakfast, soup, stew.
Coffee shop & home bakery.

Thatch Inn ⚑
57 Main St. ☎ 861223. 1200-
1415 Mon-Fri. Pub grub.

Tullymore House ⚑
2 Carnlough Rd. ☎ 861233.
Carvery 1200-1500 Mon-Sun,
1900-2130 Mon-Sat, 1800-
2130 Sun. Bistro 1700-2130
Mon-Sun. E££.

BUSHMILLS
(STD 012657)

Ahimsa
243 Whitepark Rd. ☎ 31383.
Vegetarian. Must book. £.

★ **BUSHMILLS INN** ⚑
25 Main St. ☎ 32339. Last
orders 2130. Restaurant:
beef fillet strips in cream &
Bushmills whiskey. E£££.
Brasserie: weekends &
summer only. Ballyblue brie
& beef tomatoes. £.

Causeway Flowers & Tea Shop
61 Main St. ☎ 32560. 0900-
1800 Mon-Sun, until 2000
July-Aug. Soup, Irish stew,
toasties, salads. Craft shop,
art gallery.

Coffee Shop
65 Main St, The Diamond.
☎ 31706. 0900-1730 Mon-Sat,
until 1900 in summer.
Sandwiches, grills, cakes.

Distillers Arms ⍭
140 Main St. ☎ 31044. 1230-
2100 Mon-Sun. Pub grub.

Killen's ⍭
28 Ballyclough Rd. ☎ 41536.
1900-2200 Tues-Sun.
A la carte.

Scotch House Tavern ⍭
51 Main St. ☎ 331642. 1130-
2330 Mon-Sun. Pub grub.

Valerie's Pantry
125 Main St. ☎ 31145. 0930-
1730 Mon-Sat. Ulster fry, Irish
stew, pies.

CARNLOUGH
(STD 01574)

Bridge Inn
2 Bridge St. ☎ 885669. 1200-
2000 Mon-Sun. Set lunch.

Glencloy Inn ⍭
2 Harbour Rd. ☎ 885226.
1130-2100 Mon-Sat.
Bar snacks.

Harbour House Tea Rooms
11c Harbour Rd. ☎ 885056.
1000-2030 Mon-Sun, until
1800 in winter. All-day
breakfast, teas.

★ LONDONDERRY ARMS ⍭
20 Harbour Rd. ☎ 885255. Last
orders 2100 Mon-Thur, 2130
Fri & Sat, 2015 Sun. Fresh
lobster, scallops, home-made
wheaten bread. M£, E££.

Marine Café
9 Marine Rd. ☎ 885509.
1100-2030 Mon-Sun.
Fish & chips.

Waterfall Bar ⍭
1 High St. ☎ 885606. 1230-
1730 Mon-Sat summer, until
1500 winter. 1230-1430 Sun.
Pub grub.

CARRICKFERGUS
(STD 01960)

Anne's Pantry
3 North Street. ☎ 355103.
0900-1730 Mon-Sat.
Breakfast. Snacks, lunch.
In home bakery.

Brown Cow ⍭
9 Woodburn Rd. ☎ 364815.
1215-1400 & 1700-2100
Mon-Sat, 1900-2030 Sun.
Steaks, salads.

Café No 10
10 West St. ☎ 360306. 0900-
1600 Mon-Sat. Snacks, grills.

Carrickfergus Castle
☎ 351881. 1000-1800 Mon-
Sat, 1400-1800 Sun. Muffins,
tray bakes, sausage rolls.
Coffee shop in castle.

Castle Fast Food
10 Castle St. ☎ 351859. 1030-2400 Mon-Wed, until 0100 Thur, 0200 Fri & Sat, 1400-2330 Sun. Fast food.

Chandlers ⌛
13 High St. ☎ 369729. 1200-1430 Mon-Sat, 1700-2200 Thur-Sat, 1400-2000 Sun. (à la carte). Breakfast, bar snacks.

Chestnut Inn ⌛
126 Lurgan Rd. ☎ 453165. 1130-2300 Mon-Sat, 1230-1430 & 1900-2200 Sun. Pub grub.

Coast Road Hotel ⌛
28 Scotch Quarter. ☎ 351021. Last orders 2045. Closed 25-26 Dec. Steak, scampi, chicken. £££.

Courtyard Coffee House
38 Scotch Quarter. ☎ 351881. 1000-1630 Mon-Sat. Pies, lasagne, salads.

Dobbins Inn Hotel ⌛
6 High St. ☎ 351905. Last orders 2115. Closed 25-26 Dec. Set lunch, bar meals. Bistro last orders 2000 Thur & Sat. Flambé steak, sweets. £££.

ECU Café Bar ⌛
63 North St. ☎ 360161. 1700-2200 Mon-Thur, from 1200 Fri-Sat, 1700-2200 Sun. Steaks, cajun chicken, pasta, salads, vegetarian.

Golden Fortune 🍸
14 Joymount. ☎ 351038. 1200-1400 Mon-Sat, 1700-2400 Mon-Thur, 1700-0100 Fri & Sat, 1200-1500 & 1700-2400 Sun. Chinese & European.

Indian Ocean ⌛
Unit 4, Belfast Rd. ☎ 355422. 1200-1400 Mon-Fri, 1700-2330 Mon-Sat, 1700-2300 Sun. Indian.

Knockagh Lodge ⌛
236 Upper Rd, Greenisland. ☎ (01232) 861444. 1200-1430 & 1700-2130 Mon-Sat, until 2000 Sun. Bar snacks. Evening à la carte.

La Casa Pizzeria
2 Woodburn Rd. ☎ 361399. 1700-2300 Mon-Thur, until 2400 Fri-Sat, 1600-2300 Sun. Pizzas, seafood, chicken, pasta. £££.

Leisure Centre
Prince William Way. ☎ 351711. 1030-2200 Mon-Fri, until 1530 Sat. Snacks.

Maud's Choc Shop
52 Scotch Quarter. 0830-2100 Mon-Sun. Scones, pancakes, pastries, hot chocolate. Ice-cream parlour in video shop.

McDonald's
Marine Highway, Shore Rd. ☎ 359990. 0800-2300 Mon-Thur & Sun, until 2400 Fri-Sat. Fast food

Mermaid ♒
2 Governor's Place.
☎ 351257. 1130-1430
Mon-Sat. Soup, bakes.

New Four Seas ♒
9 Governor's Place. ☎ 351226.
1200-1400 & 1700-2400
Mon-Thur & Sun, until 0100
Fri & Sat. Chinese &
European. E£.

Northgate ♒
59 North St. ☎ 364136. 1200-
1445 & 1700-2145 Mon-Sat,
1230-1400 & 1700-2000 Sun.
Steaks, chicken. E£.

Number 10
10 West St. ☎ 360306. 0900-
1600 Mon-Sat. Snacks, grills.

O'Neill's
27 North St. ☎ 351546. 0900-
1630 Mon-Sat. Café in home
bakery. Breads, soups, pies.

Oasis
10 Cheston St. ☎ 355337.
0900-1700 Mon-Sat, until
2100 in summer. Grills,
chicken, steaks, salads. £.

Old Tech Griddle
20 High St. ☎ 351904. 0900-
1730 Mon-Sat. Stew, curries,
home-baked bread.
In bakery shop.

Paradigm Café
16 West St. ☎ 361531. 1000-
2200 Mon-Sat. Baked
potatoes, salads, filled pitta
pockets, baguettes, scones.
Internet café .

Pheasant Inn ♒
77 Woodburn Rd. ☎ 361094.
1230-1430 Wed-Sat, 1700-
2030 Mon & Wed-Sat, 1200-
1400 Sun. Pub grub.

★ **QUALITY HOTEL** ♒ ⊘
75 Belfast Rd. ☎ 364556.
1200-1430 & 1730-2100
Mon-Sat, 1230-1500 & 1730-
2000 Sun. Bar food, à la carte,
Sunday carvery. E££.

Tamarind Restaurant ♠
32 West St. ☎ 355579. 1200-
1400 & 1730-2330 Mon-Sat,
1730-2300 Sun. Indian &
European.

Tourist Inn ♒
149 Larne Rd. ☎ 351708.
1230-1430 Mon-Sat. Pub grub.

★ **WIND-ROSE** ♒
Rodgers Quay. ☎ 364192.
1200-1430 & 1730-2100
Mon-Sun, until 2000 Sun.
A la carte bistro. E£££.

YMCA
Lancastrian St. ☎ 351223.
1030-1400 Mon-Wed & Fri,
0800-1400 Thur. Soup, stew.

CLOUGHMILLS
(STD 012656)

Roadside Restaurant
Logan's Fashion Store,
232 Frosses Rd. ☎ 38080.
1000-1800 Mon, Tues & Sat,
1000-2100 Wed-Fri. Teas,
salads, sandwiches, pastries.
Set lunch May-Sept.

CRUMLIN
(STD 01849)

Airport Road Café
11 Tully Rd, Nutts Corner.
☎ (01232) 825711. 0730-1730
Mon-Fri, until 1400 Sat.
Breakfast, soup, salads, stew.

Breadbasket
78 Main St. ☎ 423073. 0900-
1730 Mon-Sat. Home baking,
toasties, pies.

Bushe ⚲
47 Main St. ☎ 452411. 1200-
1400 Mon-Sat, 1800-2130 Fri
& Sat, 1230-1400 & 1900-
2100 Sun. Pub grub.

Fiddlers Inn ⚲
36 Main St. ☎ 452221. 1200-
1500 & 1800-2100 Mon-Sat,
1230-1400 & 1900-2100 Sun.
Pub grub.

CULLYBACKEY
(STD 01266)

Village Inn ⚲
76 Main St. ☎ 881290. 1230-
1430 Mon-Fri, 1700-2100 Fri-
Sat. Set lunch, grills.

Wylie's ⚲
93 Main St. ☎ 880200. 1500-
2100 Mon-Sun. Pub grub.

CUSHENDALL
(STD 012667)

Gillan's
6 Mill St. ☎ 71404. 0900-1730
Mon-Sat (closed 1400 Tues)
plus 1200-1800 Sunday in
summer. Salads, sandwiches,
hot dogs.

Half Door Restaurant ⚲
6 Bridge St. ☎ 71300. 1700-
2100 Mon-Sun. Shorter winter
hours . French-style cooking.
££.

Harry's Restaurant ⚲
10 Mill St. ☎ 72022. 1230-
2100 Mon-Sat, 1200-1500 &
1800-2100 Sun. Smoked
mackerel mousse, lamb,
scampi. M£. E££.

Lurig Inn ⚲
Bridge St. ☎ 71527. 1130-
2300 Mon-Sat, 1230-1430 &
1900-2200 Sun. Chicken,
curries, steak.

Thornlea Hotel ⚲
6 Coast Rd. ☎ 71223. Last
orders 2115. Set lunch, high
tea, carvery. A la carte. M£,
E££.

CUSHENDUN
(STD 012667)

Bay Hotel ⚲
20 Strandview Park. ☎ 61267.
Last orders 2045. Garlic
mushrooms, steak in whiskey
sauce. A la carte. E££.

Mary McBride's ⚲
Main St. ☎ 61511. 1200-2100
Mon-Sun. Home made steak &
Guinness pie, Cushendun
salmon, sea trout, sea bass in
tarragon sauce.

National Trust Tea Room
1 Main St. ☎ 61506. Easter-
Sept 1100-1900 Mon-Sat, until
2000 Sun. In winter 1100-
1800 Sat & Sun only. Soup,
quiche, salads, home-baking.
Teas in garden.

Villa Farm House ▮
185 Torr Rd. ☎ 61252. 1300-
1930 Mon-Sun. Salmon in
season, home baking.
Must book.

DERVOCK
(STD 012657)

North Irish Horse Inn ⚲
15 Carncullagh Rd. ☎ 41205.
1200-2130 Mon-Sun. Own
smoked trout & eel, dressed
crab & lobster. E££.

DOAGH
(STD 01960)

Doagh Factory Shop
6 Black Mill Row. ☎ 352501.
1000-1430 Mon-Sat.
Coffee shop.

McConnell's ⚲
4 Main St. ☎ (01960) 352352.
1230-1430 Mon-Sat. Soups,
scampi.

DUNADRY
(STD 01849)

Dunadry Inn ⚲
2 Islandreagh Drive. ☎
432474. Last orders 2145, Sun
2045. Closed 24-25 Dec.
Smoked eel, veal, partridge,
salmon. E£££.

Ellie May's ⚲
252 Belfast Rd. ☎ 433796.
Bar snacks, open sandwiches
1200-1800 Mon-Sat. Sunday
lunch & high tea. A la carte
1800-2130 Mon-Sun, later on
Sat. Ellie May chicken
specials, spare ribs, fish.

★ **LANDSCAPE CENTRE**
24 Donegore Hill. ☎ 432175.
0900-1700 Mon-Sat, 1300-
1700 Sun. Soup, salads, filled
rolls, scones. Coffee shop in
garden centre.

DUNMURRY
(STD 01232)

Beechlawn Hotel ⚲
4 Dunmurry Lane. ☎ 612974.
1200-1430 & 1800-2130
Mon-Sat. Seafood, steaks.
A la carte. E££.

Cobblestone Coffee Shop
236 Kingsway. ☎ 612324.
0900-1700 Mon-Sat. Coffee,
quiche, lasagne.

Derby House ⅀
2 Lagmore Rd, Stewartstown
Rd. ☎ 625352. 1200-2130
Mon-Sat, until 1900 Sun.
Bellybuster grills, fresh soups,
salads, vegetarian dishes. Quiz
night Wed, live entertainment
weekend. Irish-American style.
Pub grub in bar.

Dunmurry Inn ⅀
195 Kingsway. ☎ 611653.
1130-1430 Mon-Sat.
Sandwiches, stew, salads.

Farmer's Inn ⅀
91 Colinglen Rd. ☎ 600135.
1200-1430 & 1700-1900
Mon-Sun. Pub grub.

Forte Posthouse ⅀ ⊘
300 Kingsway. ☎ 612101.
0800-2200 Mon-Sun.
Vegetable soups, Irish salmon,
duck. Sun carvery lunch. E££.

Jeffer's
174 Kingsway. ☎ 617938.
0830-1700 Mon-Sat. Coffee
shop in home bakery.

Kentucky Fried Chicken
181 Kingsway. 1100-0100
Sun-Thur, until 0200 Fri-Sat.
Fast food.

Pizza Bellezza
232 Kingsway. ☎ 600202.
1600-2400 Mon-Thur, 1600-
0100 Fri & Sat, 1700-2400
Sun. Pizzas.

Skandia ♣
Kingsway Shopping Centre.
☎ 612268. 0930-2200 Mon-
Sat, 1200-2000 Sun. Creole
chicken, steak, cheesy leeks.

Sportsman Inn ⅀
101 Queensway. ☎ (01846)
663994. 1200-1430 Mon-Sat,
1730-2030 Fri-Sun.
Pub grub. E£.

Stagecoach Inn ⅀
52 Queensway, Derriaghy.
☎ 625141. Grills 1200-1430 &
1800-2045 Mon-Fri. Meal-for-
two until 2145 Fri & Sat.
1200-1600 traditional Sun
lunch. Steaks. E£.

Swillybrin Inn ⅀
12 Suffolk Rd. ☎ 614754.
1230-1430 Mon-Sat, 1900-
2130 Sun. Pub grub.

The Pyramids
180 Kingsway. ☎ 624972.
1200-1400 Mon-Sat, 1700-
2300 Mon-Thur, until 2400 Fri
& Sat. Kebabs, pizza, lasagne.

GIANT'S CAUSEWAY
(STD 012657)

Causeway Hotel ⅀
40 Causeway Rd. ☎ 31226.
Last orders 1630-2100 Mon-
Sun. Steaks, fish, duckling,
salad, bar snacks.

Hillcrest Country House ♉
306 Whitepark Rd. ☎ 31577.
Summer 1200-2130 Tues-Sun.
Winter 1700-2100 Thur-Sat &
Sunday lunch. Home cooking,
local seafood, game in season.
££.

★ **NATIONAL TRUST TEA
ROOM**
Giant's Causeway Centre.
☎ 31582. Mon-Sun March-
June & Sept, until 1845
July & Aug. Soup, snacks,
home baking.

GLARRYFORD
(STD 01266)

Crankhill Stores Café
133 Crankhill Rd. ☎ (01266)
85507. 0900-1700 Mon-Sat.
Hot dogs, sandwiches,
pastries.

Glen Tea House
99a Glen Rd. ☎ 71402. 1400-
1800 Mon-Sun in summer, Sat
& Sun only rest of year. Home
baking, pastries.

GLENARIFF
(STD 012667)

Glenariff Tea House
Glenariff Forest Park. ☎ 58769.
1100-1800 Mon-Sun Easter-
Sept. Quiche, salads.
In craftshop.

Manor Lodge ♉
120 Glen Rd. Glenariff Glen.
☎ 58221. 1200-2100 Mon-Sat,
until 2030 Sun. Lunch, high
teas, dinner.

GLENARM
(STD 01574)

Coast Road Inn ♉
3 Toberwine St. ☎ 841207.
1200-1500 Mon-Thur, 1200-
1500 & 1700-2130 Mon-Sat.
Grills, salads. Pub grub.

Drumnagreagh Hotel ♉
408 Coast Rd. ☎ 841651. Last
orders 2100. A la carte. £££.

Gallery Coffee Shop
5 Toberwine St. ☎ 841470.
0900-2100 Mon-Sun. Coffee,
snacks. Quiches, pasties,
soups, stews. Coffee shop in
art gallery.

Poacher's Pocket ♉
1 New Row. ☎ 841221. 1200-
1500 Mon-Sat. Bar snacks,
salmon, steaks, stews.

Schooner ♉
1 Castle St. ☎ 841690. 1100-
2300 Mon-Sat, 1230-1430 &
1900-2200 Sun. Pub grub.

GLENAVY
(STD 01849)

★ McGEOWN'S ♿
22 Main St. ☎ 422467. 1130-
2100 Mon-Sun. Lough shore
salmon, citrus chicken,
Portuguese salad. Bar snacks.

GLENGORMLEY
(STD 01232)

Beck's
329 Antrim Rd. ☎ 833854.
0900-1700 Mon-Sat.
Coffee, snacks.

Bellevue Arms ♿
129 Antrim Rd. ☎ 777138.
1200-2200 Mon-Sat, 1230-
1430 & 1900-2130 Sun.
Pub grub. Set meals.
A la carte. £££.

Cavalier
8 Portland Avenue. ☎ 836759.
1000-2300 Mon-Thur, until
0100 Fri-Sat. Grills, fish &
chips, coffee.

Chimney Corner Hotel ♿
630 Antrim Rd. ☎ 844925.
Last orders 2130. A la carte.
£££.

Glen Inn ♿
305 Antrim Rd. ☎ 833356.
1200-1500 Mon-Sat. Pub grub,
à la carte. £££.

Huckleberry's ♿
8 Farmley Shopping Centre.
☎ 838282. 1200-1430 &
1700-2200 Mon-Thur, 1200-
2300 Fri-Sat, 1400-2130 Sun.
Modern American. ££.

Jasmin House ♿
17a Ballyclare Rd. ☎ 840352.
1200-1400 & 1700-2400
Mon-Thur, until 0100 Fri-Sat,
1300-2400 Sun. Chinese &
European.

Kentucky Fried Chicken
376 Antrim Rd. ☎ 843040.
1100-0100 Sun-Wed, until
0230 Thur-Sat. Fast food.

Kyber ♿
373 Antrim Rd. ☎ 849414.
1100-1400, 1700-2315 Mon-
Sat, 1700-2245 Sun. Indian &
European. £££.

Madaghan's ♿
350 Antrim Rd. ☎ 836077.
1200-1430 Mon-Sat. Soups,
Peppered chicken, pasta,
open sandwiches.

Pizza Hut
Olivia Centre, Antrim Rd.
☎ 842299. 1200-2400 Mon-
Sat, 1200-2300 Sun. Pizza,
pasta, salad. ££.

Swiss Chalet ♿
81 Ballyclare Rd. ☎ 848630.
1230-1430 Mon-Sat. Chicken,
fish, open sandwiches. £.

ISLANDMAGEE
(STD 01960)

Millbay Inn ⬭
77 Millbay Rd. ☎ 382436.
1200-1430 Mon-Sun, 1900-
2130 Fri-Sat. Home-made
Hunter's broth, champ &
sausages, cottage pie. A la
carte: seafood, home-made
desserts, cheeseboard. E££.

KELLS
(STD 01266)

Country House Hotel ⬭
20 Doagh Rd. ☎ 891663.
Last orders 2115. Buffet lunch,
Sunday high tea, à la carte.
Lobster, zabaglione. E£££.

★ **JOURDAN'S** ⬭
50 Main St. ☎ 891258. 1200-
1415 &1700-2100 Mon-Fri,
until 2100 Sat. Pub grub.
Dublin Bay prawns, duck in
red wine sauce. E££.

LARNE
(STD 01574)

Ann's Pantry
64 Main St. ☎ 260474. 0900-
1730 Mon-Sat. Quiche, baked
potatoes.

Apsley's Scullery ⊖
11 Main St. ☎ 260510. 0700-
2100 Mon-Sat, until 1800 Sun.
Breakfast. Stew, sandwiches,
pastries.

Ardella
3 Upper Cross St. ☎ 270908.
0930-1730 Mon-Thur & Sat,
0900-1900 Fri. Chicken, fish,
grills, desserts.

Ballyboley Inn ⬭
125 Shane's Hill Rd.
☎ (01266) 831293. 1230-1430
& 1800-2100 Tues-Fri, 1230-
1800 Sat, 1800-2100 Sun.
Pub grub.

Bengal Cuisine
6 High St. ☎ 260000. 1200-
1400 Mon-Sat, 1730-2330
Mon-Sun. Chef's special balti.
Indian and European.

Big Sandwich Company
27 Point St. ☎ 260410. 0900-
1730 Mon-Sat. Sandwiches,
ice cream, pastries.

Bric-à-brac
4 Riverdale. ☎ 275657. 0900-
1630 Mon-Sat, until 1300
Tues. Home-made broth,
coffee. In antiques shop.

Butter Churn
61 Main St. ☎ 260575. 0700-
1700 Mon-Sat. Quiche, baked
potatoes.

Captain's Kitchen
Harbour Terminal. ☎ 270284.
0630-2230 Mon-Sun.
Fast food.

Carnfunnock Country Park
☎ 275947. Easter-Sep: 0800-2000 Mon-Sun and Oct-March: 1000-1800 Sat & 0900-1800 Sun. Lasagne, salads, sandwiches, scones, mince pies.

Carriages ⚲
105 Main St. ☎ 275132. 1700-2300 Mon-Sun. Grills, pizza. E£.

Central Bakery & Cottage Restaurant
21 Lower Cross St. ☎ 260293. 0900-1730 Mon-Sat. Home-made bread, pastries, grills, snacks.

Chekkers Wine Bar ⚲
29 Lower Cross St. ☎ 275305. 1200-1430 & 1730-2130 Mon-Thur, 1200-2130 Fri-Sat, 1230-1400 & 1900-2130 Sun. Steaks, lasagne, salads.

Country Kitchen
96b Main St. ☎ 275811. 0815-1700 Mon-Sat. Stew, salads, sandwiches.

Curran Court Hotel ⚲
84 Curran Rd. ☎ 275505. Last orders 2115 Mon-Sat, Sun 2015. Set lunch, Sunday high tea. A la carte. E££.

Dan Campbell's ⚲
2 Bridge St. ☎ 277222. 1200-1500 Mon-Sat, 1900-2130 Wed-Sat. Seafood chowder, baked stuffed chicken, steak & Guinness pie.

Eagle Bar ⚲
1 Station Rd. ☎ 273817. 1130-2300 Mon-Sat. Snacks.

Highways Hotel ⚲
Donaghy's Lane, Ballyloran. ☎ 272272. Last orders 2100, Sun 2130. Roast ham, mixed grill. A la carte. E££.

Kiln ⚲
Old Glenarm Rd. ☎ 260924. 1200-1430 & 1700-2100 Mon-Sat, 1230-1430 & 1700-2000 Sun. Seafood a speciality. Daily specials.

Loafers ⊗
8 Penny Lane, Point St.
☎ 273322. 0900-1700 Mon-
Sat, until 1500 Tues.
Sandwiches, salads, lasagne.

Lotus Flower
117 Main St. ☎ 272102.
1700-0030 Mon-Sat, 1200-
1430 Thur-Fri, 1600-2400 Sun.
Chinese & European.

Magheramorne House Hotel ⌁
59 Shore Rd. ☎ 279444. Last
orders 2100, 2130 Sat, 2000
Sun. A la carte. £££.

Maud's Ice Cream Parlour & Coffee Shop
79 Main St. ☎ 278065. 1100-
2100 Mon-Sat, until 2000 Sun.
Speciality ice cream.

Rafters ⌁
13 Point St. ☎ 274368. 1200-
1500 Mon-Sat. Soup, Irish
stew.

Rumbles ▮
116 Main St. ☎ 274445. 1000-
2200 Tues-Sat, 1300-1900
Sun. Grilled salmon, steak,
tagliatelle, chicken & broccoli
bake, cheesecake. Half
portions for children.

Silver Lounge
124 Main St. ☎ 260040. 0900-
1800 Mon-Sat ex Tues pm in
winter. Fish & chips, chicken,
mince-and-onion pie, toasted
sandwiches.

Upper Crust
28 Main St. ☎ 277795. 0830-
1730 Mon-Sat. Breakfast.
Ulster fry, steak. Home bakery.

LISBURN
(STD 01846)

Andrews
23a Market Square. ☎ 673189.
0900-1830 Mon-Sat. Ulster fry,
baked potato, salads, chips,
roast beef.

Angelo's Ristorante
3a Market Lane. ☎ 672554.
1700-2200 Tues-Sat, 1400-
2130 Sun. Pizza, pasta, fish.

Bow Street Brasserie
Bow Street Mall. ☎ 661650.
0900-1700 Mon & Tues, until
2100 Wed-Fri, 1730 Sat.
Grills, salads, pastries.

Brodie's
Bow Street Mall. ☎ 605406.
0900-1700 Mon-Sat. Until
2000 Thur-Fri. Scones, tray
bakes, salads, sandwiches.

Bruno's Café
11 Lisburn Enterprise Centre,
Ballinderry Upper. ☎ 603313.
0900-1600 Mon-Fri. Breakfast,
lasagne, gammon, fish.

Cairnmore Antiques
39 Lambeg Rd. ☎ 673115.
1400-1700 Mon-Fri, 1100-
1700 Sat. Scones, pastries.
Tea shop in antiques shop.

Carol's
13 Market Square. ☎ 673158.
0830-1700 Mon-Sat. Breakfast.
Grills, pastries.

★ COCO'S ⊖

21a Railway St. ☎ 668066.
0800-1800 Mon-Wed, until
2200 Thur-Sat. Breakfast.
Italian, Mexican.

Cooke Pot
134 Longstone St. ☎ 671204.
0900-1630 Mon-Sat. Irish
stew, pies.

Country Kitchen ⊖
57 Sloan St. ☎ 671730. 0830-
1530 Mon-Sat. Breakfast.
Omelettes, baked potatoes,
pizzas fish, salad. In home
bakery.

Dalton's
14 Market Square. ☎ 605355.
0830-1600 Mon-Sat. Baked
potatoes, sandwiches.

Down Royal ⊻
62 Ballinderry Rd. ☎ 602870.
1200-2100 Mon-Sat. Sunday
snack menu 1230-1930. Pork
in cider, pan-fried chicken,
peppered beef, salmon. Chilli,
open sandwiches, salads. £.

Eats
25 Market Square. ☎ 662960.
1000-1800 Mon-Sat. Fast food.

Family's Restaurant ⊖
46 Market Square. ☎ 603033.
0800-1730 Mon-Sat, until
2130 Thur. Grills, bakes,
salads, pies.

Franklin's
8b Graham Gardens.
☎ 666498. 0830-1700 Mon-
Sat. Sandwiches to order,
pastries, freshly ground coffee.
Café in bakery.

Gaffe Cutter ⊻
25 Market Place. ☎ 666950.
1200-1430 Mon-Fri, until
1800 Sat. Bakes, open
sandwiches. A la carte Sat. E£.

Golden Garden ⊻
140 Longstone St. ☎ 671311.
1200-1400 Thur-Sat, 1700-
2400 Mon-Sat. Chinese &
European. E£.

Grooms ⊻
Down Royal Park,
6 Dunygarton Rd, Maze.
☎ 621668. 1200-2200 Mon-
Sat, 1230-1430 & 1900-2200
Sun. Steaks, chicken, salads.
E££.

Hague's Bar ⊻
32 Chapel Hill. ☎ 663224.
1230-1430 Mon-Sat.
Chicken, plaice, home-made
bread, teas.

Harry Ramsden's
The Omniplex, Governor's Rd.
☎ 667838. 1200-2300 Mon-
Thur, from 1100 Frit-Sat,
1230-2230 Sun. Gourmet fish
& chips, desserts.

Hedley's ⊗
43 Bow St. ☎ 681337. 0900-
1700 Mon-Sat. Savoury pies,
curries, home baking,

Homestead Inn ⊔
314 Hillhall Rd. ☎ (01232)
826273. Until 1945 Mon-Thur
and until 2045 Fri-Sun.
Chicken balti with garlic naam
bread, smoked haddock.

Indian Cottage
13 Bachelors Walk.
☎ 665000. 1200-1400 &
1700-2330 Mon-Sat, until
2230 Sun. Indian & European.

Inglenook ⊗
17 Market St. ☎ 665401.
0930-1700 Mon-Wed, until
2145 Thur-Sat. Lemon
chicken, casseroles, chocolate
cake. £££.

Irish Linen Centre
Café Crommelin, Market
Square. ☎ 663377. 0930-
1700 Mon-Sat, 1400-1730
Sun. Soups, salads, bakes,
pastries. In linen centre.

Jacob Marley's
2 Haslem's Lane. ☎ 605868
0900-1630 Mon-Sat. Quiche,
lasagne, scones.

Jeffers ⊗
20 Market Square. ☎ 663210.
0845-1700 Mon-Sat. Soups,
grills, salads.

Kentucky Fried Chicken
Omniplex, Governor's Rd.
☎ 666391. 1100-2400 Mon-
Sun. Fast food.

★ **LAUREL INN** ⊔
99 Carryduff Rd. ☎ 638422.
1230-1400 Mon-Sat, until
1430 Sun, 1730-2130 Mon-
Sun. A la carte. ££.

Lisnoe Cottage
Duneight, 37 Lisnoe Rd.
☎ 663565. Morning coffee,
light teas by arrangement in
historic cottage at plant
nursery.

Lotus House ⊔
58 Bow St. ☎ 678669. 1200-
1415 Mon-Sat, 1700-2400
Mon-Thur & Sun, until 0100
Fri-Sat. Chinese & European.
£££.

Manor Inn ⊔
29 Longstone St. ☎ 662386.
1200-1430 Tues-Sat. Pub grub.

Margarita's Cantina ⊔
Lisburn Leisure Centre,
Omniplex, Governor's Rd.
☎ 628873. 1230-1430 &
1700-2200. Mexican.

Maze Station ⊔
228 Moira Rd, Maze.
☎ 621538. 1200-1430 Mon-
Sat, 1700-2045 Wed-Sat,
1900-2045 Sun. Scampi,
chicken, salads.

McDonald's
54 Bow St. ☎ 660222. 0800-
2300 Mon-Sat, 0900-2300
Sun. Fast food.

Peking Palace ⚌
58 Chapel Hill. ☎ 670445.
1200-1400 & 1700-2400
Mon-Sun. Chinese &
European. E£.

Pipers Quay ⚌
88 Bridge St. ☎ 628816. 1200-
1430 Mon-Sat, 1700-1900
Mon-Fri, 1230-2100 Sun.
Mackerel mousse, duck liver
terrine with onion compote.

Pizza Hut ⚌
Omniplex, Governor's Rd.
☎ 604272. 1200-2300 Mon-
Thur, until 2400 Fri-Sun.
Pizzas, salad bar.

Pizzarelly's ⚱
10 Bachelor's Walk.
☎ 671980. 1000-2200
Mon-Sat. Pizzas, pasta, grills.

Quincy's Restaurante
Omniplex, Governor's Rd.
☎ 605151. 1100-2300 Mon-
Sun. Steaks, chicken, lasagne,
salads, vegetarian.

Racecourse Inn ⚌ ⊘
60 Gravel Hill Rd. ☎ 621249.
1230-1430 & 1700-2030
Mon-Fri, 1200-2100 Sat,
1230-1430 & 1900-2030 Sun.
High tea, à la carte.
Sunday carvery.

Restbite
Lisburn Leisure Centre.
☎ 679564. 1030-2130 Mon-
Fri, until 1800 Sat, 1400-1800
Sun. Fish & chips, salads

Roadside Café
1 Glenavy Rd. ☎ 651379.
0900-1700 Mon-Sat. Toasties,
salads, pastries.

Robin's Nest ⚌
41 Railway St. ☎ 678065.
1130-2300 Mon-Sat. Pies,
scampi. Pub grub.

Rumbles
42 Longstone St. ☎ 676292.
1100-0100 Mon-Sun. Fish,
chicken.

Sprucefield ⊘
☎ 661244. 1000-2000 Mon &
Tues, 0930-2100 Wed-Fri,
until 1900 Sat. Pastries, coffee,
lasagne, beef stroganoff. Café
in out-of-town shopping centre
off A1.

Stepping Stones
29 Seymour St. ☎ 667124.
1000-1600 Tues-Sat. Tray
bakes, curry toasties, pitta
bread.

Super Fry
19 Antrim St. ☎ 675857.
1100-1800 Mon-Sat, ex Wed.
Fast food.

Tap Room ♿
Hilden Brewery Visitor Centre.
Grand St. ☎ 660800. 1200-
1430 Tues-Sat. Trout, lasagne,
steak, baked potatoes.
(Evening group bookings).

**Temple Golf
  & Country Club** ♿
60 Church Rd, Boardmills.
☎ 639213. 1200-1430, 1730-
2030 Tues-Fri. 1200-2030 Sat,
high tea 1530-2030. Sun.
Baked mussels on the shell,
prawn cocktail, stir fries,
steaks.

The In Plaice
79a Sloan St. ☎ 605653. 0900-
1400 & 1630-2230 Mon-Fri.
Breakfast. Salads, fish & chips.

Tidy Doffer ♿
133 Ravarnet Rd. ☎ 689188.
1200-1430 Mon-Sun, 1700-
2130 Mon-Thur, later Fri &
Sat, until 2100 Sun. Garlic
prawns, ribs, steaks, fish. E£.

Toffs
6 Railway St. ☎ 671369.
0930-1630 Mon-Sat. Curry,
lasagne, quiche.

Tormore
Temple Shopping Centre,
Carryduff Rd, The Temple.
☎ 638633. 0900-1730 Mon-
Sat. Fries, steak pie, pastries.
On A24.

Treasure Inn ♿
58 Bow St. ☎ 678669. 1200-
1400 Mon-Sat, 1700-2400
Mon-Sun. Chinese.

MALLUSK
(STD 01232)

Cottonmount Arms ♿
128 Mallusk Rd. ☎ (01232)
832006. 1700-2030 Fri-Sun.
Grills, steak, fish, vegetarian.

Roughfort Inn ♿
230 Mallusk Rd. ☎ (01849)
432963. 1200-1500 Thur-Sat.
Grills, snacks.

MUCKAMORE
(STD 01849)

Barleycorn ♿
103 Seven Mile Straight.
☎ 463450. 1200-1800 Wed,
until 2100 Thur, 2200 Fri-Sat,
1900 Sun. Pub grub.

NEWTOWNABBEY
(STD 01232)

Burnfield House Golf Club ♿
10 Cullyburn Rd. ☎ 838737.
March-Sept 1230-2100 Wed-
Sat, until 1900 Sun. Pub grub,
à la carte £.

Café Creme
Abbey Centre, Longwood Rd.
☎ 868058. 0900-1730 Mon,
Tues & Sat, until 2100 Wed-
Fri. Fast food.

Cloughfern Arms 🍷
214 Doagh Rd. ☎ 862387. 1230-1500 Tues-Thur, until 1800 Fri-Sat. Pub grub.

Corr's Corner Hotel 🍷
315 Ballyclare Rd. ☎ 849221. 1200-2200 Mon-Sat, 1230-1400 & 1900-2100 Sun. Carvery. A la carte. E££.

★ **GINGER TREE** 🍷
29 Ballyrobert Rd. ☎ 848176. 1200-1400 Mon-Fri, 1900-2200 Mon-Sat. Japanese. E£££.

Glenavna House Hotel 🍷
588 Shore Rd. ☎ 864461. Last orders 2200, Sun 1930. Tender fillet of chicken cooked in richly flavoured sauce with chillies & chocolate, creamy coconut ice cream.

Khyber 🍷
Olivia Centre, 373 Antrim Rd. ☎ 849414. 1200-1345 & 1700-2315 Mon-Sat, 1700-2045 Sun. Indian.

Kinara Restaurant 🍷
675 Shore Rd. ☎ 365800. 1700-2300 Mon-Sat, until 2200 Sun. Chinese.

Lady Love 🍷
158 Antrim Rd. ☎ 771383. 1200-1400 & 1700-2400 Mon-Sun. Chinese & European. E££.

Maggie's Kitchen
14 Abbotts Cross. ☎ 863045. 0900-1700 Mon-Sat. Fries, toasties, sandwiches, stews.

McDonald's
Longwood Rd. ☎ 866551. 0800-2300 Mon-Thur, until 2300 Fri-Sat, 0900-2300 Sun. Fast food.

McMillen's 🍷
15 Kiln Rd. ☎ 837144. 1200-1500 Tues-Sat, 1830-2130 Wed-Sat, 1200-2000 Sun. Seafood, game, steak, vegetarian, salads.

Rory's 🍾
611 Shore Rd, Whiteabbey. ☎ 865234. 1030-1430 & 1700-2100 Mon-Sat. Steaks, beef stroganoff, vegetarian curries. Snacks.

Royal Thai 🍷
377 Antrim Rd. ☎ 830007. 1200-1400 & 1700-2400 Mon-Sat, 1230-2400 Sun. Chinese & Thai.

Skandia 🍾
Abbey Centre, Longwood Rd. ☎ 365960. 0900-1730 Mon-Tues, until 2130 Wed-Fri, 1800 Sat.

Valley Leisure Centre
40 Church Rd. ☎ 861211. Bistro: 1000-2200 Mon-Fri, until 1800 Sat -Sun. Grills, sandwiches, snacks.

Whittley's ♀
401 Ballyclare Rd. ☎ 832438.
1200-1430 & 1700-2130
Mon-Fri, 1200-2130 Sat,
1900-2130 Sun. Steaks, garlic
prawns, vegetarian. E£££.

Woody's ♀
607 Shore Rd, Jordanstown.
☎ 863206. 1200-1430 Mon-
Sat. Pub grub.

Bayview Hotel ♀
2 Bayhead Rd. ☎ 31453.
Last orders 2130. Set meals.
A la carte. E££.

Beach House Hotel ♀
61 Beach Rd. ☎ 31214. Last
orders 2130. Set meals.
A la carte. ££.

PORTBALLINTRAE
(STD 012657)

Sallie's
47 Beach Rd. ☎ 31328.
Easter-end June 1100-1800 Fri-
Sun, plus Tues-Thur July-Aug.
Crafts/coffee shop. Pizzas,
baked potatoes, pastries.

★ **SWEENEY'S WINE BAR** ♀

6b Seaport Avenue. ☎ 32405.
1200-2000 Mon-Sat, 1230-
1430 & 1900-2100 Sun.
Char- grilled steaks, pork ribs,
vegetarian.

PORTGLENONE
(STD 01266)

Bann Restaurant
30 Main St. ☎ 821267. 0900-
1800 Mon-Sat. Pizzas,
hamburgers.

Golden Hill ♀
11 Clady Rd. ☎ 822168.
1700-2400 Mon-Sun.
Chinese & European. £.

Hawthorne Inn ♀
54 Kilrea Rd. ☎ 821523.
1900-2130 Thur-Sat. Pub grub.

Pat's Bar ♀
71 Main St. ☎ 821231. 1130-
2300 Mon-Sat, 1230-2200
Sun. Pub grub.

Teague's Bar ♀
46 Glenowen Rd, Clady.
☎ 822617. 1200-1430 Mon-
Sat, 1800-2100 Sun. Grills,
bar snacks.

Wild Duck ♀
93 Main St. ☎ 821232. 1200-
2130 Mon-Sat, until 2100 Sun.
Pub grub, à la carte. E£.

PORTRUSH
(STD 01265)

Beetles Bistro ♀
Golf Links Hotel, Bushmills
Rd. ☎ 822288. 1200-2130
Mon-Sun. Steak, chicken, fish,
vegetarian. Live entertainment.
E££.

Bethel
7 Lansdowne Crescent.
☎ 822354. Lunch, dinner.
Must book.

Bread Shop
21 Eglinton St. ☎ 823722.
0830-1730 Mon-Sat, 1000-
1700 Sun, in summer daily
until 1900. Breads, pies, Irish
stew, champ, Ulster fry, all
freshly prepared and baked
on premises.

Café-de-Lux
4 Main St. June-Sept 1100-
1900 Mon-Sun. Fish & chips,
ice cream, cakes.

Carousel
6 Main St. ☎ 824411. 0900-
2200 Mon-Sun, until 2100
winter. Set lunches, chicken,
grills.

Causeway Coast Hotel ♈
36 Ballyreagh Rd. ☎ 822435.
1230-1400 & 1730-2130
Mon-Sun. Garlic mushrooms
with smoked bacon, darne of
salmon. ££.

Don Giovanni's ♈
9 Causeway St. ☎ 825516.
1730-2300 Mon-Sun. Pizza,
pasta, fish. E£.

Donovan's ♈
92 Main St. ☎ 822063. 1230-
1500 & 1700-2200 Mon-Sun.
Pub grub, pasta, salads.

Dunluce Centre
☎ 824444. May-Aug 1000-
2200 Mon-Sun, shorter hours
Sept. In winter 1400-2100 Fri-
Sun only. Ulster fry, chicken,
fish. E£.

Eglinton Hotel ♈
49 Eglinton St. ☎ 822371.
Last orders 2130. Fresh
haddock, Ulster fry, black
pudding. A la carte. ££.

Golden Eagle
48 Main St. ☎ 825615. 0900-
1800 Mon-Sun. Weekends
only in winter. Fast food.

Graham's
48 Main St. ☎ 822427. 1030-
2200 Mon-Sun. In winter
1200-1830 Sat-Sun. Fresh fish,
chicken & ham pie, roast beef
with Yorkshire pudding, salads.
In gift shop, self service.

Harbour Inn ♈
5 Harbour Rd. ☎ 825047.
1130-2100 Mon-Sat, 1230-
1900 Sun. Fresh seafood. E£.

Kentucky Fried Chicken
54 Main St. ☎ 824689. Sept-
June 1100-2400 Mon-Wed,
until 0200 Thur-Sun. Fast food.

★ **MAGHERABUOY HOUSE
   HOTEL** ♈ ⊘
41 Magheraboy Rd.
☎ 823507. Last orders 2130.
Fresh baked salmon, game
terrine, roast breast of
duckling, baked alaska on
blackcurrant sauce. E££.

McLaughlin's Bar ♀
50 Ballyreagh Rd. ☎ 823509.
1200-2130 Mon-Sun.
Snacks, pub grub.

Morelli's
7 Eglinton St. ☎ 824848. 1100-
2200 Mon-Sun. Pizza,
lasagne, toasties, home-made
ice cream.

Peninsula Hotel ♀
15 Eglinton St. ☎ 822293.
Last orders 2030. A la carte.

Port Hotel ♀
53 Main St. ☎ 825353. 1200-
2100 Mon-Sun. A la carte E£.

★ RAMORE ♀

The Harbour. ☎ 824313.
Wine bar 1200-1400 & 1730-
2100 Mon-Sat. Restaurant
1830-2230 Tues-Sat. Thai
chicken, tempura prawn, hot
fresh fruit & grand marnier
souffle. £££.

Royal Court Hotel ♀
233 Ballybogey Rd, White
Rocks. ☎ 822236. Last orders
2130, Sun 2100. Grill bar.
Steaks, open sandwiches,
vegetarian. A la carte ££.

Shirley's Diner
26 Causeway St. ☎ 823581.
1100-2200 Mon-Sun, shorter
hours winter. Scampi, steaks.

Silver Sands
27 Eglinton St. ☎ 824113.
0900-2300 Mon-Sun, until
1900 in winter. Fish & chips,
Ulster fry.

Some Plaice Else ♦
21 Ballyreagh Rd. ☎ 824945.
1700-2130 Mon-Thur & Sun,
until 2200 Fri-Sat, 1230-1430
Sun. Seafood. E££.

Spinnaker ♀
25 Main St. ☎ 822348. 1030-
2130 Mon-Sun, shorter hours
in winter. Home-baked cakes.
Set lunch, à la carte E£.

Station Bar ♀
16c Eglinton St. ☎ 822112.
1200-2100. Mon-Sat. Coffee,
sandwiches. In nightclub.

Taj ♀
53 Eglinton St. ☎ 823855.
1700-2300. Mon-Sat. Indian &
European.

Uncle Saams
35 Eglinton St. ☎ 824796.
0900-2100 Mon-Sun. Chicken,
steaks, salads.

Waterworld
The Harbour. ☎ 822001.
1000-2200 Mon-Sat, from
1400 Sun. Closed winter. Fish
& chips, salads, coffee.

RANDALSTOWN
(STD 01849)

Corner House Bar ♀
30 Main St. ☎ 472488. 1130-
2400 Mon-Sat, 1430-2200
Sun. Pub grub.

Cranfield Inn 🍷
34 Cranfield Rd. ☎ 472342. 1800-2300 Mon-Fri, 1300-2300 Sat, 1230-1430 & 1900-2200 Sun. Fish, eel suppers, sausages.

Granagh House 🍷
9 New St. ☎ 472758. 1200-2200 Mon-Sun. Bar snacks. Fish, gammon with pineapple, chicken charlotte.

Marrion's 🍷
10 Main St. ☎ 472487. 1130-2300 Mon-Sat, 1230-1430 & 1900-2200 Sun. Pies.

O'Kane's 🍷
22 Main St. ☎ 473101. 1230-1430 & 1800-2100 Mon-Sat. Ulster fry, plaice, breadcrumbed hokey, toasties.

Waves
56 Main St. ☎ 472680. 1130-2400 Mon-Thur, longer hours Fri-Sat, 1630-2330 Sun. Fish & chips, curry.

RATHLIN ISLAND
(STD 012657)

Chip-a-Hoy Restaurant 🍴
The Harbour. ☎ 63907. 1100-
1800 Mon-Sun, weekends
only in winter. Speciality
seafood.

Manor House
Rathlin Island. 63964. 1000-
1730 Mon-Sun. Home-made
soup, wheaten bread,
sandwiches, scones. Evening
meals available. National Trust
property.

McCuaig's Bar ♀
The Harbour. ☎ 63974. 0900-
2100 Mon-Sun. Breakfast.
Plaice, champ.

Rathlin Guesthouse 🍴
The Quay. ☎ 63917.
Open Mon-Sun. Soup,
sandwiches. Must book high
tea, dinner. E£.

STONEYFORD
(STD 01846)

Ballymac ♀
7a Rock Rd. ☎ 648313. 1130-
2200 Mon-Sat, 1230-2100
Sun. A la carte. E££.

TEMPLEPATRICK
(STD 01849)

Airport Inn ♀
745 Antrim Rd. ☎ 432775.
1230-2145 Mon-Sat, 1230-
1430 Sun. Carvery. A la carte.
££.

Ellie May's ♀
252 Belfast Rd, Muckamore.
☎ 433796. 1800-2130 Mon-
Fri, 1900-2200 Sat, until 2100
Sun. Special chicken, salmon,
steaks. ££

Happy Inn ♀
8 Twelfth Milestone.
☎ 433717. 1200-1400 &
1730-2330 Mon-Sat, 1300-
1500 & 1700-2400 Sun.
Cantonese & European. ££.

Lyle Hill Tavern ♀
96 Lylehill Rd. ☎ 432451.
1200-1500 Thur-Sat.
Ulster fry, stew, pies.

Serendipity
Twelfth Milestone, 945 Antrim
Rd. ☎ 433475. 0900-1700
Mon-Thur, until 2100 Fri-Sat,
1000-1700 Sun. Stew, quiches,
toasties, coffee, home baking.
Grill room ££.

Stakis Park Hotel ♀
Castle Upton Estate,
Templepatrick. ☎ 435500.
1230-1400 & 1830-2145
Mon-Sun. Hot peppered
mackerel fillet, escalope of
pork, leak & potato bake,
Armagh lattice tart.

★ **TEMPLETON HOTEL** ♀

882 Antrim Rd. ☎ 432984.
Last orders 2145, 1945 Sun.
Grill room hours vary. Roasted
salmon with saffron & dill,
ostrich fillet. A la carte E£££.

Wayside Inn ♀
25 New Mill Rd, Ballywee.
☎ (01960) 324276. 1200-2300
Mon-Sat. Chicken, salads,
grills.

TOOMEBRIDGE
(STD 01648)

Drumderg Café
177 Moneynick Rd. ☎ 50306.
0800-1830 Mon-Sat. Grills,
home-baked cakes, coffee.

Elver Inn ♀
100 Moneynick Rd. ☎ 50362.
1230-1430 Mon-Sat. Pub grub.

O'Neill Arms Hotel ♀
20 Main St. ☎ 50202. Last
orders 2030. Breakfast, high
tea. Fish, roast beef, chicken
with prawn & salmon. Sunday
carvery 1230-1900. £.

T-Junction Café
62 Hillhead Rd. ☎ 50095.
0930-1900 Mon-Sat. Fish &
chips, Irish stew, sandwiches.
On A6.

WATERFOOT
(STD 012667)

Angela's Restaurant & Bakery
32 Main St. ☎ 71700. 0900-
1800 Mon-Sat & 1000-1900
Sun. Breakfast. Scones,
lasagne, prawn salad, toasties.

Mariners Bar ♀
7 Main St. ☎ 71330. 1200-
1500 Mon-Sat, 1230-1430
Sunday lunch. Salads, soups,
rolls, steaks.

Village Tea Room
32 Main St. ☎ 71700. 1000-
1900 Mon-Sun. Hot meals and
snacks. All home cooked.

WHITEHEAD
(STD 01960)

Bentra Roadhouse ♀
1 Slaughterford Rd. ☎ 353666.
1200-1445 Mon-Sat, from
1230 Sun, 1700-2045 Sun-
Thur, until 2145 Fri-Sat. Beef,
chicken, steak, fish. E£.
Whitehead

Coffee & Cream
10 King's Rd. ☎ 378757.
0900-1900 Mon-Sat. Chicken,
fish, salads, sandwiches,
scones coffee.

Ocean City
2 Marine Avenue. ☎ 353276.
1145-1400 Mon-Sat, 1700-
2200 Tues-Thur, until 2400 Fri
& Sat, 2000 Sun. Chinese &
European.

ARMAGH
(STD 01861)

★ ARCHWAY
5 Hartford Place, The Mall.
☎ 522532. 1000-1700 Tues-Sat.
Pastries, apple pie.

Basement Café
Market St (below cinema).
☎ 524311. 0900-1900 Mon-
Sat. Steak sandwiches, bakes,
salads.

Bramley Family Kitchen
Orchard Centre, Folly Lane.
☎ 515920. 1000-2200 Mon-Fri,
until 2200 Sat, 1400-1800 Sun.
Home-made soup & snacks.

Cafe Papa
15 Thomas St. Freshly baked
scones, hot snacks, gourmet
sandwiches, soup, pastries.
Freshly ground coffee, Maud's
ice cream.

Calvert's Tavern ⚲
3 Scotch St. ☎ 524186. 1200-
1430 & 1800-2200 Mon-Sun.
Pub grub.

Cellar Lounge ⚲
55 Thomas St. ☎ 525147.
1200-1500 Fri & Sat. Pub grub.

Charlemont Arms Hotel ⚲
63 Upper English St. ☎ 522028.
Last orders 2130. Set lunch.
Steak, scampi, chicken. E£.

Cottage Restaurant ⊘
Gazette Arcade, Scotch St.
☎ 528582. 0830-1730 Mon-
Sat, until 1400 Wed. Morning
coffee, lunch, home baking.

Damper Murphy's ⚲
48 Lower Irish St. ☎ 528134.
1230-1430 Mon-Sun ex Tues.
Pub grub.

De-Averell Guesthouse ▲
47 Upper English St.
☎ 511213. 1030-1500 Mon-
Sat, coffee, lunch. 1800-2200
Mon-Sun. Steak, fish, Mexican,
Italian. E££.

Diamond Bar ♆
21 Lower English St.
☎ 522645. 1200-1430 Mon-Sat. Soup, Irish stew.

Downtown Café
13 Dobbin St. ☎ 523538.
0900-1800 Mon-Sat, until
1400 Wed. Fast food.

Drumsill House Hotel ♆ ⊙
35 Moy Rd. ☎ 522009. Last
orders 2200. Salmon, steaks.
Lunch-time carvery. £££.

Fat Sam's
7 Lower English St. ☎ 525555.
0845-1800 Mon-Fri, 0915-
1700 Sat. Lasagne, salads,
sandwiches.

Glencoe ♆
72 Scotch St. ☎ 522994. 1200-
1400 Mon-Fri. Pub grub.

Harry Hoots ♆
143 Railway St. ☎ 522103.
1230-1430 & 1900-2130
Mon-Sun. Pub grub.

Hester's Place
12 Upper English St.
☎ 522374. 0900-1730 Mon-
Sat, closed Wed. Irish stew,
bacon & cabbage, home-
baked Armagh apple tart &
cream.

Jodie's ♆
37 Scotch St. ☎ 527577.
1200-1500 Mon-Fri, 1730-
2145 Wed-Fri, 1000-2200 Sat,
until 2000 Sun. Steaks, fish.
A la carte £££.

Johnston's Coffee Lounge
9 Scotch St. ☎ 522995. 0900-
1730 Mon-Sat, closed Wed.
Irish stew, salads, sandwiches,
pastries.

Ken's
16 Barrack St. ☎ 525692.
0900-2100 Mon-Sat. Grills,
snacks, pies.

Mandarin House ♆
30 Scotch St. ☎ 522228. 1200-
1400 & 1700-2300 Tues-Sat.
1700-2300 Sun. Chinese &
European. ££.

McAnerney's
Irish St. ☎ 522468. 0900-1730
Mon-Sat. Coffee, salads, rolls.

★ **NAVAN CENTRE** ⊙

Killylea Rd. ☎ 525550. 1000-
1700 Mon-Fri, later start Sat-
Sun. Hot meals, snacks. In
interpretive centre.

Northern Bar ♆
100 Railway St. ☎ 527316.
1230-1430 Mon-Sun.
Pub grub.

Orr's Corner ♆
36 Barrack St. ☎ 522052.
1130-2200 Mon-Sun.
Traditional Sunday lunch,
steaks.Cellar restaurant/coffee
house.

Our Ma's
2 Lower English St. ☎ 511289.
0900-1730 Mon-Sat. Breakfast.
Steak, fish, salads, vegetarian.

Palace Demesne
Friary Rd. ☎ 529629. 1000-
1630 Mon-Sat, 1230-2130
Sun. Last orders Thur-Sat 2130.
Antrim turkey, home-made
bread, quiches, salads, fish,
ham. In heritage centre.

Pat-a-Cake
27 Upper English St.
☎ 522862. 0830-1730 Mon-
Sat, until 1400 Wed. Salad
rolls, soda farls, soup.
In bakery.

Pub With No Beer
30 Thomas St. ☎ 523586.
0900-2230 Mon-Sat. Chicken
pie, savoury mince, champ,
salads. Soft drinks, tea, coffee.

Rainbow ⊘
13 Upper English St.
☎ 525391. 0830-1730. Mon-
Sat. Fish, ham, peppered
chicken.

Shambles Bar ⊻
9 Lower English St. ☎ 524107.
1230-1430 Mon-Sat. Fish,
duck, steak, vegetarian.

St Patrick's Trian
Pilgrim's Table, 38 English St.
☎ 521814. Open Mon-Sun.
Potato & leek soup, steak,
hotpot. In heritage centre.

Station Bar ⊻
3 Lower English St. ☎ 523731.
1230-1430 Mon-Sat. Chicken,
fish in batter, salads.

Strawberry Bar ⊻
23 Lower English St.
☎ 523865. 1230-1430 Fri-Sun.
Soup, steaks, salads.

BELLEEKS
(STD 01693)

Glenside Bar & Lounge ⊻
15 Main St. ☎ 878280. 1900-
2200 Mon-Sat. Soup, steak,
chips, salads, sweets.

Mountain House ⊻
Drumilly. ☎ 838766. 1900-
2100 Thur-Sat. Scampi, plaice,
steak, mixed grills, savoury
omelettes.

BLACKWATERTOWN
(STD 01861)

Portmor House ⊻
44 Main St. ☎ 548053. 1230-
1430 Wed-Sun, 1800-2200
Fri-Sun. Pub grub. Steaks, beef
& chicken poivrade, fillet of
trout. E££.

CAMLOUGH
(STD 01693)

Finnegan's ⊻
25 Main St. ☎ 830044. 1230-
1430 Mon-Sat. Pub grub.

Village Inn ⊻
21 Main St. ☎ 838537. 1200-
1430 & 1700-2100 Mon-Sat.
Pub grub. Chicken, steak, fish,
Irish stew.

Toucan's Perch ⅊
33 Main St, Charlemont.
☎ 84808. 1130-2300 Mon-Sat,
1230-1430 & 1900-2200 Sun.
Grills, salads, stews.

CRAIGAVON
(STD 01762)

Craigavon Leisure Centre ⊘
Brownlow Rd. ☎ 341333.
1200-1400 & 1700-2130
Mon-Fri, 1000-1700 Sat.
Grills. In recreation centre.

Loughside Café
Lough Neagh Discovery
Centre, Oxford Island.
☎ 322205. 1000-1430 Mon-
Sun. Soup, pies, lasagne.

Mr Pickwick's Kitchen
Craigavon Shopping Centre,
15 Market Lane. ☎ 341025.
0900-1730 Mon-Wed & Sat,
until 2100 Thur-Fri. Grills.

Number 7
Craigavon Shopping Centre,
15 Market Lane. ☎ 342629.
0845-2100 Wed-Fri, until
1730 Mon-Tues & Sat. Home-
made shepherd's pie, breaded
fish, salads, fresh-baked
scones, pastries.

CROSSMAGLEN
(STD 01693)

Ashfield Golf Club ⅊
Freeduff, Cullyhanna.
☎ 868180. 1200-2100 Tues-
Sun, from 1400 Mon. Soups,
steak, fish, salads.

Cartwheel ⅊
20 The Square. ☎ 861285.
1800-2300 Mon-Sat. Pub grub.
E£.

Chums ⅊
46 The Square. ☎ 868413.
1230-1430 Mon-Sat. Soup &
roll, pork chops, gammon.

Conalig House ⅊
124 Concession Rd.
☎ 861517. 1900-2200 Mon-
Sat. Pub grub.

Hearty's Folk Cottage
Glassdrummond. ☎ 868188.
1400-1800 Sun. Home-baked
cakes, scones. Traditional
music. Antiques/crafts on sale.

JB's Cabin ⅊
4 Donaldson Rd. ☎ 868424.
1900-2200 Thur-Sat. Pub grub.

Keenan's ⅊
42 The Square. ☎ 868071.
1900-2100 Fri-Sat. Pub grub.

Kerryman ⅊
36 The Square. ☎ 861589.
1900-2200 Mon-Sat. Irish
stew, chips.

Lima Country House
16 Drumalt Rd, Silverbridge.
☎ 861944. 1800-2200 Mon-
Sat. High tea, dinner. Chicken,
steak, fish. Must book.

Lite & Easy ⏴
Tullynavall Rd. ☎ 868262.
1200-1700 Mon-Sat. Bar
snacks. 4 miles NE of village.

Murtaghs ⏴
15 North St. ☎ 861378. 1230-
1430 Mon-Sat. Pub grub.

CULLYHANNA

**Cardinal O'Fiaich
Heritage Centre**
Slatequarry Rd, Cullyhanna.
Mon-Fri lunch only. Teas,
coffees by arrangement.

HAMILTONSBAWN
(STD 01762)

Bawn Inn ⏴
25 Main St. ☎ 871239. 1130-
2330 Mon-Sat. Pub grub.

Corner Bar ⏴
Main St. ☎ 871070. 1500-
2330 Mon-Fri, 1130-2330 Sat.
Hamburgers, stew.

JONESBOROUGH

Flurrybridge Inn ⏴
☎ (01693) 848181. 1800-2230
Thur-Sun, 1230-1530 Sun.
European, Chinese & Indian.

KEADY
(STD 01861)

Callan River Inn ⏴
2 The Square. ☎ 539679.
1230-1500 Mon-Sat. Chicken,
scampi, plaice.

Carnagh Country House ⏴
121 Castleblaney Rd.
☎ 538935. Bar snacks. Sunday
carvery 1230-1530. 1900-
2130 Thur-Sun à la carte.
Oysters, trout, salmon, steaks.
E££.

Old Mill
Kinelowen St. ☎ 539959.
0900-1830 Mon-Sun. Home
cooking. In heritage centre.

Rock Bar ⏴
Granemore. ☎ 538758. 2000-
0100 Fri-Sat, 1900-2200 Sun.
Pub grub.

The Trap ⏴
37 Kinelowen St. ☎ 538889.
1230-1430 Mon-Sun. Pub
grub. A la carte.

KILLYLEA

Digby's & Red Grouse ⏴
53 Main St. ☎ (01861)
568330. 1230-1430 Tues-Sun,
1830-2400 Wed-Sun. Lemon
sole, scampi, steak. M£. E££.

LOUGHGALL
(STD 01762)

★ FAMOUS GROUSE ♐

6 Ballyhagan Rd. ☎ (01762) 891778. Bar snacks 1200-2100 Mon-Sat. 1900-2200 Wed-Sat, 1230-1430 & 1730-2015 Sun. Irish salmon, duckling. E££.

LURGAN
(STD 01762)

Alpine Lodge
Ski Centre, Turmoyra Lane, Silverwood. ☎ 326606. 1100-1900 Mon-Fri, 0900-1800 Sat-Sun. Chicken, salads, vegetarian.

Andrea's Coffee House
64 Belfast Rd. ☎ 324950. 0800-1700 Mon-Sat, until 1900 Thur-Fri. Scones, salads.

Ashburn Hotel ♐
81 William St. ☎ 325711. Last orders 2100, Fri-Sat 2130. Bar food. A la carte E££.

Brindle Beam Tea Rooms
20 Windsor Avenue. ☎ 321721. 1000-1430 Mon-Sat. Chicken & broccoli crunch, salads. £.

Cafolla
2 Carnegie St. ☎ 323331. 1000-1730 Mon-Sat. Fish & chips, home-made ice cream.

Cafolla Bros
51 Church Place. ☎ 324022. 1000-1730 Mon-Wed, until 1800 Thur-Sat. Breakfast. Fish & chips, sandwiches, home-made ice cream.

Castle Park Inn ♐
Robert St. ☎ 322726. 1200-1430 & 1700-2100 Mon-Sat (ex Sun evening). Pub grub.

Cellar Lounge ♐
50 Church Place. ☎ 327994. 1200-1500 Mon-Sat. Pub grub.

Corner House ♐
93 Silverwood Rd, Derrymacash. ☎ 341817. 1200-1430 Mon-Sat, until 1500 Sun. 1900-2200 Fri-Sat, 1730-2100 Sun. Steak & Guinness pie, poached salmon, baked ham. E£.

Cosy Corner
2 Church Place. ☎ 349678. 0900-1700 Mon-Thur, 0900-2100 Sat-Sun. Grills, salads.

Crocadero Restaurant ♐
Belfast Rd, Dollingstown. ☎ 322260. 1200-1430 daily ex Mon, 1700-1900 Tues, until 1800 Wed, 2130 Thur-Fri, 2100 Sat-Sun. A la carte, high tea. Chicken curry, Mexican cod with parsley sauce. £.

Derryhirk Inn ♐
Derryhirk Rd, Aghagallon. ☎ (01846) 651251. 1800-2130 Mon-Sun, 1230-1430 Sun. Chicken, steaks, salads. Bar snacks from 1130 Fri-Sun.

Ed's Bistro ♦
9 North St. ☎ 324985. 0900-
1800 Mon-Wed, until 2100
Thur, 2300 Fri-Sat. 1100-2000
Sun. All-day breakfast, steaks,
seafood, salads.

Kebab King
62 William St. ☎ 325200.
1200-2400 Mon-Sun. Indian,
fish, snacks.

Long Hall
22a High St. ☎ 328974. 0930-
1700 Mon-Sat, closed Wed.
Broccoli quiche, scones,
afternoon tea.

Old Yard ♦ ⊘
Edenmore House, 70
Drumnabreeze Rd. ☎ (01846)
619199. 0930-1630 Mon-Sat.
Caribbean chicken, seafood
crunch. At golf course.

Peking Chinese ♦ ⊻
86 William St. ☎ 342290.
1700-2200 Tues-Sun. Chinese
& European. ££.

Pizza Pasta Hut ♦
42 Church Place. ☎ 326444.
1700-2300 Mon-Sat, until
2200 Sun. Pizza, pasta.

Rumpoles
High St. ☎ 321747. 0800-1730
Mon-Sat. Fast food.

Silverwood Hotel ⊻
Kiln Rd. ☎ 327722. Last orders
2130, Sun 2030. Bar snacks
from 1130. Carvery lunch
Mon-Fri, Sunday lunch 1230-
1430. Beef stroganoff, steaks.
££.

Simply Enchanting
23a High St. ☎ 349207. 0930-
1630 Mon-Sat ex Wed.
Scones, traybakes, toasted
sandwiches. In craft shop.

Spades
Stewarts Shopping Complex,
Windsor Avenue. ☎ 343558.
0900-1730 Mon-Wed & Sat,
until 2100 Thur-Fri. Quiche,
lasagne, pie.

Stables ⊻
Old Portadown Rd. ☎ 323974.
1900-2200 Tues-Fri,1100-2230
Sat, 1200-1400 Sun. Pub grub.
Grills, salads.

The Mall
Waves Complex, Robert St.
☎ 322906. 1000-2130 Mon-
Sat, closed Thur. Pies, Irish
stew, salads.

Vintage ⊻
31 Church Place. ☎ 328757.
1230-1430 Mon-Sat, until
1500 Sun. Pub grub.

White Wren
45 Market St. ☎ 325418.
0900-1800 Mon-Sat.

Wilton Cross ⊻
38 Church Place. ☎ 322076.
1200-1500 Mon-Thur, 1800-
2100 Thur, 1200-2100 Fri-Sat,
1230-1430 Sun. Scampi,
plaice, minute steak, pork
chops. ££.

MARKETHILL
(STD 01861)

The Buttery ⚲
103 Main St. ☎ 551237. 1230-
1430 Tues-Fri, 1900-2130
Wed-Sat. Chicken, grills, steaks,
salads.

Corner Bar ⚲
110 Main St. ☎ 551887. 1230-
1500 Tues-Fri, 1900-2200 Fri-
Sat. Pub grub.

Gosford Forest Park
☎ 551277. 1200-1700 Mon-
Sun July-Aug. Easter-Sept
weekends only. Scones,
pastries, chocolate cake.
Teashop in forest park. Off B28.

★ OLD THATCH
3 Keady St. ☎ 551261. 1000-
1645 Mon-Sat ex Wed.
Morning coffee, lunch,
afternoon tea. Home-made
jam, chocolate fudge cake,
carrot cake. Coffee shop in
Alexander's department store.

MIDDLETOWN
(STD 01861)

Commercial Bar ⚲
Main St. ☎ 568407. 1230-1430
Mon-Sat. Pub grub.

Fedara's
4 Main St. ☎ 568189. 1030-
2230 Mon-Sat, until 2100 Sun.
Steaks, grills.

NEWTOWNHAMILTON
(STD 01693)

Vallendale ⚲
16 The Square. ☎ 878984.
1200-1500 Mon-Sun, until
2100 Sat. 1900-2100 Sun.
Pub grub.

PORTADOWN
(STD 01762)

Bengal Tandoori ⚲
121 Bridge St. ☎ 350922.
1200-1400 & 1700-2400
Mon-Sat, 1700-2300 Sun.
Indian & European. ££.

Bennett's Bar ⚲
4 Mandeville St. ☎ 350778.
1200-1430 Mon-Fri. Pub grub.

Boardwalk 🍴
15 Mandeville St. ☎ 337814.
0900-2130 Mon-Sat, 1230-
1430 & 1730-1930 Sun. Grills,
steaks, chicken. '60s music.

Brambles
2 Borough Place, Magowan
Buildings. ☎ 351000. 0900-
1700 Mon-Sat. Lasagne,
shepherd's pie, quiche.

Buttercup
47 William St. ☎ 333388.
0900-1730 Mon-Sat. Quiche,
chicken & ham pies. In
delicatessen shop.

C McKeever & Sons ⚲
28 Woodhouse St. ☎ 332054.
1200-1500 Mon-Sat. Pub grub,
set lunch.

Carngrove Hotel 🍷
2 Charlestown Rd. ☎ 339222.
Last orders 2130, Sun 2030.
Duckling, paella. E£££

Cascades
Swimming Pool, Thomas St.
☎ 332802. 1500-2030 Mon-
Fri, 0930-1730 Sat. Café in
pool complex.

Chalet 🍷
111 Armagh Rd. ☎ 336980.
1200-1430 Mon-Sat. Pub grub.

Chandlers Café Bistro
First Floor, 16 West St.
☎ 392998. 0900-1700 Mon-
Thur, 0700-1700 & 1900-2130
Fri-Sat.Chargrilled chicken on
bruschetta with mango salsa
and coriander dressing. Baked
potato, bread varieties.

Cookery Nook
42 High St. ☎ 351535. 0830-
1700 Mon-Sat. Home-made
soup, pies, quiches.

Dragon Inn 🍷
34 Carleton St. ☎ 350761.
1700-2400 Mon-Sun, 1200-
1500 Sun. Chinese &
European. E£.

El Porto Café & Restaurant
10 Market St. ☎ 394343.
0900-1730 Mon-Sun.
Breakfast, fish, steak, salad,
baked potato, sandwiches.

Ells 🍷
42 Dobbin Rd. ☎ 336326.
0900-2200 Mon-Sat. Breakfast,
lunch, grills, daily specials. E£.

Gaynor's
3 Church Lane. ☎ 337117.
0800-1830 Mon-Sat. Fish,
steaks, salads, desserts.

Golden Bridge 🍷
71 Bridge St. ☎ 333028. 1200-
1400 & 1700-2400 Mon-Thur,
1200-0100 Fri-Sat, 1300-2400
Sun. Chinese & European. E£.

J D Tipler 🍷
58 Killycomain Rd. ☎ 339288.
1200-1430 & 1730-2030
Mon-Sun. Creamy peppered
chicken, salad, fresh tuna
steak, vegetable fajitas.

McCann's
250 Obin St. ☎ 332668. 0900-
2400 Mon-Sat, until 2100 Sun.
Fish & chips, steak, salads,
sandwiches.

Minella
22 Market St. ☎ 332660.
0900-1700 Mon-Sat, until
1400 Thur. Grills, sandwiches.

New Mandarin House 🍷
34 West St. ☎ 351034.
1200-1400 & 1700-2330
Mon-Thur, until 0030 Fri-Sat,
1730-2300 Sun. Cantonese &
European. E£££.

No. 7 ☺
7 High St. ☎ 350808. 0900-
1730 Mon-Sat. Lasagne,
curries, home-baked pastries.

Pie Man ⊘
74 Woodhouse St. ☎ 330743.
0930-1645 Mon-Sat. Savoury
& sweet pies (28 varieties),
pizza, teas.

Royal Oak ⏳
8 Woodhouse St. ☎ 335204.
1200-1500 Mon-Sat. Pub grub.

Savoy Restaurant
Savoy Buildings, West St.
☎ 337581. 0830-1700 Mon-Sat.
Steak, poultry, pasta, salads.

Seagoe Hotel ⏳
Upper Church Lane.
☎ 333076. Last orders 2200.
Irish brotchan, planter's beef.
Carvery. E££.

Spades
Portadown Shopping Centre.
☎ 339420. 0900-1730 Mon-
Sat, until 2100 Fri. Breakfast.
Irish stew, sweets.

Wee Barney's
4 Bridge St. ☎ 362166. 0830-
1800 Mon-Wed, 1000-1930
Thur, until 2100 Fri. Fish,
chicken, sandwiches, scones.

Whistles Coffee Lounge
43 High St. ☎ 331696. 0900-
1500 Mon-Thur, until 1700
Fri-Sat. Breakfast. Chicken pie,
casseroles, salads, pastries,
coffee.

RICHHILL
(STD 01762)

Lyness ♀
1 The Square. ☎ 871874.
1200-2000 Tues-Wed & until
2100 Thur-Sat. 1230-1430
Sun. Deep fried brie on a bed
of salad with red currant
sauce, darne of salmon.

Normandy Inn ♀
6 Main St. ☎ 871386. 1230-
1430 Mon-Sat, 1800-2100 Fri-
Sat. Toasted sandwiches, grills,
steaks.

Ye Olde House Bar ♀
9 Irish St. ☎ 871616. 2000-
2200 Fri-Sat. Pies.

TANDRAGEE
(STD 01762)

Paddock ♀
2 Mill St. ☎ 840928. 1130-
2300 Mon-Sat, 1230-1400 &
1900-2200 Sun. Pub grub.

Park View Bar ♀
12 Church St. ☎ 840219.
1200-1430 & 1900-2115.
Pub grub.

Talk of the Town ♀
65 Market St. ☎ 849974.
1230-1430 Mon-Fri, 1800-
2100 Mon-Sun. Prawns, pork
in barbecue sauce, steaks. E£.

The Mall Restaurant ♦
Church St. ☎ 840219. 1230-
1500 Mon, Wed & Sat. Steaks,
salads, grills.

WHITECROSS

Rockerfellas ♀
114 Tullyah Rd,
Drumnahuncheon. ☎ (01693)
830230. 1800-2300 Fri-Sat.
Pub grub.

ANAHILT
(STD 01846)

Bauhinia Palace
Village Centre. ☎ 613603.
1700-2330 Mon-Thur, 1700-
2400 Fri-Sat, 1300-2200 Sun.
Chinese.

ANNALONG
(STD 013967)

★ GLASSDRUMMAN LODGE

85 Mill Rd. ☎ (01396) 768451.
1930-2100 Mon-Sun. Seafood
soup with lemon and fennel,
Spanish chicken, garden salad.
£££.

Halfway House
138 Glassdrumman Rd.
☎ 68224. 1230-1430 & 1900-
2100 Mon-Sun. Pub grub.

Harbour Inn
6 Harbour Drive. ☎ 68678.
1230-2130 Mon-Sun. Pub
grub, grills. £.

Marlino's
224 Glassdrumman Rd.
☎ 67080. 1030-2230 Mon-
Sun, in winter 1100-1800.
Soup, sandwiches, toasties,
ice cream.

Mill Coffee Shop
Marine Park. ☎ 68736. 1000-
2000 Mon-Sun, in winter
1000-1700 Sat-Sun only.
Snacks.

Aldo's
7 Castle Place. ☎ 841315.
1700-2200 Tues-Sun, in winter
1730-2100 Thur-Sun. Fresh
fish, steak, varied menu.

Angus Cochrane's
The Harbour. ☎ 841551.
0800-2200 Mon-Sun.
Sandwiches, prawns, potted
herrings, cockles, mussels.

Chapeltown Bar
83 Strangford Rd. ☎ 841332.
1330-2200 Mon-Sat, 1230-
1430 & 1900-2200 Sun.
Scampi, chicken, fish.

BALLYGOWAN
(STD 01238)

Deerstalker Inn
15 The Square. ☎ 528712.
1230-1730 & 1830-2200
Mon-Sun. Steaks, fish,
chicken. E£.

Nookie's Diner
19 Belfast Rd. ☎ 528007.
0900-1530 Mon-Thur, until
2000 Fri, 1700 Sat. Soup,
stew, fish & chips, scones,
sandwiches.

BALLYNAHINCH
(STD 01238)

Corner Restaurant ⊖
1 Main St. ☎ 562264. 0900-
1400 Mon, until 1900 Tues-
Thur, 2200 Fri-Sat. Grills,
self-service.

Foo Kwai
25 Dromore St. ☎ 563214.
1700-2400 Mon-Sat. Cantonese.

Fortune ♈
25 High St. ☎ 561030. 1700-
2400 Mon-Sun. Chinese &
European. E££.

Ginesi ♦
34 Main St. ☎ 562653. 1130-
2300 Mon-Sat ex Tues, from
1430 Sun. Steak, scampi, fish &
chips.

Matt's Bar ♈
3 Dromore St. ☎ 562627. 1200-
1500 Tues, until 1900 Wed-Sat,
1230-1700 Sun. Vegetable
soups, baked potato, plaice,
scampi, steak.

Maud's ⊖
10 Main St. ☎ 565252. 0900-
2100 Tues-Sat, from 1400 Sun.
Shorter winter hours. Soup,
stew, ice cream, sandwiches.

Millbrook Lodge Hotel ♈
5 Drumaness Rd. ☎ 562828.
Last orders 2115. A la carte,
high tea, bar snacks. M£, E££.

★ **PRIMROSE BAR** ♈ ⊖
30 Main St. ☎ 563177. 1200-
1430 & 1700-2045 Mon-Fri,
1200-2045 Sat, 1230-1430
Sun. Open sandwiches, pub
grub, daily specials. E£.

Ruffles Coffee Shop
2 The Square. ☎ 563091.
0930-1700 Mon-Sat. Ulster
fries, home-made desserts.

Shelly's
Unit 7, Windmill Shopping
Centre. ☎ 563903. 1000-1200
Mon-Fri, until 1430 Sat.
Fish & chips, chicken.

Victor's
6 Dufferin Avenue. ☎ 271088.
1100-2300 Mon-Sat. Fish &
chips.

White Horse Hotel ⬚
17 High St. ☎ 562225. Last
orders 2115. Bar snacks. Fresh
Ardglass scampi, chicken
Maryland. E££.

BALLYWALTER
(STD 012477)

Ballywalter Factory Shop
80 Main St. ☎ 58393. 0930-
1700 Mon-Sat. Savoury snacks,
soup, wheaten bread. Coffee
shop in factory shop.

Greenlea Farm
48 Dunover Rd. ☎ 58218.
Evening meals. Farmhouse
cooking. Must book.

BANBRIDGE
(STD 018206)

Banbridge Swimming Pool
Victoria St. ☎ 62233. 1000-
1400 & 1600-2030 Mon-Sun.
Fast food.

Bannville House ⬚
174 Lurgan Rd. ☎ 28884.
1230-1430 & 1730-2130 Wed-
Sat, 1730-2030 Sun. Fresh
salmon, duckling.

Belmont Hotel ⬚
Rathfriland Rd. ☎ 62517. 1230-
1430 Mon-Sun, 1730-2130
Tues-Sun, until 2030 Mon. Pub
grub. Scampi, steaks. ££.

Café Caille
15 Newry St. ☎ 62604.
0900-1730 Mon-Sat. Roast
vegetables in pitta bread,
quiche, sandwiches.

Captain Cooks
17 Castlewellan Rd. ☎ 62112.
1100-2400 Mon-Sun.
Fast food.

Coach Inn ⬚
13 Church Square. ☎ 62763.
1230-1430 Tues-Sun, 1830-
2130 Tues-Sun. Bar snacks,
beef stroganoff, duckling. E£.

Downshire Arms Hotel ⬚
95 Newry St. ☎ 62638. 1230-
1430 & 1800-2100 Mon-Sun.
Steak, chicken tikka, scampi,
salmon. E££.

Friar Tucks
57 Bridge St. ☎ 28282. 1100-
2400 Mon-Sat. Fish, vegetable
burgers, pizzas, garlic bread.

Half Way House ⬚
80 Half Way Rd. ☎ (01846)
692351. 1200-1430 & 1800-
2130 Mon-Sat. Steaks, hot &
cold buffet.

★ **HARRY'S BAR** ⬚ ⊙
7 Dromore St. ☎ 62794.
1200-1430 & 1730-2030 Tues-
Sat, 1900-2130 Sun. Bar
lunches, Ulster gammon,
salad bar, speciality desserts.

Imperial Inn ⬚
38 Bridge St. ☎ 22610. 1230-
1430 Mon-Sat. Bar snacks.

119

Jim's Plaice
Banbridge Motor Company,
101 Dromore Rd. ☎ 28241.
1000-1930 Mon-Thur, until
2130 Fri-Sun. Fish, Ulster fry,
mixed grills, salads.

Maud's Ice Cream Shop
37 Church Square. ☎ 28645.
1100-2200 Mon-Sun. Ice
cream, coffee, soup,
sandwiches, pastries.

Patrisse Coffee Lounge
48 Newry St. ☎ 28595. 0730-
1630 Mon-Sat, until 1330 Thur.
Soups, cakes, coffee.

Piggott's Sandwich Bar
2 Rathfriland St. ☎ 69119.
0900-1730 Mon-Sat.
Sandwiches.

Superbite
Supervalu Shopping Centre,
Scarva St. ☎ 62200. 0900-1700
Mon-Sat, until 1900 Thur. Grills.

The Food Exchange
200 Newry Rd. ☎ 23344.
1000-1630 Mon-Sat. Salads,
savoury dishes, freshly baked
scones, wheaten bread.

The Loft
3 Scarva St. ☎ 62929. 0900-
1730 Mon-Wed, until 2145
Thur-Sat. Breakfast. Snacks.
Scampi, chicken curry, salads.

The Ranch ⬚
41 Newry St. ☎ 62446. 1130-
1430 Mon-Sat, 1730-2100
Tues-Sun. Scampi, ham, chips,
scones, pastries.

Top Notch Catering
Unit 10, BEC Scarva Rd
Industrial Estate. ☎ 62260.
0830-1530 Mon-Fri. Breakfast,
fish, salad, sweets, home
baked scones.

Top of the Town ⬚
86 Newry St. ☎ 62170. 1200-
1500 Mon-Fri, until 1730 Sat,
1700-2030 Sun. Champ with
boiled Irish ham, seafood
tagliatelli, lemon-stuffed trout.

BANGOR
(STD 01247)

Avant Garde Café Bar ⬚
132 Main St. ☎ 454428.
1200-1500 & 1730-2100
Mon-Sat. Modern
mediterranean cuisine. £££.

Back Street Café ⬚
14 Queen's Parade.
☎ 453990. 1900-2230 Tues-
Sat. Baked turbot, barbary
duck fillets, bramble ice
cream. £££.

Bamboo Tree ⬚
22 High St. ☎ 467826. 1200-
1400 Mon-Sat, 1700-0030
Mon-Thur & Sun, later Fri-Sat.
Cantonese & European. £££.

Bangor Bay Inn ⬚
10 Seacliff Rd. ☎ 270696.
Last orders 2115, Sun 2000.
Portavogie prawns, garlic
mushrooms. £££.

Bewley's

Bloomfield Shopping Centre, South Circular Rd. ☎ 272079. 0900-2100 Mon-Fri, 0900-2000 Sat. Breakfast. Soups, stews, sweets, coffee.

Bokhara

2a King St. ☎ 452439. 1200-1430 & 1700-2400 Tues-Thur, until 0100 Fri & Sat, 1700-2330 Sun. Indian. £££.

Bryansburn

151 Bryansburn Rd. ☎ 270173. 1200-1430 & 1700-2100 Sun-Thur. Salmon in hollandaise sauce, peppered fillet steak. £££.

Café Brazilia

13 Bridge St. ☎ 272763. 0900-1800 Mon-Sat. Filled baguettes, salads, coffee,

Castle Garden

Heritage Centre, Town Hall. ☎ 270371. 1100-1630 Tues-Sat, 1400-1730 Sun, closes earlier in winter. Morning coffee, afternoon tea.

★ CLANDEBOYE LODGE HOTEL

10 Estate Rd, Clandeboye. ☎ 852500. Last orders 2200 Mon-Sat, 2100 Sun. Bar food. Sunday lunch 1200-1500. Fish dishes, sirloin steak, lamb, venison. £££.

Coffee Pot

88a Groomsport Rd. ☎ 271765. 0930-1700 Mon-Sat. Soup, salads, sandwiches, coffee.

Cosy Tea Pot

28 Dufferin Avenue. ☎ 466572. 1000-1630 Mon-Thur, until 1900 Fri-Sat. Soups, pies, scones, .

Cybernet Café

21 Hamilton Rd. ☎ 479703. 1000-2200 Mon-Sat & 1200-2000 Sun. Varied menu, speciality coffees. Internet Café.

Donegan's

44 High St. ☎ 270362. 1230-1430 & 1700-2200 Mon-Sat, 1200-1430 & 1900-2100 Sun. Galgorm salmon, steak, stir fry, salads, £££.

Dragon House

76 High St. ☎ 459031. 1700-0030 Mon-Thur, until 0130 Fri-Sat, 1700-2400 Sun. Chinese & European.

Dragon Palace

5 Crosby St. ☎ 457817. 1200-1400 & 1700-2400 Mon-Sat. 1700-2330 Sun. Chinese & European. ££.

Dunkin Donuts

2 Main St. ☎ 473901. 0900-2200 Mon-Sun. doughnuts, baguettes, ice-cream.

Fountain Coffee Shop

2 Queen's Parade. ☎ 455188. 1000-1600 Mon-Fri, 1000-1700 Sat. Coffee, scones, lasagne, chicken bakes, fish. Inside Methodist church.

Ganges ♦
9 Bingham St. ☎ 453030.
1200-1400 & 1730-2330
Mon-Sat, 1700-2300 Sun.
Indian. £££.

Genoa Bistro
1a Seacliff Rd, Bangor.
☎ 469253. 1200-1430 Wed-
Sun, 1830-2100 Wed-Thur,
1000-1230 & 1500-1800 Sun,
1830-2130 Fri-Sat. Herbed
olives, Palak lamb with spiced
couscous, glazed lemon tarte
with lime dressing. £££.

Gray's
20a Gray's Hill. ☎ 270339.
0900-1700 Mon-Sat, 1100-
1900 Sun. Sandwiches,
toasties.

Green Bicycle
6 Hamilton Rd. ☎ 271747.
1000-1630 Mon-Sat.
Vegetarian, afternoon tea.

★ **HEATHERLEA** ⊘
TEA ROOMS

94 Main St. ☎ 453157. 0900-
1730 Mon-Sat. Home-made
quiche, pies, pizza, salads,
desserts.

Imperial ⊻
4 Central Avenue. ☎ 271133.
1200-1700 Mon-Sat, 1230-
1430 & 1900-2200 Sun.
Pub grub.

Jamaica Inn ⊻
188 Seacliff Rd. ☎ 274674.
1130-1500 & 1700-2130 Wed-
Sat, 1230-1430 Sun. Warm
beef salad, pork marsala,
chargrilled swordfish. £££.

Jenny Watt's ⊻
41 High St. ☎ 270401. 1200-
2130 Mon-Sat, 1230-1430 &
1900-2100 Sun. Champ, stew,
burgers, club sandwiches.

Kentucky Fried Chicken
1 Main St. ☎ 452686. 1100-
2400 Sun-Thur, until 0200
Fri-Sat. Fast food.

King Jade ⊻
22 Dufferin Avenue.
☎ 270662. 1200-1400 &
1800-2130 Mon-Sat, 1700-
2330 Sun, closed Tues.
Cantonese & European. £££.

Knuttel's ♦
7 Gray's Hill. ☎ 274955.
1800-2130 Tues-Thur, 1800-
2200 Fri-Sat (& Mon June-
Aug). Pork in sherry sauce,
mignon of beef fillet, scallops.
££.

Legends ⊻
The Arcade, Main St.
☎ 467539. 1200-1900 Mon-
Thur, 1200-2000 Fri-Sat.
Baked potatoes, mixed grills,
open sandwiches.

Leisure Centre
Castle Park. ☎ 270271. 0930-
2200 Mon-Fri, until 1800 Sat,
1400-1800 Sun. Fast food.

Los Amigos ⚱
9-11 Crosby Street. ☎ 274060.
1700-2300 Sun-Thur, 1700-
2330 Fri & Sat. Mexican. £££

Marerosa ⚱
14 Abbey St. ☎ 471106. 1200-
1400   Mon-Sat. 1700-2400
Mon-Sun. Chinese &
European. £££

Marine Court Hotel ⚱
18 Quay St. ☎ 451100. Last
orders 2200 Mon-Sat, 2100
Sun. Bistro/coffee shop.
Omelettes, scampi, gammon.
Sunday lunch. A la carte, rack
of lamb, beef stroganoff EE

McBurney's Bars ⚱
41 Queen's Parade. ☎ 271462.
1230-1430 Mon-Fri, 1200-
1900 Sat. Pub grub.

McDonald's
Bloomfield Shopping Centre.
☎ 273300. 1000-2300 Mon-
Sun. Fast food.

McElhills
37 High St. ☎ 463928. 1000-
2200 Mon-Sat, until 2100 Sun.
Seafood, filled baguettes,
scones, coffee.

Mrs Bun's Coffee Shop
108 Abbey St. ☎ 466294.
0900-1730 Mon-Sat. Ulster fry,
stew, toasties, milk shakes.

New Orleans Restaurant ▮
7 Hamilton Rd. ☎ 461529.
1130-2230 Mon-Thur, until -
2300 Fri-Sat. Fajitas, southern
fried chicken, pasta. £££

Penguin Coffee Shop
5 King St. ☎ 271682. 0900-
1700 Mon-Sat. Breakfast. Fish,
stew, vegetarian, pies, toasties.

Pizza Hut ⚱
115 Main St. ☎ 271272. 1200-
2400 Mon-Sat, until 2300 Sun.
Pizza. ££

Rose & Chandlers ⚱
2 High St. ☎ 271540. 1200-
1500 Mon, until 2100 Tues-
Sat. Home-made soup,
pub grub.

★ **ROYAL HOTEL** ⚱
26 Quay St. ☎ 271866. Quay's
Restaurant. Last orders 2115,
grill room 21.45. Passion fruit
& lime sorbet, fillet of beef
with scallion mash, pac choy,
roast shallots and celeriac.

Rumblin' Tum
6 Dufferin Avenue. ☎ 271088.
0930-2100 Mon-Sat. Breakfast,
fish & chips, champ.

Sampan ⚱
2a Market St. ☎ 460470.
1200-1400 & 1700-2330
Mon-Sat, until 2300 Sun.
Cantonese. £££

★ **SHANKS** ⚱
Blackwood Golf Club
Crawfordsburn Rd. ☎ 853313.
1200-1400 & 1900-2130 Tues-
Sat, 1200-1400 Sun, 1230-
1600 Mon. Langoustine with
orza pasta, wild salmon with
smoked chilli & pecan crust.
£££

Springers
Springhill Shopping Centre. ☎ 469802. 0900-1730 Mon-Sat, until 2100 Thur-Fri. Breakfast. Pizzas, fish & chips, salads.

Steamer Bar 🍷
30 Quay St. ☎ 467699. 1200-1430 & 1730-2130 Mon-Thur, until 2200 Fri-Sat, 1230-1400 Sun. Seafood, chicken, steaks, pasta. E£.

The Castle Restaurant 🍷
Castle Street. ☎ 465808. 1200-1400 & 1700-1900 Mon-Wed, later Thur-Sun. Lunch, high tea, a la carte.

Vesuvio Italia Pizzeria 🍷
8 Quay St. ☎ 274804. 1200-1500 Thur-Sun, 1700-2330 Tues-Thur, until 0030 Fri-Sat, 2230 Sun. Italian, pizza, pasta.

★ VILLA TOSCANA 🍷
Toscana Park, West Circular Rd. ☎ 473737. 1700-2330 Mon-Sat, until 2200 Sun. 1200-1430 Sun. Pizza, pasta, steaks. E££.

Viscount of Clandeboye 🍷
Springhill Shopping Centre. ☎ 271545. 1200-1500 Mon-Sat, 1900-2200 Thur-Sat. Pub grub.

★ WHEATEAR
108 Main St. ☎ 467489. 0830-1730 Mon-Sat. Chicken & broccoli, soups, Irish stew, cauliflower cheese, apple sponge & custard, all homemade.

Windsor 🍷
24 Quay St. ☎ 473943. 1200-2130 Mon-Sat, 1230-1430 & 1900-2100 Sun. Ulster fry, seafood, vegetarian, salads. E££.

Wolsey's 🍷
24 High St. ☎ 460495. 1200-1900 Mon-Thur, until 2000 Fri-Sat, 1230-1430 Sun. Chicken & ham pie, smoked haddock, scampi, salads.

Wongs 🍷
37 Queen's Parade. ☎ 452893. 1200-1400 Mon-Sat, 1700-2400 Mon-Sun, until 0100 Fri-Sat. Chinese & European. E£.

CARROWDORE
(STD 01247)

White Horse Inn 🍷
39 Main St. ☎ (01247) 861212. 1230-1430 & 1730-2030 Mon-Wed, until 2130 Thur-Sun. Salmon, steaks, salads, vegetarian.

CARRYDUFF
(STD 01232)

Ivanhoe Inn ⚲
556 Saintfield Rd. ☎ 812240.
1200-1430 & 1730-2100
Mon-Sun. Fish, ham, pasta,
light snacks.

Little Chef
Town & Country Shopping
Centre. ☎ 812097. 0930-2200
Mon-Sat. Chicken, salads.

Oriental Garden ⚲
Town & Country Shopping
Centre. ☎ 812755. 1700-2400
Mon-Sun. Chinese &
European. E£.

Pizza Hut
Town & Country Shopping
Centre. ☎ 815060. 1200-2400
Mon-Sat, until 2300 Sun.
Pizzas, garlic bread, salads. £.

Rick's ⚲ ⊘
Carryduff Shopping Centre.
☎ 814558. 0900-2300 Mon-
Sat, 1000-2100 Sun. Breakfast.
Grills, salads, snacks.

Rockmount Golf Club ⚲
28 Drumalig Rd. ☎ 812279.
0900-2100 Mon-Sat, until
2000 Sun. Chicken, scampi,
steak. Restaurant in golf club.

Royal Ascot ⚲
46 Hillsborough Rd.
☎ 812127. 1130-2330 Mon-
Sat, 1200-1430 & 1800-2200
Sun. Fish, steaks, chicken. E£.

CASTLEWELLAN
(STD 013967)

Chestnut Inn ⚲
28 Lower Square. ☎ 78247.
1200-2100 Mon-Thur, 1200-
2130 Fri-Sat, 1200-1430 &
1700-2030 Sun. Pub grub.
Duckling with grand marnier,
salmon, turbot, salads,
vegetarian. E£.

Dolly's Brae Inn ⚲
15 Gargary Rd. ☎ (018206)
50213. 1700-2230 Mon-Sat,
1900-2130 Sun. Pub grub.

Grange Coffee Shop
Castlewellan Forest Park.
☎ 71447. 1000-1800 Mon-
Sun. Breakfast, home baking.

★ **HILLYARD HOUSE**
1 Castle Avenue. ☎ 70141.
1100-2100 Mon-Sun. Daily
specials, high tea, scones.

Maginn Bros. ⚲
9 Main St. ☎ 78359. 1200-
1500 Mon-Sun. Scampi, chilli,
salads.

McElroy's ⚲
151 Ballylough Rd. ☎ 78238.
1800-2330 Mon-Sat. Pub grub.

Oak Grill
35 Main St. ☎ 78616. 1000-
0100 Mon-Sun. Fast food,
steaks.

Slieve Croob Inn ♁
119 Clonvaraghan Rd.
☎ 71412. Bistro 1230-2100
Mon-Sun. Restaurant 1800-
2100 Mon-Sat, 1230-1500 &
1800-2000 Sun. Italian,
Mexican, daily specials. £££.

Zebedees
74 Main St. ☎ 71410. 1100-
1230 Mon-Thur, until 0200 Fri-
Sat, 1600-0100 Sun. Fast food.

CLOUGH
(STD 01396)

Clough Inn ♁
28 Main St. ☎ (01396) 811209.
1200-1430 & 1700-2100 Mon-
Sat, until 1900 Sun. Set meals,
à la carte.

COMBER
(STD 01247)

★ **CASTLE ESPIE**
78 Ballydrain Rd. ☎ 872517.
1030-1700 Mon-Sat, 1130-
1800 Sun. In winter 1130-1600
Mon-Sat & 1130-1700 Sun.
Home-made soup, fisherman's
pie, scones.

Cooperage Coffee Shop ⊘
3a Killinchy St. ☎ 873063.
1000-1630 Mon-Sat. Bakes,
potatoes, salads, scones.

Express Pizza ♁
39 Castle St. ☎ 874488. 1700-
2200 Tues-Thur, until 2300
Fri-Sat.

Harry Fraser's
11 Castle St. ☎ 872546. 0830-
2230 Tues-Fri, until 1900 Sat.
Grills.

Mayflower ♁
47 Castle St. ☎ 873254. 1200-
1400 & 1700-2400 Mon-Sat,
1630-2330 Sun. Chinese &
European. £E.

McBride's
1 The Square. ☎ 878703.
1145-1430 Mon-Sat. Stuffed
steak, ham with parsley sauce.

★ **OLD SCHOOL HOUSE** ♁
100 Ballydrain Rd.
☎ (01238) 541182. 1900-2230
Mon-Sat, 1230-1430 Sun.
Steaks, seafood, desserts. £££.

Salem's Tea Rooms
29 Mill St. ☎ 873624. 1000-
1630 Mon-Sat. Salads, baked
potatoes, daily specials,
pastries.

The Willow Tree
12 The Square. ☎ 878307.
0900-1645 Mon-Sat. Breakfast,
silverside of beef, scampi,
soup.

★ **TOURIST
TROPHY LOUNGE**
101 Mill St. ☎ 874554. 1200-
1500 Mon-Sat, 1915-2330
Mon-Thur, 1800-2330 Fri-Sat.
Home-made paté, steak
sandwiches, chilli, chicken.

**Venice Pizza &
Ice Cream Parlour**
24 Mill St. ☎ 878777. 1500-2300
Mon-Sun. Pizza, ice cream.

Willow Tree 🍴
12a The Square. ☎ 878307.
0900-1700 Mon-Sat. Silverside
of beef, deep baked apple pie,
filled baguettes.

CONLIG
(STD 01247)

Martha's Vineyard
105 Main St. ☎ (01247)
820219. 0930-1630 Mon-Sat.
Morning coffee, shepherd's pie,
fish, lasagne, pastries.

CRAWFORDSBURN
(STD 01247)

Crawfordsburn ⊘
Country Park
☎ 852725. 1030-1730 Mon-
Sun, shorter hours in winter.
Fish & chips, nut cutlets,
sandwiches, pastries.

★ **OLD INN** ⏛
15 Main St. ☎ 853255. Last
orders 2130, 2000 Sun. Roast
beef, sole, Portavogie scampi,
salmon, sherry trifle. E££.

Postage Stamp
7 Main St. ☎ 852649. 0730-
1630 Mon-Fri, 0930-1330 Sat.
Home-made soup, toasted
sandwiches, baked potatoes,
salads, cakes, scones, ice cream
in summer. Coffee shop in post
office.

CROSSGAR
(STD 01396)

★ **ROSEMARY JANE
TEA ROOM**
81 Killyleagh St. ☎ 831185.
0930-1630 Tues-Sat, 1230-
1430 Sunday carvery.
Vegetarian dishes, home-made
soups, bakes, cakes.

CULTRA
(STD 01232)

★ **CULLODEN HOTEL** ⏛
Craigavad. ☎ 425223. Last
orders 2145, Sun 2030. Sundried tomato & brie tart,
shrimps with red pepper
coulis, steak & lobster. E£££.

Cultra Inn ⏛
Culloden Hotel, Craigavad.
☎ 425840. 1230-1415 &
1800-2145 Mon-Sat. Salmon,
turkey, steak & kidney pie.
E££.

Cultra Manor ⏛
Ulster Folk & Transport
Museum. ☎ 427097. 1100-
1700 Mon-Sat, 1230-1500
Sun, longer hours in summer.
Sunday carvery, snacks. Inside
open-air museum.

DONAGHADEE
(STD 01247)

Captain's Table
22 The Parade. ☎ 882656.
1200-1400 Mon-Fri, until
2100 Sat-Sun. Fish & chips.

★ COFFEE PLUS

Market House, New St.
☎ 882641. 0900-1630 Mon-
Sat. Pies, lasagne, bakes.

Connoisseur ☖
31 High St. ☎ 882656. 1200-
2100 Mon-Sat, until 2000 Sun.
Fast food.

Copelands Hotel ☖
60 Warren Rd. ☎ 888189. Last
orders 2130 Mon-Thur, 2130
Fri-Sat, 2200 Sun. Sirloin steak
in Bushmills whiskey, lamb
noisettes. E££.

Dunallan Hotel ☖
27 Shore St. ☎ 883569. 1200-
2045 Mon-Sun. A la carte. E£.

★ GRACE NEILL'S ☖

33 High St. ☎ 882553. 1130-
2300 Mon-Sat. Pub grub,
potted herrings. Beer garden at
rear 17th-century bar. 1200-
1430 (bistro food), 1700-1900
(snacks), 1900-2130 Tues-Sat.
E£.

Moat Inn ☖
102 Moat St. ☎ 883297. 1230-
1430 & 1730-2100 Mon-Sun,
Sunday lunch 1230-1400.
Grills. E£.

Old Pier Inn ☖
33 Manor St. ☎ 882397. 1200-
2100 Mon-Sat, 1230-1930
Sun. Peppered steaks, pork
escalope. E£.

Tivoli Bar ☖
32 Manor St. ☎ 882961. 1230-
1430 & 1630-2100 Mon-Sun.
Roast lamb, steak & kidney
pie, open sandwiches.

DOWNPATRICK
(STD 01396)

Abbey Lodge Hotel ☖
38 Belfast Rd. ☎ 614511.
Last orders 2115 Mon-Sat,
2000 Sun. M£, E££.

Arts Café
Down Arts Centre, Irish St.
☎ 615283. 1000-1630 Mon-
Sat. Soup, salads, pastries.

Brendan's ☖
94 Market St. ☎ 615311.
1200-1500 Mon-Sat, 1700-
2100 Wed-Sat, 1230-1430 &
1700-2030 Sun. Chicken kiev,
Irish lamb, lasagne, open
sandwiches, daily specials.

Castle Inn ☖
109 Ballynoe Rd. ☎ 612116.
1230-1430 Mon-Sat. Pub grub.

China Garden ☖
16 English St. ☎ 613364.
1200-1400 Mon-Sat, 1630-
2400 Mon-Sun. Chinese &
European. E£.

Country Fried Chicken
26 St Patrick's Avenue.
☎ 617766. 1200-2400 Mon-
Thur, until 0200 Fri-Sat, 2300
Sun. Grills.

Denvir's ⚲
14 English St. ☎ 612012.
1200-1430 Mon-Sun, 1800-
2000 Mon-Fri, 1900-2100 Sat.
Home-cooking with fresh
organic vegetables.

Fry Inn
13 St Patrick's Avenue.
☎ 616033. 0930-1730 Mon-
Sat. Poached egg, scrambled
egg on toast, soups, stew,
baked potatoes, rhubarb pie,
scones, pastries.

Golden Dragon
21 Scotch St. ☎ 612596. 1200-
1400 & 1700-2400 Mon-Thur,
until 0100 Fri-Sat, 1630-2400
Sun. Chinese & European.

Harry Afrika's ♦
102 Market St. ☎ 617161.
0830-2030 Mon-Sun.
Breakfast, grills, daily specials.

Jack Robinson's ⚲
37 Mearne Rd, Saul.
☎ 615750. 1200-1430 Mon-
Sat, 1800-2000 Mon-Tues,
until 2100 Wed-Fri, 1230-
1430 & 1700-2000 Sun. 1900-
2100 Fri-Sat. Bistro menu.
High tea, Sunday lunch.

Museum Tea Room
The Mall. ☎ 615218. 1100-
1630 Tues-Fri, 1400-1630 Sat.
June-Aug: 1100-1630 Mon-Fri,
1400-1630 Sat-Sun. Light
refreshments. Teashop in
museum.

Pepper Pot
38 St Patrick's Avenue.
☎ 615165. 0930-1730 Mon-
Sat. Roast beef, chicken.

Slaney Inn ⚲
64 St Patrick's Rd, Raholp.
☎ 612093. 1200-1430 Mon-
Sun, 1800-2100 Wed-Sat, until
2000 Sun. Bar food all day.
Seafood specialities. £££.

The Forge Bar ⚲
14 Church St. ☎ 612522.
1100-1430 Mon-Sat, 1200-
1500 Sun. Chicken Maryland,
lasagne, open sandwiches.

DROMARA
(STD 01238)

O'Reilly's ⚲
7 Rathfriland Rd. ☎ (01238)
532209. 1200-2200 Wed-Sat,
until 2030 Sun. Salmon with
dill, duck with blueberry &
ginger. £££.

Wendy's Coffee Shop
36 Market Square. ☎ 693149.
0900-1700 Mon-Sat. Pies,
chicken, salads, desserts.

DROMORE
(STD 01846)

Country Cottage
273a Ballygowan Rd.
☎ 698383. 1030-1700 Tues-Sat. Light meals, fresh scones, pastries, coffee.

La Patisserie & Deli
30 Market Square. 0900-1730 Mon-Sat. Sandwiches, homebakes, Ulster fry, tea, coffee.

River Café
12 Bridge St. ☎ 699211. 0930-1700 Mon-Sat. Filled croissants, patisseries, scones. In restored Georgian auction rooms overlooking river.

DUNDRUM
(STD 013967)

★ BUCK'S HEAD ⚲
77 Main St. ☎ 51868/51859. 1700-1900 High tea and 1900-2100 dinner Mon-Sat. Traditional Sunday lunch 1200-1430.

Murlough Tavern ⚲
143 Main St. ☎ 51211. 1200-1430 Mon-Sun, 1700-2030 Mon-Sat, until 1900 Sun. Home-made patés, soups, prawns in filo pastry with spicy dip. Snacks all day.

GILFORD
(STD 01762)

★ GILBERRY FAYRE ⊗
92 Banbridge Rd. ☎ 832098. 0900-1630 Mon-Sat. Quiche, salads, home baking.

★ HALLS MILL INN ⚲
Banbridge Rd, Lawrencetown. ☎ 25565. 1200-1430 & 1730-2100 Mon-Fri, 1730-1900 Sat, 1900-2100 Sun. Quail eggs, grilled sardines, oriental spicy duck, ostrich steak, wild boar stroganoff. £££.

Honey Pot
40 Dunbarton St. ☎ 831497. 0900-1700 Mon-Sat. Breakfast. Soup, Irish stew.

Pot Belly ⚲
59 Banbridge Rd, Tullylish. ☎ 831404. 1800-2200 Tues-Sat, 1200-1500 Sun. Pot Belly chicken, smoked salmon parcel, pork fillet. £££.

★ THE YELLOW DOOR ⚲
1 Bridge St. ☎ 831543. 1200-1430 & 1800-2200 Tues-Sun. Pasta filled with minced lamb, roast wild boar. M£. ££££.

GREYABBEY
(STD 012477)

Hoops
7 Main St. ☎ 88541. 1000-1700 Wed-Sat. Sandwiches, pizza, stew. In crafts/antiques shop.

Wildfowler 🍷
1 Main St. ☎ 88260. 1100-1500 & 1700-2130 Mon-Sat, 1230-2130 Sun. Fish, roast beef, salads. Pub grub, high tea. A la carte E££.

GROOMSPORT
(STD 01247)

ADELBODEN LODGE 🍷
38 Donaghadee Rd. ☎ 464288. Last orders 2100, 1900 Sun. Salmon, gammon, roast duck, lamb cutlets. Bar snacks. E£.

Anchorage 🍷
49 Main St. ☎ 465757. 1900-2200 Wed-Sat, 1200-1500 Sun. Pigeon & pheasant salad with blackberry vinaigrette, chicken liver paté with geranium jelly. E£££.

Groomsport House Hotel 🍷
12 Donaghadee Rd. ☎ 270449. 1215-2100 Mon-Sat, 1600-1900 Sun. Bar snacks. Seafood platter, vegetarian crepes. £.

Lock & Quay 🍷
26 Main St. ☎ 271518. 1130-2300 Mon-Wed, until 0100 Thur-Sat, 1230-1430 & 1900-2200 Sun. Snack-in-a-basket. Music.

The Stables 🍷
1 Main St. ☎ 464229. 1230-1430 Mon-Sun, 1700-2130 Mon-Sat, from 1900 Sun. Grills, steaks, seafood. A la carte. E££.

HELEN'S BAY
(STD 01247)

Bay Café 🍷
Station Square. ☎ (01247) 852841. From 1800 Tues-Sat, 1200-1430 Sun. Mediterranean. Must book.

HILLSBOROUGH
(STD 01846)

★ HAMPTON'S COFFEE SHOP
5 Harry's Rd. ☎ 682500. 0930-1700 Mon-Sat. Home baking, cakes, scones. Restaurant in furniture shop.

★ HILLSIDE 🍷
21 Main St. ☎ 682765. 1200-1430 Mon-Sat. Pub grub. Restaurant 1900-2130 Tues-Sat. Oysters, duck breast in brandy. Children's area. E£££.

Marquis of Downshire 🍷
Main St. ☎ 682095. 1200-1430 Mon-Sat (from 1230 Sun), 1930-2200 Tues-Thurs, from 1730 Fri-Sat. Grills, salads.

Pheasant 🍷
410 Upper Ballynahinch Rd. ☎ 638056. 1200-1415 & 1700-2100 Tues-Sat, 1230-1415 & 1700-2000 Sun. Gourmet bistro.

★ PLOUGH INN ⬚

3 The Square. ☎ 682985.
1200-1415 Mon-Sun pub
grub. Bistro 1200-1415 &
1700-1900 Tues-Sat, until
2000 Sun. Seafood, steak. £££.

★ RED FOX ◯

6 Main St. ☎ 682586. 1015-
1400 & 1445-1700 Tues-Sat.
Salads, quiche, home baking.

Revival ⬚
41 Old Coach Rd. ☎ 689624.
1700-2130 Tues-Thur, until
2230 Fri-Sat, 1200-2030 Sun.
Indian.

Ritchie's ⬚
3 Ballynahinch St. ☎ 683601.
1200-1430 Mon-Tues, until
2100 Wed-Sat. Lasagne, pies,
club sandwiches.

The Pheasant ⬚
410 Upper Ballynahinch Rd.
☎ 638056. 1200-1430 Tues-
Sun, 1700-2100 Tues-Sat, later
Sun. Fresh basil and herb
pasta, Portavogie monkfish.

Traveller's Kitchen
163 Dromore Rd. ☎ 683956.
0745-1800 Mon-Fri, until
1700 Sat. Ulster fry, gammon,
fish, salads.

White Gables Hotel ⬚ ◯
14 Dromore Rd. ☎ 682755.
Last orders 2115 Mon-Sat,
2030 Sun. Local vegetables,
game in season. M£, £££.

HILLTOWN
(STD 018206)

Downshire Arms ⬚
Main St. ☎ 38899. 1230-1430
Mon-Sun, 1830-2200 Mon-
Thur, until 2230 Fri-Sat, 1900-
2100 Sun. Salmon, chicken,
steaks. £££.

Shamrock ⬚
Main St. ☎ 30045. 1600-2200
Tues-Thur, 1130-2330 Fri-Sat,
1200-1430 Sun. Pub grub.

Village Inn ⬚
43 Main St. ☎ 38649. 1230-
1430 & 1800-2200 Mon-Sat,
1900 Sun. Pub grub,
traditional Sunday lunch.

HOLYWOOD
(STD 01247)

Akropolis ▮
110 High St. ☎ 422009. 1200-
1430 Tues-Sat & 1700-2200
Tues-Sun. Traditional Greek.

★ BAY TREE
  COFFEE HOUSE ▮

Audley Court, 118 High St.
☎ 421419. 1000-1630 Mon-
Sat. Cinnamon scones,
vegetarian dishes, salmon
plait. Restaurant open from
1930 1st & last Fri in month –
must book £££.

Bokhara ⬚
149 High St. ☎ 427989. 1700-
2300 Mon-Sun, until 2330 Fri-
Sat. Indian. £££.

Carmichael's ♆
25 Hibernia St. ☎ 424759.
1200-1430 & 1700-2030
Mon-Sat. Steak, kebabs,
seafood. E£.

Dirty Duck ♆
2 Kinnegar Rd. ☎ 596666.
From 1230 daily. Bistro menu
from 1830. Daily specials,
grills. Beer garden.

Fontana
High St. ☎ 809908. 1200-1430
Mon-Fri, 1830-2200 Mon-Sat,
1100-1600 Sunday brunch.
Nouvelle cuisine with an
Italian twist. E£££.

Lapananzi ♦
49b High St. ☎ 427552. Coffee
shop 1100-1500 Tues-Sat.
1900-2400 Tues-Sat. Gammon,
steak, lasagne, egg and chips.

★ **OLDE PRIORY INN** ♆
13 High St. ☎ 428164. 1200-
2230 Mon-Sat, 1230-1430 &
1900-2130 Sun. Grills, steaks,
Mexican, Indian.

Panini's
125 Church Rd. ☎ 427774.
0815-1900 Mon-Fri, until
1800 Sat, 1200-1700 Sun.
Coffee bar in delicatessen.
Pastries, snacks.

★ **RAYANNE HOUSE** ♆
60 Demesne Rd. ☎ 425859.
1900-2100 Mon-Sat. Roast
suckling pig. A la carte. Must
book. E£££.

Seaside Tavern ♆
19 Stewart's Place. ☎ 423152.
1130-1430 & 1730-2000 Mon-
Fri, 1130-2000 Sat 1230-1430
Sun. Fish, Cajun steak, pitta
pockets, vegetarian.

Silver City
124 High St. ☎ 428766. 1700-
2400 Tues-Sun. Chinese &
European. E£.

Sullivan Coffee Shop
117 High St. ☎ 427467. 0900-
1700 Mon-Sat. Lasagne, pie,
salads, bakes.

★ **SULLIVANS** ♦
5a Sullivan Place. ☎ 421000.
1000-1600 Mon-Sat, 1900-
2130 Mon-Sat. Seafood with
leeks & saffron, game. E£££.

The Bistro ♦
27 Church Rd. ☎ 425655.
1830-2400 Mon-Sat. Pork with
peppercorns, coffee ice cream.
££.

The Jiggery ♆
30 High St. ☎ 421769. 1200-
1415 & 1730-2130 Mon-Sat.
Deep fried brie, Cumberland
pâté. E££.

Wilson's
58 High St. ☎ 427419. 0800-
1630 Mon-Sat. Snacks,
toasties, pies.

Wine & Company ♆
57 High St. ☎ 426083. 1000-
2100 Mon-Sat. Baked trout
with roasted vegetables.

KATESBRIDGE
(STD 018206)

Angler's Rest ⚲
42 Aughnacloy Rd. ☎ 71515.
1230-1430 & 1800-2100
Wed-Sun. Fish, poultry, salads.

KILKEEL
(STD 016937)

Archways ⚲
23 Newry St. ☎ 64112. 1230-
1400 Mon-Sat. Pub grub.

Captain's Table
24 Newcastle St. ☎ 64555.
1100-1800 Mon-Fri, until
2100 Sat. Fish & chips.

Coffee Shop
25a Greencastle St. ☎ 64370.
1000-1730 Mon-Sat. Chicken
& ham pie, chicken &
broccoli, quiche, sausage rolls,
pastries, coffee.

Cranfield House Hotel ⚲
57 Cranfield Rd. ☎ 62327. Last
orders 2045, Sun 2000. E££.

The Fisherman ⚲
68 Greencastle St. ☎ 62130.
1200-1430 & 1800-2130
Mon-Sun. Local clams, lobster,
turbot. E££.

Harbour Café
5 Harbour Rd. ☎ 62207. 1030-
1900 Mon-Wed, until 2000
Fri-Sat. Fish, chicken, salads.

Jacob Hall's ⚲
8 Greencastle St. ☎ 64751.
1200-1430 & 1700-2000
Mon-Sat, summer only. Grills.

Kilmorey Arms Hotel ⚲
41Greencastle St. ☎ 62220.
Last orders 2100. A la carte.
E££.

Mourne Grange
169 Newry Rd. ☎ 62228.
1000-1230 Mon-Sat, 1400-
1700 Mon-Sun. Scones, cakes.
In craft shop.

Old Mill ♨
12 Knockchree Avenue.
☎ 65993. 1000-2300, until
1900 winter. Traditional &
Eastern dishes. £.

Port Inn ⚲
3 The Square. ☎ 62453. 1130-
2300 Mon-Sat.

Port O Call
13 Bridge St. ☎ 62621. 0930-
1730 Mon-Wed, until 1400
Thur, 1800 Fri, 2030 Sat.
Ulster fry, steaks, chicken.

Quick Stop Chippee
16 Newcastle St. ☎ 63059.
1200-0100 Mon-Sat, from
1430 Sun. Fast food.

Riverside Tavern ⚲
2 Bridge St. ☎ 65316. 1200-
1400 Mon-Fri & Sun. Grills.

Silent Valley Reservoir
☎ (01232) 746581. 1130-1830
Mon-Sun summer only. Home
baking, lasagne, pies. Café in
interpretive centre (6 miles
from Kilkeel).

Silver Herring ⚲
4 The Square. ☎ 62491. 1200-
1400 Mon-Fri & Sun.

KILLINCHY
(STD 01238)

★ BALLOO HOUSE ⚲
☎ 541210. 1100-2200 Mon-Sat, from 1230 Sun. Chargrilled salmon, steaks, game. Hot & cold buffet. E££.

Daft Eddy's ⚲
Sketrick Island, Whiterock. ☎ 541615. 1700-2130 Mon-Sat, 1230-1500 & 1700-2100 Sun. Grills, salads. Pub on island across causeway. E£.

★ LISBARNETT HOUSE ⚲
181 Killinchy Rd, Lisbane. ☎ (01238) 541589. 1130-2300 Mon-Sat, 1230-1700 & 1830-2200 Sun. Chicken, salmon, steaks, vegetarian. E££.

Tide's Reach ⚲
Whiterock Bay. ☎ 541347. 1200-1500 & 1700-2130 Mon-Sun. Seafood.

KILLYLEAGH
(STD 01396)

Corner Home Bakery
1 Catherine St. ☎ 821087. 0900-1730 Mon-Sat. Stews, salads, scones, home baking.

Cross Fish
17 Cross St. ☎ 828266. 1030-2000 Mon-Thur, until 2100 Fri-Sun. Fish & chips, Ulster fry, chicken.

★ DUFFERIN ARMS ⚲
35 High St. ☎ 828229. 1800-2030 Mon-Wed, until 2100 Thur-Sat, 1230-1430 Sat-Sun. Poached salmon kebab. Live music. E££.

Finnegan's Bar ⚲
1 Cooks Brae. ☎ 38282. 1200-1500 Mon-Thur, 1200-1700 & 1900-2100 Fri-Sun. Pub grub.

KIRCUBBIN
(STD 012477)

Mermaid's Bar ⚲
49 Main St. ☎ 38215. 1130-2300 Mon-Sat, 1230-1430 & 1900-2200 Sun. Pub grub.

Saltwater Brig ⚲
43 Rowreagh Rd. ☎ 38435. 1230-1430 Mon-Sun, 1700-2100 Mon-Sat, from 1900 Sun. Bistro menu. £.

LOUGHBRICKLAND
(STD 018206)

Brontë Steakhouse ⚲
71 Ballynafoy Rd, Ballinaskeagh. ☎ 51338. 1730-2100 Tues-Sat. Steaks, duck with Cointreau sauce, chicken stir-fry. E£.

Road Chef
179 Dublin Rd. ☎ (01762) 318366. 0800-2000 Mon-Sat, 1230-2000 Sun. Breakfast, lunch. Grills.

Seven Stars ♉
4 Main St. ☎ 26461. 1800-
2130 Tues-Sat, 1230-1430 &
1700-2100 Sun. Steak,
chicken.

MAGHERALIN
(STD 01846)

Byrne's ♉
2 Newforge Rd. ☎ (01846)
611506. 1200-1430 & 1700-
2000 Mon-Sat. Irish stew,
soup, chicken, desserts.

Edenmore Golf Club
70 Drumnabreeze Rd.
☎ (01846) 619199. 0930-1630
Mon-Sat. Morning coffee,
lunch, afternoon tea.

MILLISLE
(STD 01247)

Dorothy's
53 Main St. ☎ 861852. 1100-
2200 Mon-Sun. Shorter hours
in winter. Fast food.

Windmill Grill
57 Main St. ☎ 861461. 1100-
2100 Mon-Thur, until 2200
Fri-Sat, 2000 Sun. Grills.

MOIRA
(STD 01846)

Ballycanal Manor
2 Glenavy Rd. ☎ 611923.
Traditional cooking.
Must book.

Chestnut Lodge ♉
6 Chestnuthill Rd. ☎ 611409.
1200-1430 & 1700-2100
Mon-Sun. Chicken & smoked
bacon terrine, wild salmon
cushions, brandied baskets
with fruit. E££.

Country Kitchen
21 Main St. ☎ 612787. 1000-
1700 Mon-Sat. Snacks, salads.

The Croft
101 Main St. ☎ 619788. 1000-
1630 Mon-Sat. Home-made
lunches, scones, traybakes.
Wide choice of coffees.

Four Trees ♉
61 Main St. ☎ 611437. 1230-
1430 Mon-Sat, 1730-2030
Thur-Sat. Bar menu.

Glenavy Road Restaurant
BP Service Station, 500 yd
beyond Moira roundabout
towards airport. ☎ 611909.
0800-2000 Mon-Sat, from
0900 Sun. Set lunch. Grills.

**Graham's Traditional
Fish & Chips**
67 Main St. ☎ 613030. 1200-
2400 Mon-Sat, 1600-2300
Sun. Traditional style.

J's Fried Chicken
87 Main St. ☎ 619718. 1200-
2400 Mon-Sat, 1700-2200
Sun. Fast food.

Maghaberry Arms ⚲
23 Maghaberry Rd. ☎ 611852.
1130-1430 Mon-Fri, 1730-
2000 Tues-Thur, until 2100 Fri,
1130-2100 Sat, 1800-2100
Sun. Pub grub.

Midnight Haunt ⚲
90 Main St. ☎ 611391. 1700-
2330 Mon-Sun. Chinese &
European. £.

Norman's Inn ⚲
86 Main St. ☎ 611318. 1230-
1900 Mon-Sun. Restaurant:
1930-2200 Mon-Sun. A la
carte, bar food.

Old Yard
70 Drumnabreeze Rd.
☎ 619199. 0900-1640 Mon-
Sat. Traditional home cooking.
Evenings by appointment.

Rose Lodge
74 Main St. ☎ 611185. 0830-
1900 Mon-Fri, later Sat. Fish &
chips, steaks, lasagne.

★ **SCULLERY MOYRAH**
101 Main St. ☎ 619788. 1000-
1700 Mon-Sat. Home-made
soups, salads, casseroles,
scones. Café in craft shop.

MONEYREAGH
(STD 01247)

Auld House ⚲
27 Church Rd. ☎ 448446.
1130-2300 Mon-Wed, until
0100 Thur-Sat, 1230-1430 &
1900-2200 Sun. Baked
potatoes, home-made pies.
A la carte E£.

The Lodge
4 Moneyreagh Shopping
Centre. ☎ 448595. 0900-1800
Mon-Thur, until 1930 Fri, 1700
Sat. Grills.

NEWCASTLE
(STD 013967)

Anchor Bar ⚲
9 Bryansford Rd. ☎ 23344.
1200-1430 Mon-Fri, until 1800
Sat. Home-cooked pub grub.

Avoca Hotel ⚲
93 Central Promenade.
☎ 22253. Bar food from 1200
daily. High tea. Last orders
1900 Mon-Fri, 2000 Sat, 2030
Sun. Mixed grill, gammon, fish,
steak, omelettes, salads. £.

Briers
39 Middle Tollymore Rd.
☎ 24347. 1700-2100 Mon-
Sun. Local fish, lamb, beef.

Broadway Café ⚲
47 Central Promenade.
☎ 22263. 1100-2300 Mon-Sun.
Grills, salads, pasta, snacks.

Brook Cottage Hotel ⚲
58 Bryansford Rd. ☎ 22204.
1230-1430 & 1730-2100 Mon-
Sat, until 2000 Sun. Steak au
poivre, crispy roast duckling,
lamb cutlets. E££.

★ **BURRENDALE HOTEL** ⚲ ⊙
51 Castlewellan Rd. ☎ 22599.
1230-1430 & 1700-2100 Mon-
Sat, until 2030 Sun. A la carte.
E££.

Central Park ⚲
121 Central Promenade.
☎ 22487. 1230-1430 & 1700-
2100 Mon-Sat, from 1900
Sun. Grills, salads.

Cookie Jar ⊖
121 Main St. ☎ 22427. 0900-
1730 Mon-Sat. Cakes, pastries,
sandwiches.

Cookie Jar
4 The Shopping Centre.
☎ 22045. 0900-1730 Mon-Sat.
Cakes, pastries, sandwiches.

Country Fried Chicken
119 Main St. ☎ 23900. 1100-
2400 Mon-Thur & Sun, until
0130 Fri-Sat. Fast food.

Cygnet Coffee Shop ⊖
2 Savoy Lane. ☎ 24758. 1000-
1730 Mon-Sat, until 1800 Sun.
Stew, salads, soup, scones.

Donard Hotel ⚲
27 Main St. ☎ 22203. Last
orders 2045. Closed Jan-Feb.
A la carte. ££.

Enniskeen Hotel ⚲
98 Bryansford Rd. ☎ 22392.
Last orders 2030, closed Dec-
Feb. Stuffed pork & apple
sauce, steak chasseur, scampi,
salmon. £££.

Harbour Inn ⚲
4 South Promenade. ☎ 23445.
1230-2100 Mon-Sun. Bar
snacks, oysters, plaice, scampi.
Blackboard specials: cod in
beer batter, hot chocolate
fudge cake.

★ **MAPLE LEAF COTTAGE**
149 Bryansford Rd. ☎ 23500.
1100-1800 Tues-Sat, 1200-
1900 Sun. From 1 Sept-Easter
weekends only. Closed Dec-
Jan. Home-made snacks in
craft shop.

Mario's ⚲
65 South Promenade.
☎ 23912. 1830-2200 Tues-Sat,
1230-1430 & 1700-2100 Sun.
Italian. ££.

Maud's Ice Cream
137 Main St. ☎ 26184. 0900-
2300 Mon-Sun. Closes earlier
in winter. Ice cream, Italian
gâteaux.

McGlennon's Hotel ⚲
59 Main St. ☎ 22415. Last
orders 2100. High tea, mixed
grill, steaks, scampi, chicken,
desserts.

Newcastle Centre
10 Central Promenade.
☎ 25034. 1100-1900 Mon-Sat,
1400-1900 Sun summer only.
Grills.

Pavilion ⚲
36 Downs Rd. ☎ 26239.
1200-2100 Mon-Wed, 1200-
2145 Thur-Sat, until 2030 Sun.
Salmon, steaks, gâteaux. £££.

★ **PERCY FRENCH** ⚲
Downs Rd. ☎ 23175. 1230-
1430 & 1730-2130 Mon-Sun.
Ploughman's lunch. Chicken
chasseur, poached haddock,
salads. £££.

Pizza Palazzo
98 Main St. ☎ 26444. 1600-2400 Mon-Thur & Sun, until 0200 Fri-Sat. Pizzas, fish, garlic bread.

Quinn's ⚲
62 Main St. ☎ 26400. 1200-1600 Mon-Sun. Pub grub.

Robinson's
72 Main St. ☎ 26259. 0800-2100 Mon-Sun. Grills, chicken, salads, sweets.

Sea Palace ⚲
135 Main St. ☎ 23626. 1700-2400 Mon-Thur, until 0130 Fri-Sat, 1600-2400 Sun. Chinese & European.

Shimna Diner ⬧
2 Main St. ☎ 23010. 0830-1900 Mon-Sun. Fresh Kilkeel fish, steak, toasted sandwiches.

Slieve Donard Hotel ⚲
Downs Rd. ☎ 23681. Last orders 2130. Must book. £££.

Stone Boat
4 South Promenade. ☎ 24118. 1700-2130 Mon-Sun. Locally caught fish, steaks, pasta, strawberries, chocolate fudge cake.

Strand Coffee Shop ⊖
3 Main St. ☎ 23924. 0830-1730 Mon-Sat, 0900-1730 Sun. Open until 2200 in summer. Sandwiches, soup, bakes, cakes, coffee.

Strand Palace
53 Central Promenade. ☎ 23472. 0900-2300 Mon-Sun summer, until 1800 Mon-Sat winter. Snacks, lunch, high tea. Irish ham, salads, sweets.

The Stone Boat ⚲
4 South Promenade. ☎ 24118. 1700-2130 Mon-Sun. Locally caught fish. Steaks, pasta, strawberries, chocolate fudge cake. Restaurant with fishing theme.

Tollymore Teahouse
Tollymore Forest Park. ☎ 24067. 1030-1830 Mon-Sun. Oct-Feb 1200-1800 Sat-Sun only. Grills.

Top of the Town
1 Main St. ☎ 24328. 1000-0100 Mon-Wed, 0215 Thur-Sun. Fast food.

Toscano ⚲
47 Central Promenade. ☎ 22263. Easter-Oct 1230-2200 Mon-Sun. Ice cream, snacks, high tea.

Wadsworths
38 Main St. ☎ 22626. 0930-1700 Mon-Sat, ex Thur in winter. Snacks, lunch. In store.

Zebedee's
81 Main St. ☎ 22985. 1200-0030 Mon-Thur, until 0215 Fri-Sun. Fast food.

NEWRY
(STD 01693)

Ambassador
81 Hill St. ☎ 65307. 0800-1900 Mon-Wed, until 2000 Thur-Sat. Breakfast, grills, vegetarian, children's menu.

Arts Centre
1a Bank Parade. ☎ 61244. 1100-1600 Mon-Fri. Sandwiches, cakes.

Blueprint Pizza Company ♈
Ballybot House, Cornmarket. ☎ 250596. 1100-2300 Mon-Sat, from 1400 Sun. Garlic mushrooms, pizza, pasta, salad, chocolate fudge cake.

Boulevard
1 Margaret Square, Hill St. ☎ 66555. 0800-1830 Mon-Wed & Sat, until 2000 Thur-Fri. Chicken curry, fish.

Boyd's
14 John Mitchell Place. ☎ 62424. 0900-1700 Mon-Sat. Snacks, grills. Restaurant in store.

★ BRASS MONKEY ♈
1 Sandy St. ☎ 63176. 1030-2130 Mon-Sun. Morning coffee, salads, seafood, steaks, chicken. A la carte M£. E£££.

Bridge Bar ♈
53 North St. ☎ 62240. 1230-1500 & 1800-2100 Mon-Sat. Pub grub.

Canal Court Hotel ♈
Merchant's Quay. ☎ 251234. 0730-1030 Breakfast, 1230-1500 lunch, carvery, 1730-2130 dinner Mon-Sun. Selected pieces of seafood in mustard & white wine sauce, chocolate mousse cup.

Carriage ♨
Warrenpoint Rd. ☎ 250000. 0800-1900 Mon-Sat, 1000-1900 Sun. Breakfast. Chicken, salads, desserts. M£.

Cavern ♈
28 Church St. ☎ 62124. 1230-1500 & 1700-2200 Mon-Sat. Pub grub.

Cheers ♈
1 Trevor Hill. ☎ 64888. 1230-1500 Mon-Sun, 1800-2200 Thur-Sat, 1700-2100 Sun. Steaks, barbecued chicken, pavlova, apple pie. M££.

Clarke's ♈
73 Kilmorey St. ☎ 63960. 1230-1500 Mon-Sat. Pub grub.

Coach House
Abbey Yard. ☎ 68114. 0900-1700 Mon-Fri. Salads, open sandwiches.

Crusty Corner
22 Margaret St. ☎ 67708. 0830-1730 Mon-Sat. Quiche, rolls, tray bakes, scones.

Cupids ♈
25 Merchants Quay. ☎ 63221. 1230-2100 Mon-Sun. Irish stew, sweets.

143

Deli*Lites
12 Monaghan St. ☎ 61770.
0800-1730 Mon-Sat. Breakfast.
Gourmet sandwiches, pitta
breads.

Donnelly's ⊻
33 Silverbridge Rd. ☎ 861410.
1230-1430 Mon-Sat. Pub grub.

Florintine
4a Lower Catherine St.
☎ 63161. 0900-2100 Mon-Sat,
1600-2100 Sun. Traditional
fish & chips.

Friar Tuck's
3 Sugar Island. ☎ 69119. 1100-
2400 Mon-Sat, from 1500 Sun.
Fast food.

Glenside House
22a Tullynavall Rd. ☎ 861075.
1200-1430 & 1800-1930
Mon-Sat. Steaks, home baking.

Good Food Shop
Buttercrane Shopping Centre.
☎ 68655. 0900-1730 Mon-
Wed, until 2100 Thur-Fri,
1800 Sat. Salads, scones.

Hermitage Bar ⊻
1 Canal St. ☎ 64594. 1230-
1430 Mon-Sat. Grills.

Jake McCoy's ⊻
8 John Mitchell Place.
☎ 62413. 1130-2100 Mon-
Sun. Bar snacks. Chicken,
steak, beef, fish. E£.

Kylemore Café
10 Buttercrane Centre.
☎ 65555. 0900-1730 Mon,
Tues, Sat, until 2100 Wed-Fri.
Grills, snacks.

Lite 'n' Easy ⊻
Tullynavall Rd, Cullyhanna.
☎ 868262. 1300-1800 Mon-
Sat. Set meals, pub grub.

Mall View
60 Lower Mill St. ☎ 66236.
0900-1800 Mon-Sat. Snacks.

Mister B's ⊻
8 Water St. ☎ 250205. 1200-
1800 Mon-Sat. Pub grub.

Mourne Country Hotel ⊻
52 Belfast Rd. ☎ 67922. 1200-
1430 & 1700-2100. Restaurant
1830-2100 Mon-Sat, 1700-
2100 Sun. High tea.

Murtaghs ⊻
25 Bridge St. ☎ 62558. 1230-
1430 Mon-Sat. Pub grub.

Newry Golf Inn ⊻
11 Forkhill Rd. ☎ 63871.
1230-1400 & 1700-2100
Mon-Fri, 1130-2300 Sat. Set
lunch: turkey & ham, roast
lamb, steak, salmon, poached
cod, pasta. E£.

Olive Grove ⊻
5 Cornmarket ☎ 250575.
1700-2200 Mon-Sun. Pizzas,
pasta, steak, seafood.

Orchard Bar ⊻
114 Rathfriland Rd. ☎ 64911.
1930-2130 Mon-Sat. Pub grub.

Quayside Inn ♀
55 Merchants Quay. ☎ 62143.
1200-2230 Mon-Sun. Carvery,
high tea, bar snacks.

Riverside ♀
3 Kildare St. ☎ 67773. 1200-
1430 & 1900-2330 Sun-Thur,
1200-1430 & 1700-0030 Fri-
Sat. Chinese.

Rose Garden ♀
3 Sugar Island. ☎ 68702.
1200-1400 Mon-Fri, 1700-
2330 Mon-Thur, until 0030
Fri-Sat, 2315 Sun. Chinese &
European. E£.

Satellite
13 Kilmorey St. ☎ 62657.
1200-2330 Mon-Sat, 1700-
2400 Sun. Grills.

Sheepbridge Inn ♀
143 Belfast Rd. ☎ 60000.
1200-2030 Mon-Sat – bar
snacks, soup, stew. Upstairs
restaurant 1800-2130 Fri-Sat –
high tea, fish, steaks. 1200-
2030 Sunday carvery.

Shelbourne
69 Hill St. ☎ 62006. 0900-
1730 Mon-Sat ex Wed. Soup,
stews, pies.

Snaub's Coffee Shop ♀
15 Monaghan St. ☎ 65381.
0900-1800 Mon-Sat. Home
cooking, salads, hot & cold
buffet.

Sports Centre
61 Patrick St. ☎ 67322. 0900-
2200 Mon-Fri. Snacks.

Tall Man ♀
2 Water St. ☎ 68654. 1200-
1800 & 1900-2200 Mon-Sat.
Pub grub.

Terrace
6 Marcus St. ☎ 65396. 0830-
1800 Mon-Sat. Breakfast. Fish,
toasted sandwiches, salads.

The Cove ♀
33 Hilltown Rd. ☎ 67193.
1230-1700 Mon-Sun.
Pub grub.

NEWTOWNARDS
(STD 01247)

Ballyharry Roadhouse ♀
151 Donaghadee Rd.
☎ 820808. Bistro 1230-1430
Mon-Sun, 1730-2000 Mon-
Thur, until 1830 Fri-Sat, 1930
Sun. Restaurant 1930-2100
Fri-Sat E£.

Broadway Café
1 Pound St. ☎ 817970. 1200-
1900 Sun-Thur & 1200-1930
Fri-Sat.

Café Two
10 Regent St. ☎ 820131.
0930-1730 Mon-Sat.
Baguettes, salad, pasta,
baked potato.

Cafolla's
15 Conway Square.
☎ 812185. 0745-1800 Mon-
Fri, 0830-1800 Sat & Sun.
Fish & chips, ice cream.

Cafolla's Premier Café
10a Regent St. ☎ 814999.
0830-1730 Mon-Sat.

Connors ⊗
12 Regent St. ☎ 813359. 0900-
1630 Mon-Sat. Baked potatoes,
sandwiches.

Eastern Tandoori ⊻
16 Castle St. ☎ 819541. 1200-
1400 Mon-Sat, 1700-2330
Mon-Sun. Indian & European.
E££.

Finnegan's ⊻
1 Cooks Brae, Kircubbin.
☎ 38282. 1200-1400 Mon-Sun
(ex Tues.) 1900-2100 Fri-Sun.
Escalope of salmon, pan fried
with prawns and Thai dressing.

Foon Yee ♪
38 Regent St. ☎ 814346. 1200-
1400 & 1700-2300 Tues-Thur,
1200-1400 & 1700 2400 Fri-
Sat & 1700-2400 Sun. Chinese.

Ganges ⊻
69 Court St. ☎ 811426. 1200-
1400 & 1700-2330 Mon-Sat.
Indian. E££.

Giuseppe's Ristorante ⊻
31a Frances St. ☎ 812244.
1700-2230 Tues-Sun. Roast
pheasant, fish kebab, peach ice
cream with liqueur. E£.

Honey Pot ⊗
25 High St. ☎ 819591. 0815-
1630 Mon-Fri, until 1700 Sat.
Home-made quiche, lasagne,
vegetarian menu.

Huntsman ⊻
10 Castle St. ☎ 813073. 1200-
1430 Mon-Sat, 1700-2100 Fri-
Sat, 1300-1800 Sun. Pub grub.

Interno
Regent House, Regent St.
☎ 821030. 0900-1630 Mon-
Sat. Portavogie prawns, fish
pie, chilli, lasagne, baked
potato, cakes, pastries.
In Department Store.

Jolly Judge ⊻
54 Regent St. ☎ 819895.
1200-1415 & 1700-1930
Mon-Thur, 1200-2030 Fri-Sat,
1200-1415 Sun. Pub grub.

Knightsbridge Inn ⊻
Scrabo Rd. ☎ 813221. 1230-
2100 Mon-Fri, until 2030 Sat-
Sun. Hickory-smoked ribs,
black tiger prawns, smoked
chicken. A la carte E£.

★ **KNOTT'S COFFEE SHOP**
45 High St. ☎ 819098. 0900-
1730 Mon-Sat. Quiche, salads,
pastries, home baking, coffee.

Menary's Café
99 East St. ☎ 812870. 1100-
2400 Mon-Sat. Fish & chips.

Menary's - The Scrabo Room
53 High St. ☎ 813279. 0900-
1730 Mon-Sat. Restaurant in
store.

Ming Court ⊻
63 Court St. ☎ 815073. 1200-
1400 & 1730-2330 Mon-Fri,
1200-2330 Sat, 1230-2300
Sun. Chinese. E££.

Minstrels
7 Lower Mary St. ☎ 811760.
0900-1645 Mon-Sat. Quiche,
open sandwiches.

Mount Stewart
Mountstewart. ☎ (012477)
88387. May-Sept & Easter
1300-1730 Mon-Sun. April &
Oct 1300-1800 Sat-Sun only.
Cakes, coffee. National Trust
house.

New Dragon Palace ⚲
61 Portaferry Rd. ☎ 816800.
1230-1430 & 1700-2330
Mon-Fri, 1230-2330 Sat-Sun.
Peking & Cantonese. E££.

Old Cross Inn ⚲ ⊘
47 South St. ☎ 820212. & Sun.
1200-1500 & 1730-2100
Tues-Sat. 1200-1500 Sun-Mon
Steaks, fish. A la carte. E£.

Peking Garden ⚲
17 Castle St. ☎ 813903. 1200-
1400 Mon-Sat, 1700-2300
Mon-Sun. Chinese &
European. E££.

Pied Piper
11 High St. ☎ 818140. 0900-
1730 Mon-Sat. Savoury pies,
lasagne.

Regency
5 Regent St. ☎ 814347. 0800-
1700 Mon-Thur 0800-1900
Fri-Sat. Breakfast, sandwiches,
snacks.

★ **ROMA'S** ⚲
4 Regent St. ☎ 812841. 1130-
2300 Mon- Tues, 1130-0100
Wed-Sat, 1230-1430 & 1900-
2200 Sun. Italian.

Scholars
35 Regent St. ☎ 821030.
1000-1700 Mon-Sat. Soups,
salad, baked potatoes, pastries,
daily special. Coffee shop in
Gregstown department store.

Scrabo Café
187 Mill St. ☎ 810963. 1200-
1400 & 1600-1900 Mon-Wed,
1200-2200 Thur-Fri, until
1930 Sat. Grills.

Smyth's
31 West St. ☎ 812732. 1130-
2300 Mon-Thur, until 0030
Fri-Sat. Spring rolls, fish,
chicken, gammon, pizzas.

Strangford Arms Hotel ⚲
92 Church St. ☎ 814141.
Ostlers: Until 2130 Mon-Sat,
2030 Sun. Bar food. Salmon,
oysters. E££.

Temptations ⊘
31b Frances St. ☎ 820361.
1000-1700 Tues-Sat. Baked
potatoes, seafood vol-au-vents.

PORTAFERRY
(STD 01247)

Christine's Café
3 The Square. ☎ 38971. 0900-
1700 Mon-Sat. 1200-1700
Sun, July-Aug only. Grills, teas.

Cornstore ⚱
2 Castle St. ☎ 29779. 1200-
2130 Wed-Sun (until 2030 in
winter). Local seafood. £££.

Exploris
Rope Walk, Castle St.
☎ 28062. 1100-1730 Mon-Sat,
1300-1730 Sun. Snacks. Inside
aquarium.

Ferry Grill
3 High St. ☎ 28448. 1100-
2300 Mon-Sat, 1400-2130
Sun. Fish & chips.

★ PORTAFERRY HOTEL ⚱
10 The Strand. ☎ 28231. Until
2100 Mon-Sat, 2030 Sun. Bar
lunches. Stuffed mussels, fried
oysters, turbot. £££.

Scotsman ⚱
156 Shore Rd. ☎ 28024. 1230-
1430 & 1730-2030 Mon-Sun,
until 2130 Sat. Seafood,
chicken, steaks.

The Narrows ⚱ ⊘
8 Shore Rd. ☎ 28148. 1200-
1430 Tues-Sun, 1900-2130
Thurs-Sat. Seafood, salads.
£££.

RATHFRILAND
(STD 018206)

Country Fayre
1a Church Square. ☎ 38177.
0900-1730 Mon-Sat ex Thur
pm. Breakfast. Open Danish
sandwiches.

Maple Leaf Café
4 John St. ☎ 31191. 1100-
2400. Mon-Sat. Soup, scones,
salads, pastries.

Old George ⚱
2 Caddell's Lane. ☎ 30836.
1200-1900 Mon-Sat. Bar food.
A la carte, steak, gammon,
salmon. £.

Pat's Bar ⚱ ⊘
88 Castlewellan Rd, Lenish.
☎ 30439. 1900-2100 Tues-Fri,
1800-2130 Sat, 1700-2030
Sun. Pub grub.

Rosetta Inn ⚱
106 Newry Rd. ☎ 31203.
1800-2130 Fri-Sat, 1200-1430
& 1700-2030 Sun. Grills,
home-made sweets.

ROSTREVOR
(STD 016937)

Cloughmor Inn ⚱
2 Bridge St. ☎ 38007. 1930-
2230 Mon-Sat. Pub grub.

Corner House ⚱
1 Bridge St. ☎ 38236. 1200-
1430 & 1830-2130 Mon-Sat,
ex Wed. Pub grub.

Kilbroney Park
☎ 38026. 1100-2000 Mon-Sun, closes earlier in winter. Traditional Sunday lunch 1200-1600. Fish, baked potatoes, toasted sandwiches. Café in forest park.

The Kilbroney
31 Church St. ☎ 38390. 12.30-1430 & 1730-2100 Mon-Sat. 1230-1430 & 1500-2100 Sun. Avocado pear with shrimp, seafood tagliatelle & fillet of lamb with peppered herb crust.

Top of the Town ⚲
31 Church St. ☎ 38276. 1130-2200 Mon-Sat, 1230-1400 & 1900-2030 Sun. Steak, scampi.

Ye Olde Corner House ⚲
The Square. ☎ 38236. 1900-2200 Mon-Sun. Salads, baked potatoes.

SAINTFIELD
(STD 01238)

Caroline's Parlour
66 Main St. ☎ 511108. 0900-1700 Mon-Sat. Set lunch, afternoon tea.

Rosy Bar ⚲
14 Main St. ☎ 510388. 1900-2300 Mon-Thur, until 2200 Sun, 1130-2300 Fri-Sat. Pub grub.

Rowallane Gardens
Rowallane. ☎ 510131. May-Aug: 1230-1700 Mon-Fri, 1400-1800 Sat-Sun. April-Sept: 1400-1800 Mon-Fri, Cream teas. National Trust.

Rowallane Inn ⚲
1 Belfast Rd. ☎ 510466. Bar meals: 1230-1430 Mon-Sun, all day Fri-Sun. Grilled chicken salad, pork in two mustards sauce. Chocolate cheesecake. E££.

Saintfield Griddle
19 Main St. ☎ 510270. 0900-1730 Mon-Sat. Teas, coffees, sandwiches, scones, cakes.

Tasty Grill
86 Main St. ☎ 511452. 1200-2000 Mon-Thur, 0900-2100 Fri-Sat. Fish & chips.

Upper Room ♟
21 Main St. ☎ 511772. 0900-1700 Mon-Sat, until 2100 Fri. Soup, fish, chicken & ham pie, salads, pastries.

White Horse Inn ⚲
49 Main St. ☎ 510417. 1130-2230 Mon-Sat. Scampi, trout, steaks, home-baked gammon. E£.

SCARVA
(STD 01762)

Scarva Visitor Centre
1a Main St. ☎ (01762) 832163. 1100-1700 Tues-Fri, from 1400 Sat-Sun. Closed Nov-Feb. Pastries, coffee.

SEAFORDE
(STD 01396)

**Butterfly Restaurant
& Coffee Shop**
☎ 811138. 1100-1700 Mon-Sat
(ex Mon-Tues in winter),1300-
1800 Sun. Closes 1hr. earlier
in winter, no Wed opening
Jan-mid-March. Home-made
lasagne, salads, light snacks,
scones, desserts.

★ SEAFORDE INN ♉
24 Main St. ☎ 811232. 1900-
2130 Wed-Sat, 1200-1415 &
1700-2000 Sun. Dundrum
mussels, venison sausages.
E£££. Pub grub 1200-2100
Mon-Sat (2015 Sun).

STRANGFORD
(STD 01396)

★ CUAN BAR
& RESTAURANT ♉ ⊘
6 The Square. ☎ 881222.
1130-2130 Mon-Sat, 1230-
2130 Sun. Seafood chowder,
goat's cheese tartlet, ostrich,
quail, hot & cold buffet. E£££.

Lobster Pot ♉
The Square. ☎ 881288. 1100-
2130 Mon-Sat, 1200-2030 Sun
(2000 in winter). Bar food,
high tea. Seafood. Beer
garden.

WARINGSTOWN
(STD 01762)

★ THE GRANGE ⚲
Mill Hill, Main St. ☎ 881989.
1230-1430 Tues-Fri & Sun,
1930-2200 Tues-Sat. Baked
salmon, whiskey steak,
chocolate mousse. A la carte.
Must book. E£££.

Joy's Kitchen
51 Main St. ☎ 882557. 1100-
2200 Mon-Sat. Chicken, fish,
ice cream.

Planter's Tavern ⚲
4 Banbridge Rd. ☎ 881510.
Breakfast: 0730-0945, lunch
1230-1430 daily & 1500-2130
Thur-Sat. Bar snacks,
à la carte.

Village Inn ⚲
51 Main St. ☎ 881495. 1230-
1430 & 1900-2200 Mon-Sat.
Pub grub.

WARRENPOINT
(STD 016937)

Aylesforte House ⚲ ⊙
44 Newry Rd. ☎ 72255. 1230-
1430 Mon-Sun, 1800-2200
Mon-Sat, 1730-2030 Sun.
Moroccan lamb with
couscous, oriental duck with
plums & red onion. E££.

Balmoral ⚲
13 Seaview. ☎ 54093. 1230-
1430 & 1800-2130 Mon-Sat.
Pub grub.

Bennett's ⚲ ⊙
21 Church St. ☎ 52314. 1230-
1430 & 1700-2130 Mon-Sun.
Local seafood, traditional pies,
steaks.

Carlingford Bay Hotel ⚲
3 Osborne Promenade.
☎ 73521. Last orders 2130.
Steak, salmon with lemon
cream, chicken kiev. E£.

Central Café
32 Church St. ☎ 72693. 0930-
1800 Mon-Sat, until 1400
Wed. Set lunch, sweets.

Coffee House
40 Church St. ☎ 72718. 0930-
1800 Mon-Sat ex Wed, 1430-
1800 Sun. Coffee, cakes.

Crown ⚲
7 The Square. ☎ 52917. 1230-
1430 & 1730-2100 Mon-Sun.
Afternoon tea. A la carte. E£.

Diamond's
9 The Square. ☎ 52053. 1030-
1900 Mon-Thur, until 2200
Fri-Sun. Breakfast. A la carte,
high tea. Vegetarian.

Duke Bar & Steakhouse ⚲
7 Duke St. ☎ 53149. 1800-
2200 Mon-Thur, until 2230
Fri-Sat, 1700-2200 Sun.
Steaks.

Jack Ryan's ⚲
15 The Square. ☎ 52001.
1230-1430 & 1730-2130
Mon-Thur, until 2200 Fri-Sat.
Bar snacks, high tea, à la carte.
Themed nights.

Mac's Bar ♒
1 Marine Parade. ☎ 52082.
1200-1500 & 1700-2130
Mon-Sat, 1230-1430 & 1900-
2200 Sun. Pub grub.

Marine Tavern ♒
4 Marine Parade. ☎ 54147.
1230-1430 & 1730-2200
Mon-Sun. Set meals, high tea,
à la carte. £££.

Ship Lounge ♒
14 The Square. ☎ 52685.
1230-1430 Mon-Sat. Pub grub.

Silvana
29 Church St. ☎ 72714. 1000-
2200 Mon-Sun. Grills, salads.

Tai Pan ♒
1 Duke St. ☎ 52084. 1700-
2300 Tues-Thur, until 2400 Fri-
Sat, 1200-1500 & 1700-2200
Sun. Cantonese & European.

Vecchia Roma Pizzeria ♒
1 Marine Parade. ☎ 52082.
1700-2200 Mon-Thur, until
2300 Fri-Sat, 1230-1430 &
1700-2130 Sun. Italian. ££.

Victoria ♒
1 Dock St, The Square.
☎ 53687. Breakfast in pub
0800-1000 Mon-Sun. Punjabi
restaurant 1st floor 1700-2300.
Chicken jalfrezi, lamb
dopiaza. £££.

Whistledown Inn ♒
6 Seaview. ☎ 52697. 1230-
1530 & 1830-2130 Mon-Sun.
Bar snacks. A la carte.
Seafood, gammon, steak,
Mediterranean chicken.

OSCAR'S
Restaurant

29 Belmore Street, Enniskillen
☎ **(01365) 327037**

*Oscar's restaurant is dedicated to Oscar Wilde,
"the literary genius", who was educated at Enniskillen's
Portora Royal School. This beautiful, romantic restaurant
overbrimming with personality, is a warren of booked tables,
including a themed Irish writers' room, the Dorian Gray room,
and a beautiful bar dating back to the early 1800s.*

*So why not soak up the atmosphere and browse through one
of the hundreds of old books and indulge yourself with the
mouthwatering food and Fermanagh hospitality,
at its very best.*

Features include:

★ *Fully licensed bar*
★ *Les Routiers Casserole Award
  Winner 1998*
★ *Fully air-conditioned*
★ *Baby changing facilities*
★ *Excellent tea-time
  & children's menus available*
★ *Serving a wide range of
  international cuisine,
  all freshly prepared on the premises*
★ *96% rating in Good Restaurant Guide*

**Open:
1700-2230 daily**

BALLINAMALLARD
(STD 01365)

Encore Steak House ♀
66 Main St. ☎ 388606. 1730-
2200 Wed-Sun. Steaks, Italian
beef, duck, trout. E££.

Mallard Bar ♀
64 Main St. ☎ 388388.
1130-2300 Mon-Sat. 1230-
1400 pub grub.

BELCOO
(STD 01365)

Border Diner
11 Main St. ☎ (01365)
386464. 0900-0100 Mon-Sat,
1400-2400 Sun. Grills.

BELLANALECK
(STD 01365)

Moorings ♀
156 Derrylin Rd. ☎ 348328.
0930-2130 Mon-Sun. Tia
Maria duckling, home-made
sweets, scones, pastries,
children's menu. Traditional
Sunday lunch. E£.

★ **THE SHEELIN** ♀
Bellanaleck. ☎ 348232.
1000-1630 & 1800-2200
Mon-Sun. Honey-marinated
ham, Bailey's cheesecake,
soda bread. Must book. E£££.

BELLEEK
(STD 013656)

Belleek Pottery Tea Rooms
☎ 58501. 0930-1800 Mon-Sat,
1400-1800 Sun. Lasagne,
quiche, casseroles, baked
potatoes, salads, sweets.

Cleary's Corner Bar ♀
5 Main St. ☎ 58403. 1200-
2200 Mon-Sat. Pub grub.

Fiddlestone Café
Main St. Quiche, vol-au-vents,
salads.

McDonnell's
32 Main St. ☎ 58392. 1200-
1400, until 0300 Fri-Sat. Fish
& chips, sausages, burgers.

McMorrow's Bar ♀
19 Main St. ☎ 58423. 1130-
2330 Mon-Sat, 1230-1430 &
1900-2200 Sun. Tea & toasties.

Rooney's Bar ♀
Main St. ☎ 58279. 1200-1500
Mon-Sat. Pub grub.

Thatch Coffee Shop
20 Main St. ☎ 58181. 0900-
1700 Mon-Sat. Scones, cakes,
soups.

BLANEY
(STD 013656)

Restaurant Nautique ⚲
Lough Shore Rd. ☎ 41715.
1900-2400 Mon-Sun, ex Tues
in winter. Trout fillet, banana
flambé. ££.

BROOKEBOROUGH
(STD 013655)

Castle Hill Bar ⚲
58 Main St. ☎ 31424. 1700-
2300 Wed-Sun. Fish & chips,
pizzas, sandwiches.

Forest Inn ⚲
73 Main St. ☎ 31814. 1230-
2400 Mon-Sun. Hot pies,
soup, toasted sandwiches.

DERRYGONNELLY
(STD 013656)

Bond Store ⚲
75 Main St. ☎ 41254. 1300-
2400 Mon-Sat.

Drumary Farm
Glenasheever Rd. ☎ 41420.
0800-2130 Mon-Sun. Home
cooking. Must book. E£.

McGovern's ⚲
66 Main St. ☎ 41212. 1130-
2300 Mon-Sat, 1900-2200
Sun. Pub grub.

DERRYLIN
(STD 013657)

Blake's ⚲
136 Main St. ☎ 48203. 1230-
1430 & 1830-2130 Mon-Sat.
Grills, salads, game, fish.

Knockninny ▲
Corraclare. ☎ 48339. 1300-
1500 Tues-Sun. Home
cooking.

Mountview Bar ⚲
69 Main St. ☎ 48226. 1200-
1430 & 1800-2100 Mon-Sat.
Pub grub. Sunday lunch:
turkey & ham, roast beef.

EDERNEY
(STD 013656)

Roley's Bistro ⚲
19 Market St. ☎ 31506. 0730-
2400 Mon-Thur, until 0200
Fri-Sat, 1200-2400 Sun.
Steaks, fish, salads, game.
Fri-Sun E£.

Three Way Inn ⚲
9 Main St. ☎ 31615. 1130-
2300 Mon-Sat, 1230-1430 &
1900-2200 Sun. Pub grub.

ENNISKILLEN
(STD 01365)

Aisling Centre
37 Darling St. ☎ 325811.
1000-1700 Mon-Fri, until
1400 Sat. Scones, pastries,
light lunches. In coffee shop.

Anchorage
Brooke Park. ☎ 322882.
May-June & Sept Sat-Sun
1100-1800, July-Aug Mon-Sun
1100-1900. Sandwiches,
pastries.

Ardhowen Theatre ⌾
Dublin Rd. ☎ 325254. 1100-
1530 Mon-Sat. Light lunch,
coffee, pastries.

Ashberry Hotel ⌡
14-20 Temp Rd. ☎ 320333.
1200-1500 & 1800-2130
Mon-Thur, 1200-2130 Fri-Sun.
Breakfast. Morning coffee.
Prawns, steak, chicken.
Vegetarian.

Barbizon
5 East Bridge St. ☎ 324456.
0800-1800 Mon-Sat. Home
baking.

★ **BLAKE'S OF
   THE HOLLOW** ⌡
6 Church St. ☎ 322143. 1215-
1430 Mon-Sat. Pub grub,
soup, sandwiches. Live music.

Bush ⌡
26 Townhall St. ☎ 325210.
1230-1430 & 1700-1900
Mon-Sat. Pub grub.

Castle Coole
☎ 322690. 1300-1730 April-
Sept Sat-Sun, May-Aug daily
ex Thur. Tea shop in visitor
centre. Admission charge to
National Trust estate.

Castlebowlervision
21 Factory Rd. ☎ 324172.
1000-2300 Mon-Thurs, until
2400 Fri-Sat, 1200-2400 Sun.
Fast food.

Charlie's ⌡
1 Church St. ☎ 325303. 1130-
2300 Mon-Sat, until 2230 Sun.
Pub grub.

Corner Bar ⌡
22 Townhall St. ☎ 326445.
1100-2300 Mon-Sun. Pub
grub, sandwiches, tea, coffee.

Crowe's Nest ⌡
12 High St. ☎ 325252. 0900-
2100 Mon-Sun. Oysters,
smoked salmon, gammon,
cottage pie, mini-grills. E£.

Dunnes Stores
Fairgreen. ☎ 325132. 0900-
1800 Mon-Tues, Sat, until
2130 Wed-Fri, 1300-1730
Sun. Bakes, salads, cakes.
Restaurant in store.

Feast House
25 Head St. ☎ 328083. 1200-
0200 Mon-Sun. Fast food.

Fort Cavern
28 Forthill St. ☎ 324240.
1000-1900 Mon-Sun. Grills,
salads, pizzas.

Fort Lodge Hotel ⌡
72 Forthill St. ☎ 323275. Last
orders 2100 Mon-Wed, 2200
Thur-Sun. A la carte. E££.

"Traditional Irish Hospitality
and Superb Food Daily".

Set in the west of Enniskillen, Mulligans offers superb food at tremendous value for money, both at lunchtime and in the evenings. A short stroll from all the main jetties, Mulligans has a delightfully informal, rustic charm, regular live music and the great atmosphere ensures it's a lively meeting-place for all ages. Give us a call - from a quick drink to a 5-course meal, we cover the lot, and we're looking forward to meeting you!

- Bushmills Northern Ireland Bar of the Year 1994 & 1996
- Lunch midday till 3pm
- Evening menu 4pm till 9.30pm
- Live music Wednesdays, Fridays & Sundays
- Children welcome

MULLIGANS

BAR & RESTAURANT

33 Darling St., Enniskillen, Northern Ireland BT74 7DP
☎ **(01365) 322059 Fax (01365) 325319**

★ **FRANCO'S** ⅋
Queen Elizabeth Rd.
☎ 324424. 1200-2330 Mon-
Sat, 1700-2200 Sun. Mussels,
crab, seafood, pasta, pizza,
salads. ££.

Golden Arrow
23 Townhall St. ☎ 322259.
1000-1800 Mon-Sat ex Wed.
Fish & chips.

Johnston's
6 Townhall St. ☎ 322277.
0900-1730 Mon-Sat.
Sandwiches, lasagne, pastries.

Kamal Mahal ⅋
1 Water St. ☎ 325045. 1700-
2100 Mon-Sun ex Tues. Indian
& European. ££.

Kentucky Fried Chicken
1 Wellington Rd. ☎ 327143.
1100-2400 Sun-Thur, until
0200 Fri-Sat. Fast food.

Killyhevlin Hotel ⅋
Dublin Rd. ☎ 323481. Last
orders 2100, Sun 2000. Duck,
pheasant, monkfish, salmon.
£££.

Lakeland Forum
Broad Meadow. ☎ 325534.
0800-1030 Mon-Fri, 1000-
1800 Sat, 1400-1800 Sun.
Snacks, set meals.

★ **LE BISTRO** ⌾
Erneside Centre. ☎ 326954.
0900-1730 Mon-Sat, until
2100 Thur-Fri. Breakfast,
coffee, grills.

Leslie's
10 Church St. ☎ 324902.
0830-1700 Mon-Sat. Bakes,
salads, cakes.

Lily's Coffee Lounge
40 Head St. ☎ 325100. 0830-
1730 Mon-Sat. Home-baked
scones, pastries, pizzas, filled
rolls. Café in bakery.

Lough Erne House
St Catherine's, Blaney.
☎ 41216. 1200-2130 Mon-Sun.
Snacks, afternoon tea, high tea,
dinner.

Magee's Wine & Spirit Store ⅋
21 East Bridge St. ☎ 324996.
1130-2330 Mon-Sat, until 2230
Sun. Pub grub.

Maud's
26 Wellington St. ☎ 326208.
0900-2200 Mon-Sat, from
1200 Sun. Soup, pizzas, salads.

★ **MELVIN HOUSE** ⅋
1 Townhall St. ☎ 322040.
1930-2300 Mon-Sun. Morning
coffee, scones. Lunch: turkey
& ham, roast lamb, trout, 20
different sweets. Porterhouse
steak, seafood platter. £££.

★ **MULLIGAN'S** ⅋
33 Darling St. ☎ 322059.
1200-1500 & 1600-2130 Mon-
Sun. Steaks, seafood. ££.

McCartney's Inn ⅋
17 Belmore St. ☎ 322012.
1200-1500 Mon-Sat. Home-
made broth, Irish stew.

Oscar's ⚲
29 Belmore St. ☎ 327037.
1700-2230 Mon-Sun. Steaks,
pasta, Chinese dishes.

Pat's Bar ⚲
1 Townhall St. ☎ 327462.
1130-2000 Mon-Sun. Pub
grub. Live music Thurs-Sun,
every night in summer.

Peppercorn
15 Townhall St. ☎ 324834.
1200-1730 Mon-Sat. Fish,
chicken, lasagne.

Pizzerella
Dublin Rd. ☎ 320444. 1700-
2330 Tues-Sun, late Sat.
Pizzas.

Railway Hotel ⚲
34 Forthill St. ☎ 322084.
Last orders 2100. Fish,
chicken, steak, mixed grill,
gammon, vegetarian. E£.

Rebecca's
Buttermarket, Down St.
☎ 324499. 0930-1730 Mon-
Sat. Sandwiches, salads,
pastries.

Ringside Restaurant ⚲
New Agricultural Centre,
Leckaboy. ☎ 322218. 0800-
1500 Mon-Fri, 1600-1800
Thurs. Soups, Ulster fry, pies.

Roadhouse Bar ⚲
73 Cornagrade Rd. ☎ 327432.
1130-2330 Mon-Sat, until
2230 Sun. Pub grub.

Saddler's ⚲
66 Belmore St. ☎ 326223.
1100-2300 Mon-Sun.
Pub food. Sunday lunch.
A la carte E£.

Silver Swallow Bar ⚲
Drumawill, 189 Sligo Rd.
☎ 322051. 1130-2330 Mon-
Sat, until 2230 Sun. Burgers.

Three Way Inn ⚲
Ashwoods, 247 Sligo Rd.
☎ 327414. 1230-1430 Mon-
Sat. Pub grub.

Tippler's Brook ⚲
1 The Brook. ☎ 322048. 1130-
2300 Mon-Sat, 1230-1430 &
1900-2200 Sun. Pub grub.

Ulsterbus Bistro
Wellington Rd. ☎ 322633.
0845-1800 Mon-Sat. Snacks,
sandwiches, salads.

Village Inn ⚲
Scaffog, Sligo Rd. ☎ 323132.
1230-1430 Mon-Sat. Pub grub.

Vintage ⚲
13 Townhall St. ☎ 324055.
1200-1900 Mon-Sat. Turkey,
beef, lamb, chicken, pizza. E£.

Watergate ⚲
1 Ann St. ☎ 327447. 1130-
1800 Mon-Fri. Pub grub.

Welcome Inn ⚲
10 Sligo Rd. ☎ 323734. 1700-
0030 Mon-Thur, until 0130
Fri-Sat, 0100 Sun. Chinese &
European. E££.

Willy Rambler's ⚲
14 Forthill St. ☎ 327484.
1200-1800 Mon-Sat, until
1630 Sun. Pub grub, vegetable
stir fry, scampi, gammon steak.

FLORENCECOURT
(STD 01365)

Florence Court House
☎ 348249. July-Aug 1200-
1800 daily ex Tues. April-June
& Sept Sat-Sun/bank holidays
1300-1800. Quiche, stews,
wheaten bread. In National
Trust visitor centre.

★ TULLYHONA HOUSE 🍷
59 Marble Arch Rd. ☎ 348452.
Easter & June-Aug only, 1000-
1900 Mon-Sun. Buffet salads,
home baking. Must book.

Marble Arch Caves
☎ 348855. March-Sept 1100-
1630 Mon-Sun. Rolls, pastries,
coffee. Café at caves.

Regal Bar ⚲
2 Mullanaveay Rd. ☎ 348264.
1230-1430 & 1500-2200
Mon-Sat. Pub grub.

Tippler's Inn ⚲
Skea, Arney. ☎ 348214. 1130-
2330 Mon-Thur, 1130-1330
Fri-Sat, 1230-1430 & 1900-
2200 Sun. Pub grub.

GARRISON
STD (013656)

Bilberry Restaurant ⚲
Main St. ☎ 58970. 1200-2200
Thur-Sun. Steak, chicken, fries,
salads. E£.

Heathergrove Guesthouse
Meenacloybane. ☎ 58362.
Lough Melvin trout, steaks.
Must book. E££.

Lough Melvin Holiday Centre
☎ 58142. 0800-2100 Mon-Sun
April-Oct, until 1800 Nov-
March. Soup, stews, fresh fish.

IRVINESTOWN
(STD 013656)

Bawnacre Centre
Castle St. ☎ 21177. 1300-2230
Mon-Fri, 1400-1800 Sat-Sun.
Soups, sandwiches. Café in
leisure centre.

Central Bar ⚲
38 Main St. ☎ 21249. 1230-
1530 Thur-Sat. Pub grub.

Corner Café
18 Church St. ☎ 21696.
0900-1900 Mon-Sat ex Thur.
Fast food.

Devenish Bar ⚲
60 Main St. ☎ 21241. 1200-
2100 Tues-Sat. Pub grub.

the INISHCLARE

Restaurant, bar, bistro, marina & Cedars Guesthouse

For the finest cuisine in the most beautiful surroundings, it has to be the Inishclare!

Restaurant
Wed-Sat 1900-2200

Sunday
1200-1900 (booking advised)

Bar/Bistro
Open 7days a week, 12 noon until late. Extensive menu available at the most competitve prices

• Live enertainment every weekend •
Private & semi-private functions available on request
Cedars Grade A Guesthouse - 8 ensuite rooms
One deluxe with four poster

Killadeas, Irvinestown, Co Fermanagh BT94 1SF
☎ (013656) 28550 Fax (013656) 28552

★ HOLLANDER ⏛
5 Main St. ☎ 21231. 1130-
2300 Mon-Sat, 1900-2200
Sun. In winter 1230-1430
Mon-Sat, 1730-2200 Sun.
Salmon en croute, beef
Wellington. E££.

Lily House ⏛
54 Main St. ☎ 21880. 1700-
2400 Mon-Thur, until 0100
Fri-Sat, 1600-2400 Sun.
Chinese & European. E££.

Mahon's Hotel ⏛
Mill St. ☎ 21656. Last orders
2100. Garlic steak, stuffed
mushrooms. E££.

Maurizio's Coffee Shop
Savemore, Main St. ☎ 21110.
0930-1730 Mon-Sat. In store.

McCaffrey's ⏛
Main St. ☎ 21832. Bar snacks
served daily. A la carte from
1600 daily, Sun lunch from
1200.

Necarne Arms ⏛
1 Church St. ☎ 21572. 1200-
1800 Mon-Sat. Bar food.

Railway Engine Bar ⏛
Mill St. ☎ 21392. 1800-2130
Mon-Sat. Pub grub.

The Cedars ⏛
Drummal. ☎ 013656 21493.
1800-2130 Mon-Sat & 1700-
2130 Sun. Steaks, stew,
lasagne.

The In Place
31 Main St. ☎ 21965. 1100-
2400 Mon-Sat, 1200-0230
Sun. Fast food.

Woodhill Hunting Lodge ⏛
Derrynanny. ☎ 21863. 1700-
2300 Wed-Sun, until 0100 Sat.
A la carte. E££.

KESH
(STD 013656)

Drumrush Lodge ⏛
Boa Island Rd. ☎ 31578.
1730-2130 Mon-Sun. Oct-May
Fri-Sun only. Grills, à la carte.
££.

★ LUSTY BEG ISLAND ⏛
Lusty Beg, Boa Island.
☎ 31342. Bar food 1200-2100.
Smoked wild Irish salmon,
pizzas, baked potatoes. A la
carte 1830-2130 Mon-Sun. Tea
room in summer 0900-1900.

Lough Erne Hotel ⏛
2 Main St. ☎ 31275. Last
orders 2100. A la carte. E££.

May Fly ⏛
14 Main St. ☎ 31281. 1200-
1430 Mon-Sat, 1800-2200
Mon-Sun. Pub grub.

Mullynaval Lodge ♦
Boa Island. ☎ 31995. Home-
baking. Last orders 1900. Must
book £.

Welcome to
Saddler's Restaurant

**66 Belmore Street, Enniskillen,
Co Fermanagh**

Savour the freshly prepared food in Enniskillen's
award-winning restaurant. A wide choice of menu
for all the family, now including oriental.
Great quality food at reasonable prices,
with friendly service in a relaxed atmosphere
Food served 1100 - 2300, 7 days a week

☎ **(01365) 326223 / 325076**
Live entertainment every weekend

Saddler's Restaurant

Riverside Restaurant ♀
9 Main St. ☎ 32342. 1700-2130
Tues-Sat, 1200-1500 Sun.
Roast duckling, fillet of steak on
a bed of champ & bacon. £.

Sarah Jane's
41 Main St. ☎ 31940. 1030-
1700 Mon-Sat, 1200-2000 Sun.
Home baking.

KILLADEAS
(STD 013656)

Archdale Diner
☎ 28300. July-Aug 1000-2200
Mon-Sun, Sept-Oct 1700-2200
Sat-Sun. Chicken, salads. E£.

**Castle Archdale
Country Restaurant**
☎ 21345. July-Aug 0900-2230
Mon-Sun, June & Sept closes
earlier. Scampi, Lasagne,
quiche.

★ **MANOR
HOUSE HOTEL** ♀
☎ 21561. Last orders 2200.
Local salmon, game, steaks.
A la carte. M£, E££

Inishclare ♀
☎ 28550. 1200 until late Mon-
Sun. Crab claws, chargrilled
Pernod chicken, wild
mushroom soufflé.

Waterfront ♀
Rosigh. ☎ 21938. 1730-2100
Wed-Sat, 1200-2200 Sun,
longer hours July-Aug. Soup,
sandwiches.

KINAWLEY
(STD 01365)

Corrigans ♀
39 Main St. ☎ 348285. 1900-
2300 Mon-Sat. Pub grub. £.

LISBELLAW
(STD 01365)

Carrybridge Hotel ♀
Inishmore Rd, Carrybridge.
☎ 387148. Last orders 2200.
Fish, duck, steaks, vegetarian
dishes. E££.

Glencar Bar ♀
29 Main St. ☎ 387818. Bar
snacks 1230-1430 Mon-Sun,
1800-2130 Fri-Sun. Salmon,
chicken Maryland. E££.

Wild Duck Inn ♀
Farnamullan Rd. ☎ 387258.
1130-2300 Mon-Sat, 1230-
1430 & 1900-2200 Sun. Pub
grub, fish, chicken, salads.

LISNARICK
(STD 013656)

★ **CEDARS** ♀
Castle Archdale, Drumall.
☎ 21493. 1800-2130 Mon-Sat,
from 1700 Sun. Steaks, stew,
lasagne.

★ **DRUMSHANE HOTEL** ♀
☎ 21146. Last orders 2000.
Lamb kebab Drumshane, shark
steaks. A la carte. E£££.

LISNASKEA
(STD 013657)

The Barter Stone
187 Main St. ☎ 23120. 0800-1730 Mon-Sat. Toasties, baked potatoes.

Corner House ⊻
169 Main St. ☎ 21172. 1230-1430 grills, 1230-1700 snacks Mon-Sat. Pub grub.

FDH Coffee Shop
193 Main St. ☎ 21276. 1000-1700 Mon-Wed & Sat, until 2030 Thur-Fri. Quiche, pizza.

Ortine Hotel ⊻
92 Main St. ☎ 21206. Last orders 2130. Pub grub. A la carte. £££.

Shoe the Donkey ⊻
133 Main St. ☎ 21298. 1130-2330 Mon-Sun. Pub grub.

Teach a' Ceili
Inishcorkish. ☎ 21360. Snacks for holidaymakers on boats. Phone to enquire.

NEWTOWNBUTLER
(STD 013657)

Crom Estate
☎ 38118. April-Sept 1400-1700 Sat-Sun, July-Aug daily. Tea shop (National Trust) in visitor centre. Admission charge to estate.

Lanesborough Arms ⊻
6 High St. ☎ 38488. 1230-1430 & 1800-2130 Mon-Sat, in winter Fri-Sat only. 1230-2000 Sun. Steak burgers, chicken Maryland, toffee pavlova.

Mulligan's ⊻
19 Main St. ☎ 38737. 1200-1500-2130 Mon-Sat, 1230-1430 & 1900-2100 Sun. Pub grub.

Nana's Coffee Shop
Main St. ☎ 38090. 0830-1730, Mon-Sat, 0930-1330 Wed. Cakes, scones, daily specials.

ROSLEA
(STD 013657)

Carnmore Restaurant ⊻
Upper Main St. ☎ 51693. 0700-2300 Tues-Sat, 1200-1530 Sun. Steaks, chicken, fish. Sunday lunch.

Roslea Heritage Centre
Monaghan Rd. ☎ 51750. April-Sept 0900-1700 Mon-Fri, 1600-1800 Sat-Sun. Scones, pastries, coffee.

Village Inn ⊻
11 High St. ☎ 51321. 1130-2330 Mon-Sat, 1230-1530 & 1900-2230 Sun. Pub grub.

TEMPO
(STD 013655)

Milltown Manor ⊻
61 Main St. ☎ (013655) 41779. 1130-1500 Mon-Sat. Prawn cocktail, melon, soups, roast beef, fish, salads.

COUNTY LONDONDERRY

AGHADOWEY
(STD 01265)

★ BROWN TROUT GOLF & COUNTRY INN 🍷 ⊘

209 Agivey Rd, Mullaghmore.
☎ (01265) 868209. 0700-1500
& 1700-2130 Mon-Sun, open
all day June-Sept. Grills, steaks.
E£.

BALLYKELLY
(STD 015047)

Drummond Hotel 🍷
481 Clooney Rd. ☎ 22121. Last
orders 2130.

Helen's Restaurant 🍷
440 Clooney Rd. ☎ 62098.
1700-2330 Sun-Thur, until
0030 Fri-Sat. Chinese &
European. ££.

Oven Door
34 Main St. ☎ 66228. 0730-
1800 Mon-Sat. Toasties, salads,
sandwiches, cakes.

Weavers 🍷
450 Clooney Rd. ☎ 62999.
1230-1430 & 1900-2130 Mon-
Sat. Steak, curry, lasagne.

BENONE
(STD 015047)

Ballymaclary House 🍷
573 Seacoast Rd. ☎ 50283.
1200-1400 & 1700-2100 Mon-
Sun. Steaks, locally caught
lobster, salmon, vegetarian
dishes, home-made puddings.
Restaurant in historic rectory.
E££.

CASTLEDAWSON
(STD 01648)

Ditty's Home Bakery ⊘
44 Main St. ☎ 68243. 0900-
1730 Mon-Sat. Vegetarian
pies, lasagne, sandwiches.

Thatch Inn 🍷
116 Hillhead Rd. ☎ 68322.
1230-1430 & 1800-2200
Wed-Sat, 1230-1430 Sun.
Steak, fish. E£.

CASTLEROCK
(STD 01265)

Golf Hotel 🍷
17 Main St. ☎ 848204. Last
orders 2030. Fillet of sole with
green grape sauce, duckling,
pork in mild chilli sauce.
E£££.

Marine Inn 🍷
9 Main St. ☎ 848456. 1230-
1930 Mon-Sat, 1230-1500 &
1700-2200. Sun. E£.

Temple Lounge 🍷
17 Sea Rd. ☎ 848423, 1130-
2200 Mon-Sat. Snacks.

CLAUDY
(STD 01504)

Beaufort House ♒
11 Church St. ☎ 338248.
1230-2030 Mon-Sat. Snacks.

Claudy Inn ♒
60 Main St. ☎ 338515. 1200-
1430 Mon-Sat. Pub grub.

McKeever's ♒
68 Main St. ☎ 338546. 1200-
1900 Mon-Sat. Pub grub.

Rio Grande ♒
207 Learmount Rd, Park.
☎ (015047) 81210. 1900-2100
Mon-Sat. Pub grub.

COLERAINE
(STD 01265)

Belfry Restaurant
11 Church Lane. ☎ 44646.
0900-1730 Mon-Sat. Quiche,
sandwiches, salad.

Big 'O'
11 New Row. ☎ 44777. 0900-
1700 Mon-Sat. Grills.

Blackthorn Inn ♒
16 New Market St. ☎ 44514.
1200-1430 Mon-Sat. Pub grub.

**Bohill Hotel &
Country Club** ♒
69 Cloyfin Rd. ☎ 44406.
Last orders 2115. Sun 2015.
Lunches, high tea, dinner.

Bon Appetit
5 Church St. ☎ 328181. 0830-
1730 Mon-Sat. Savouries,
pastries, freshly baked bread.

Brook's Wine Bar ♒
21 Park St. ☎ 42550. 1200-
1500 & 1730-2100 Mon-Sat.
Steaks, salads, baked potatoes.

Bull's Eye ♒
9 Lime Market St. ☎ 43485.
1230-1500 Mon-Sat, 1730-
2100 Wed-Sat. Savoury pies,
open sandwiches.

Bushtown House Hotel ♒
283 Drumcroone Rd.
☎ 58367. 1200-2130 Mon-
Sun. Fish, chicken with
vegetable stuffing, rack of
lamb. E££.

Buttery ⊘
31 Kingsgate St. ☎ 52127.
0745-1745 Mon-Sat. Carvery,
casseroles, quiche, lasagne,
salads. Home baking.

Charly's ♒
34 Newbridge Rd. ☎ 52020.
1200-2200 Mon-Sun.
Closed 1500-1700 in winter.
Pub grub.

Coffee Cup
22 The Diamond. ☎ 43810.
0900-1715 Mon-Sat, until
1600 Thur. Pies, scones,
gateaux, milk shakes.

Coffee Dock ⊘
20 New Row. ☎ 52565. 0900-
1700 Mon-Sat. Baked
potatoes, salads.

Copper Room
4 Railway Rd. ☎ 53184.
1000-1700 Mon-Sat ex Thur.
Pizza, pies.

Country Club ⬚
69 Cloyfin Rd. ☎ 44406. Last
orders 2100, Sun 2000. Grill
bar, poached salmon. ££.

Dunnes Stores
Bannside Wharf, Circular Rd.
☎ 320800. 0900-1800 Mon &
Tues, 0900-2100 Wed-Fri,
0900-1900 Sat & 1300-1800
Sun. Breakfast, fish, chicken
nuggets, salads, scones,
pastries. Café in store.

Eileen's Diner
8 Station Square. ☎ 57386.
0830-1730 Mon-Sat. Quiche,
salads, toasties.

Erin Eating House
5 Long Commons. ☎ 43612.
1000-1730 Mon-Sat, 0900-
1400 Thur. Salads, curry,
baked potatoes. Set lunch.

Forum ⊘
15 Church St. ☎ 52638. 0930-
1700 Mon-Sat. Coffee shop in
department store.

Gran'ma Smyth's
9 Railway Rd. ☎ 51150. 0800-
1700 Mon-Sat. Snacks.

Kitty's of Coleraine
3 Church Lane. ☎ 42347.
0900-1730 Mon-Sat, closed
Thur. Sandwiches, pies.

Lacy's Wine Bar ⬚
2 Beresford Court. ☎ 43755.
1200-1430 & 1700-2100
Mon-Sat. Lasagne, chicken.

Leisure Centre
Racquets, Railway Rd.
☎ 56432. 1000-2130 Mon-Fri,
until 1800 Sat, 1400-1800
Sun. Soup, sandwiches.

★ LITTLE TEA SHOP ⊘
Diamond Arcade. 1030-1730
Mon-Sat ex Thur July-Aug.
Afternoon tea, set lunches.

Lily D's
31 New Row West. ☎ 51680.
0930-1700 Mon-Sat. Salads,
baked potatoes, scones.

Little Caesars ▮
45 Railway Rd. ☎ 329991.
1200-2400 Mon-Fri, 1700-
2400 Sat-Sun. Italian. E£.

Lodge Hotel ⬚
Lodge Rd. ☎ 44848. Last
orders 2100, Sun 1930.
Salmon in pineapple & ginger
sauce, chicken Maryland. £££.

Lombard Café
12 Queen St. ☎ 43041. 0900-
1730 Mon-Sat. Soup,
sandwiches, scones. Set lunch.

McCloskey's Bar ⬚
2 Shuttle Hill. ☎ 42516. 1130-
2300 Mon-Sat, 1230-1430 &
1900-2200 Sun. Pub grub.

McDonald's
Riverside Regional Centre,
Dunhill Road. ☎ 321500.
0800-2400 Mon-Sat, 0900-
2400 Sun. Burgers & fast food.

Moores
7 Church St. ☎ 44444. 0900-
1700 Mon-Sat. Fish, Irish stew,
lasagne, salads, vegetarian,
scones, pastries. Gallery
Restaurant in store.

Old Forge Inn ⍾
6 New Market St. ☎ 52931.
1200-1400 & 1700-1900
Mon-Sat. Pub grub. E£.

Pine Tree Country Club
1 Somerset Rd. ☎ 58002.
1200-1430 Mon-Sat. Snacks.

Pizza Pomodoro ♨
4 The Waterside. ☎ 43222.
1630-2330 Mon-Sun. Italian.
E£.

Red Cross Café
43 Kingsgate St. ☎ 58250.
1000-1600 Mon-Sat. Grills.

Restaurant Twenty-Two
22 Church St. ☎ 43761. 0900-
1730 Mon-Sat. Salads, quiche,
lasagne.

Sainsbury's
Riverside Regional Centre,
Dunhill Rd. ☎ 328957. 0830-
2100 Mon-Fri, until 2000 Sat.
1300-1800 Sun. Fish, chicken,
salads, vegetarian, pasta,
sandwiches, scones.
JSR restaurant in store.

★ SALMON LEAP ⍾
53 Castleroe Rd. ☎ 52992.
1130-2300 Mon-Sat, 1230-
1430 & 1900-2200 Sun. Buffet
lunch, game in season,
smoked fish, salmon. M£, E££.

Strawberry Fayre Tea Room
1 Blagh Rd. ☎ 320437. 0930-
1700 Mon-Sat. Morning
coffee, set lunch, afternoon
tea.

Sun Do
66 New Row. ☎ 53022. 1200-
1400 & 1700-0030 Mon-Sat,
1700-2400 Sun. Chinese &
European.

Teddy & Son
12 Railway Rd. ☎ 53211.
0900-1700 Mon-Sat.
Sandwiches, snacks.

The Whistlestop
4a Railway Place. ☎ 321521.
0800-1800 Mon-Sat. Home-
baked pies, lasagne, salads.

Victor's Fish Restaurant
26 Railway Rd. ☎ 56247.
1200-2300 Mon-Sat. Set
lunch. Steak, scampi.

**Water Margin
at the Boathouse** ⍾
Hanover Place. ☎ 42222.
1730-2330 Mon-Sat, 1300-
1500 & 1700-2330 Sun.
Seafood, vegetarian. Chinese.
E££.

Wellworths ⊙
2 Ring Rd. ☎ 58446. 0900-
1730 Mon-Tues & Sat, until
2100 Wed-Fri. Afternoon tea,
salad bar. Café in store.

DRAPERSTOWN
(STD 01648)

Market Inn ⊠
27 St Patrick St. ☎ 28250.
1200-1500 Friday only. Pub
grub.

Mary Pats ⊠
2 St Patrick St. ☎ 28051. 1200-
1430 Mon-Sun, 1200-2130 Fri-
Sat, 1800-2130 Sun. Corn on
the cob, melon salad, breaded
fish, chicken. A la carte.

**Plantation of Ulster Visitor
Centre**
50 High St. ☎ 28113. 1000-
1800 Mon-Sat, from 1330 Sun.
Shorter winter hours. Salads,
quiche, chips, sandwiches,
scones, pastries. Café in
visitor centre.

DUNGIVEN
(STD 015047)

Carraig Rua ⊠
40 Main St. ☎ 41682. 1200-
1430 Mon-Sat,1800-2130 Mon-
Sun. Home-made lasagne,
quiche, casseroles.

Castle Inn ⊠
Upper Main St. ☎ 41369.
1200-2130 Mon-Sat, 1230-
1430 & 1830-2100 Sun.
Pub grub.

Delaney's Restaurant ⊠
804 Feeny Rd. ☎ 41302.
1200-2030 Mon-Sun. Champ,
fish, salads, carvery.

Dolphin Bar ⊠
22 Gortnaghey Rd. ☎ 41289.
1000-0100 Sat, 1800-2200 &
1230-1430 Sun. Pub grub.

Ponderosa ⊠
974 Glenshane Rd (top of
Glenshane Pass). ☎ 41987.
1130-2130 Mon-Sat, 1230-
1430 & 1900-2200 Sun.
A la carte. Steak, seafood.

EGLINTON
(STD 01504)

★ **DECKS** ⊠
1 Campsie Business Park.
☎ 860912. 1230-1430 Tues-
Fri, 1730-2100 Tues-Sun, until
2200 Wed-Sat. Rack of Irish
lamb, steaks, fish from
Donegal. E££.

Longfield Inn ⊠
5 Longfield Rd. ☎ 810211.
1130-late Mon-Sun. Pub grub.

Station Inn ⊠
37 Station Rd. ☎ 810470.
1200-1415 Mon-Sun, 1730-
2130 Mon-Wed, until 2200
Thur-Sat, 2115 Sun. Pub grub.

The Villager ⊠
4 Main St. ☎ 810206. 1215-
1430 & 1730-2130 Tues-Sat,
until 2045 Sun. Pub grub.
A la carte. E£.

Village Bakery & Tea Rooms
6a Main St. ☎ 810970. 0730-
1630 Mon-Fri, 0800-1630 Sat.
Scones, sandwiches, pastries.

GARVAGH
(STD 012665)

The Café
111 Main St. ☎ 58374. 0900-
1700 Mon-Sat. Home-made
ice cream, wheaten scones,
buns. Lunch 1200-1330. Café
in grocery shop.

Central House
41 Main St. ☎ 58262. 0930-
2300 Mon-Thur, until 0130
Fri-Sat, 1530-2300 Sun.
Breakfast. Roast beef &
potatoes, fish. Fast food.

Imperial Hotel ⬤
38 Main St. ☎ 58218. Last
orders 2100. Steaks, fish. E£.

GREYSTEEL
(STD 01504)

Foyle View Bar ⬤
161 Clooney Rd. ☎ 810560.
1230-2200 Mon-Sun.
Pub grub.

Rising Sun ⬤
105 Killylane Rd. ☎ 810959.
1230-1430, 1630-1930 Mon-
Sun. Pub grub. Gammon &
pineapple, scampi, chicken,
steak, cod in batter. E£.

KILREA
(STD 012665)

Angie's Diner
27 Maghera St. ☎ 41247.
0900-1900 Mon-Sat. Ulster fry,
sandwiches, pies.

Arbutus ⬤
13 Bridge St. ☎ 40140. 1700-
2130 Wed-Sun. Grilled salmon
on a bed of fennel with dill
sauce. Restaurant with roof
garden. E££.

Cellars ⬤
69 Bridge St. ☎ 41351. 1830-
2300 Mon-Sun. Steaks, lobster,
salmon. Cellar restaurant at
Manor Golf & Fishing Club.

McLaughlin's ⬤
McLaughlin's Corner.
☎ 40962. 1230-2100 Mon-
Sun. Duck à l'orange, salmon,
trout, scampi. Pub grub.E£.

Old Point Inn ⬤
80 Drumagarner Rd. ☎ 40330.
1230-1430 & 1800-2100 Thur-
Sat, 1230-1430 & 1900-2130
Sun. Chicken curry, fish, melon.

Pointers ⬤
3 The Diamond. ☎ 40404.
1230-1430 & 1800-2100 Tues-
Sat. Bar snacks.

The Manor ⬤
69 Bridge St. ☎ 40205. 1200-
1500 Mon-Sat, 1600-2100
Mon-Wed, until 2200 Thur-Sat,
1230-1430 & 1900-2100 Sun.
Grills, steaks, salads, desserts.

KNOCKCLOGHRIM

Fox & Pheasant Inn ☖
69 Glenmaquille Rd. ☎
(01648) 69463. 1300-1400 &
1800-2100 Thur-Sun. Grills,
set meals. A la carte.

LIMAVADY
(STD 015047)
Alexander Arms ☖
34 Main St. ☎ 63443. 0800-
1000, 1200-1430 & 1700-
2230 Mon-Sat. Breakfast. Fish,
steak, mixed grill, pork chops,
lasagne, vegetarian dishes.

Beehive
21 Market St. ☎ 22692. 0900-
1800 Mon-Sat. Grills, snacks,
chicken, steak.

Belmont ☖
24 Linenhall St. ☎ 22514.
1130-2300 Mon-Sat. Bar
snacks. Toasties, sandwiches,
pies, stew, fish & chips.

Chats Coffee Shop
Connell Street Carpark. 0900-
1700 Mon-Fri & 0900-1640
Sat. Lunches, sandwiches,
pastries.

Coasters ☖
148 Seacoast Rd. ☎ 63562.
1230-1500 Mon-Sun, 1900-
2200 Mon-Sat, until 2100 Sun.
Steak, pizza.

Crown Bar ☖
24 Irish Green St. ☎ 62402.
1900-2300 Fri-Sat. Pub grub.

Crumpet ⊙
43 Market St. ☎ 22886. 0900-
1730 Mon-Sat, until 1630
Thur. Breakfast, grills, salads,
pastries.

Gentry's ☖
18 Main St. ☎ 22017. 1230-
2230 Sun-Wed, 1200-2400
Thur-Sat. Onion bhajis, balti
chicken & lamb, pizza, pasta,
banana tort.

Gorteen House ☖
187 Roe Mill Rd. ☎ 22333.
Last orders 2230, 2100 Sun.
Tournedos rossini, veal, fillets
of sole & scampi, chicken in
white wine. £££.

**Grace's Old Traditional
Tea Rooms**
Central Car Park. ☎ 67525.
1000-1800 Mon-Sat.
Traditional fare, also home-
baked cakes and pastries.
Antiques on show.

★ **RADISSON ROE PARK
HOTEL/GOLF RESORT** ☖ ⊙
Roe Park. ☎ 22212. Breakfast
0700-1000. Brasserie: 1000-
1800 Mon-Fri. Open salmon
sandwich, curry, grills.
Restaurant: 1900-2300 Mon-
Sun. Lamb, salmon, duck in
champagne & sesame seed
sauce. ££££.

Lucille's Kitchen ⊙
Central Carpark. ☎ 68180.
0900-1700 Mon-Sat. Home-
cooking. Lunches, teas.

The Lime Tree ♉
60 Catherine St. ☎ 64300.
1200-1415 & 1800-2130
Wed-Mon. Grills, salads. £££.

Lucille's Sandwich Bar ⊖
17c Catherine St. ☎ 68180.
0900-1700 Mon-Sat.
Sandwiches to order, snacks,
hot lunches.

Oven Door
Hunter's Bakery, 5 Market St.
☎ 22411. 0830-1730 Mon-Sat.
Toasties, salads, sandwiches,
cakes.

Rendezvous
15 Catherine St. ☎ 22272.
0900-1830 Mon-Sat. Grills,
fish & chips, Ulster fry.

Roebuck Inn ♉
25 Main St. ☎ 68558. 1200-
1430 Mon-Sat. Pub grub.

Shanvey ♉
109 Aghanloo Rd. ☎ 50229.
1200-1400 & 1700-2300
Mon-Sat. 1200-2200 Sun.
Spicy beef, grilled salmon,
pitta bread, profiteroles, fresh
fruit salad. Carvery, à la carte.

Shenandoah ♉
88 Main St. ☎ 64366. 1700-
1930 Mon-Fri, until 2100 Sat.
Pub grub.

Spinning Wheel Café
Roe Valley Country Park.
☎ 22920. 1000-1800 Mon-Fri
& 1000-2030 Sat-Sun.
Breakfast. Ulster fry, champ,
baked potatoes, salads.

Sunflower ♉
4 Catherine St. ☎ 63151.
1200-1400 Thur-Fri, 1700-
2330 Mon-Thur, until 2400
Fri-Sat, 2300 Sun. Chinese &
European.

The Old Rectory Tea Rooms
4 Duncrun Rd. ☎ 50477.
1030-1700 Tues-Sat, 1230-
1800 Sun. Garlic mushrooms,
prawns, salads, omelettes,
scones, tray-bakes.

World Café
The Classic, 48 Main St.
☎ 22406. 0900-1700 Mon-Sat.
Home-baked bread, pastries,
soup. In home bakery.

LONDONDERRY
(STD 01504)

Abrakebabra
109 Strand Rd. ☎ 281122.
1200-late Mon-Sat, 1300-late
Sun. Fast food.

Abrakebabra
50 Waterloo St. ☎ 280066.
1200-late Mon-Sat, 1300-late
Sun. Fast food.

Anne's Hot Bread Shop
8 William St. ☎ 269236. 0700-
0200 Mon-Sat, from 1800 Sun.
Fish & chips, mixed grill,
scones, breads.

★ BADGERS ♉
16 Orchard St. ☎ 360763.
1200-1900 Mon-Thur & 1200-
2130 Fri-Sat. Grills, steaks,
Salads.

Bogside Inn ⚲
21 Westland St. ☎ 269300.
1200-1430 Mon-Sat. Pub grub.
70s photographs.

Boston Tea Party
13 Craft Village, Shipquay St.
☎ 269667. 0900-1730 Mon-
Sat. Sandwiches, pies, soups.

Bowery Bar ⚲
1 Orchard Row. ☎ 260028.
1230-1430 Sun only. Steaks,
chicken & chips.

Bridge Bistro ⚲
100 Duke St. ☎ 349245. 1200-
1430 Mon & Tues, 1200-1430
& 1730-2130 Wed-Sun.
Vegetarian specialities, fish.

Bronnics
50 Clooney Terrace.
☎ 349347. 0900-1700 Mon-
Fri, until 1600 Sat. Lasagne,
salads, sandwiches.

Broomhill Hotel ⚲
78 Limavady Rd. ☎ 347995.
1200-1430 & 1830-2130
Mon-Sun. Gammon steak,
chicken Maryland. ££.

★ **BEECH HILL COUNTRY
   HOUSE HOTEL** ⚲
32 Ardmore Rd. ☎ 349279.
Last orders 2145. Lamb with
mustard, pork with rosemary,
white chocolate gateau. M££.
E£££.

★ **BROWN'S BAR &
   BRASSERIE** ⚲
1 Bonds Hill. ☎ 345180.
1230-1430 Tues-Fri, 1730-
2230 Tues-Thur, 1730-2300 Fri
& Sat. Irish lamb, Kilkeel fish,
vegetarian. Modern European.
E££.

Cappuccino
31 Foyle St. ☎ 370059. 0800-
1730 Mon-Sat. Grills, salads,
sandwiches.

Carraig Bar ⚲
121 Strand Rd. ☎ 267529.
1200-1430 & 1900-2300
Mon-Fri. Soup, grills,
sandwiches.

Chat & Chew
23 William St. ☎ 269376.
0730-1630. Soup, stew, rolls.

Chatters Coffee Shop
Lisnagelvin Shopping Centre.
☎ 345446. 0800-1800 Mon,
Tues & Sat, 0800-2100 Wed,
Thur & Fri & 1200-1730 Sun.
Salads, sandwiches.

Churn
37 Great James St. ☎ 268001.
0900-1600 Mon-Fri, until
1500 Sat. Soup, stew, scones.
Café in home bakery.

City Restaurant ⚲
27 Shipquay St. ☎ 271011.
1200-2230 Mon-Thur, until
2400 Fri-Sun. Chinese &
European.

Clarendon Bar ♀
48 Strand Rd. ☎ 263705.
1230-1430 Mon-Fri. Pub grub.

Coffee Stop
Drumahoe Shopping Centre.
☎ 301068. 0900-1700 Mon-
Sat. Lasagne, quiche.

Crusty Kitchen
304 Richmond Centre.
☎ 260637. 0900-1730 Mon-
Sat, until 2100 Thur-Fri.
Sandwiches, cakes.

Culmore Tavern ♀
161 Culmore Rd. ☎ 354497.
1700-2200 Tues-Sat & 1200-
2200 Sun. Salmon, steaks.

Da Vinci's Restaurant ♀
19 Culmore Rd. ☎ 372074.
1730-2200 Mon-Sat, 1230-
1430 & 1730-2100 Sun.
Seafood, chow mein, steaks.

Deehan's Bar ♀
5 Chamberlain St. ☎ 374796.
1200-1500 Mon-Sat. Steak,
shepherd's pie, salads, toasted
sandwiches.

Delacroix ♀
18A Buncrana Rd. ☎ 262990.
1800-2200 Mon-Thur, 1800-
2230 Fri & Sat & 1200-1430 &
1700-2100 Sun. Fish, steak,
chicken, pork. E£.

Dungloe Bar ♀
41 Waterloo St. ☎ 267716.
1130-1430 Mon-Sat. Pub grub.
Live music.

Ebrington House ♀
6 Ebrington Terrace. 1200-
1500 Mon-Sat, 2100-2400 Fri-
Sat. Pub grub.

Everglades Hotel ♀
Prehen Rd. ☎ 346722. Bar
food 1230-2100. Restaurant
1900-2145 Mon-Sun. E£££.

Fiorentini's
47 Strand Rd. 0900-2130
Mon-Fri, 0900-1730 Sat-Sun.
Closes earlier in winter. Grills,
ice cream.

The Gallery ♀
14 Dungiven Rd. ☎ 343698.
1230-1430 Mon-Fri, 1730-
2200 Mon-Sat, until 2100 Sun.
Steak, salmon.

The Galley
12a Shipquay St. ☎ 370260.
0900-1730 Mon-Sat. Baked
potatoes, roasts, lasagne.

Glue Pot ♀
36 Shipquay St. ☎ 367463.
1200-1430 Mon-Sun, 1700-
2100 Wed-Sat. Soup,
sandwiches, toasties, sweets.

Grand Central ♀
27 Strand Rd. ☎ 267826.
1200-2300 Mon-Sat, 1230-
1430 Sun. Pub grub.

Gravy ▲
32 Carlisle Rd. ☎ 360300.
0800-1800 Mon-Sat, 1800-
2300 Thur-Sat. Breakfast.
Hot and cold lunches, soups
from local ingredients.
Afternoon tea.

Henry J's ⚱
10 Magazine St. ☎ 360177.
1200-1500 Mon-Sat. Salads,
grills.

Hong Kong Garden
27 Foyle St. ☎ 373667. 0800-
2000 Mon-Sat, 0900-1900
Sun. All day breakfast, Chinese
& European.

India House ⚱
51 Carlisle Rd. ☎ 260532.
1730-2300 Sun-Thur & 1730-
2330 Fri-Sat. Indian &
European.

Inn at the Cross ⚱
171 Glenshane Rd. ☎ 301480.
1200-2115 Mon-Sun. Pub
grub, high tea, A La Carte. E£.

Iona House ⚱
19 Spencer Rd. ☎ 343529.
1230-1430 Mon-Sun.
Pub grub.

J&J McGinley's ⚱
24 Foyle St. ☎ 360066. 1200-
1430 Mon-Sat. Salads,
sandwiches, specials.

Kam House ⚱
14 William St. ☎ 372166.
1200-0200 Mon-Sat, 1630-
0030 Sun. Chinese &
European.

Kentucky Fried Chicken
2 Strand Rd. ☎ 372016. 1200-
2300 Mon-Thur, until 0200
Fri-Sat, 1200-2400 Sun. Fast
food.

Kylemore Café
Foyleside Shopping Centre.
☎ 377676. 0800-1800 Mon-
Wed, until 2100 Thur-Fri,
1900 Sat, 1200-1800 Sun.
Soups, sandwiches, salads.

La Sosta Ristorante ⚱
45a Carlisle Rd. ☎ 374817.
1800 till late Tues-Sat. Pasta,
chicken with olives. E££.

Le Café Monroe
15 Carlisle Rd. ☎ 264622.
0900-1730 Mon-Sun. All day
breakfast, lasagne, baked
potatoes, stew, salads,
sandwiches.

Leprechaun
23 Strand Rd. ☎ 363606.
0930-1730 Mon-Sat. Scones,
quiches, salads. Set lunch.

Linenhall Bar ⚱
3 Market St. ☎ 371665. 1200-
1530 Mon-Fri & 1200-1500
Sat. Home-made fish pie, pub
grub. Set menu E£.

Malibu
6 Bishop St. ☎ 371784. 0900
till late Mon-Sat & 0900 till
late (summer only). Grills,
steaks, salads.

Mandarin Palace ⚱
134 Strand Rd. ☎ 264613.
1630-0045 Mon-Thur, 1630-
0230 Fri & Sat & 1630-0030
Sun. Chinese & European.

Marlene's
33 Shipquay St. ☎ 370145.
1100-1800 & 2030-0300 Mon-
Wed, until 0400 Thur, 0430
Fri-Sat, 2030-0230 Sun. Grills,
salads, fries.

Martha's Vineyard ♀
Brunswick Superbowl,
Pennyburn Industrial Estate.
☎ 371999. 1230-2330 Mon-
Sun. Lunches, à la carte.

Maverick Steak House ♀
21 Drumahoe Rd. ☎ 342721.
1230-1430 Mon-Sun lunches
served.

McCourt's Bar ♀
91 Ardmore Rd. ☎ 342903.
1900-2300 Mon-Sun. Pub grub.

McDonald's
Foyleside Shopping Centre.
☎ 377800. 0800-2300 Mon-
Sat, 1000-2300 Sun. Fast food.

★ **METRO** ♀
3 Bank Place. ☎ 267401. 1200-
1530 Mon-Thur & 1200-1700
Fri-Sun. Soup, beef stew,
desserts.

Monico ♀
4 Customs House St.
☎ 263121. 1200-1445 Mon-
Sat. Stew, soup.

New Tower Coffee Shop
Austin's department store,
The Diamond. ☎ 261817.
0900-1730 Mon-Sat, until 2100
Fri. Soup, stews, salads,
pastries. Panoramic view.

Nicer's Café
Sackville St. ☎ 265021. 1000-
0230 Mon-Thur, 1000-0300
Fri-Sat. Burgers, chicken.

Oak Grove Bar ♀
86 Bishop St. ☎ 260856.
1230-1430 Mon-Sat. Pub grub.

Old Factory Restaurant ♀
Ebrington Gardens. ☎ 311005.
1130-1430, 1800-2100 Mon-
Sun. Ulster fry, grills, curries.

Oysters ♀
164 Spencer Rd. ☎ 344875.
1230-1430 & 1730-2200
Mon-Fri, 1730-2230 Sat &
1700-2100 Sun. Fish, duck.

Peadar O'Donnell ♀
63 Waterloo St. ☎ 372318.
1230-1430 Mon-Sat. Pub grub.
Live traditional music.

Peking Pagoda ♀
33 Foyle St. ☎ 267271. 1200-
0030 Mon-Thur, until 0200
Fri-Sat, 1400-2400 Sun.
Chinese & European. E£.

Piemonte Pizzeria ♦
2 Clarendon St. ☎ 266828.
1700-2330 Mon-Sun. Pizzas.

Pilot's Row Leisure Centre
Rossville St. ☎ 269418. 1200-
1430 Mon-Fri. Shepherd's pie,
cod & potatoes, Irish stew,
salads.

Pitchers ⌷ ⌒
Foyle Golf Centre, 12 Alder
Rd. ☎ 352222. 1200-1430
Mon, 1200-1430 & 1700-2200
Tues-Fri, 1200-2200 Sat &
1200-2100 Sun. Fish, steaks,
chilli. A la carte. E££.

Pizza Hut ⌷
Unit 21, Quayside Shopping
Centre, Strand Rd. ☎ 269696.
1200-2300 Mon-Sun. Pizza,
pasta, salad.

Rafters ⌷
122 Northland Rd. ☎ 266080.
1200-1500 & 1700-2245
Mon-Sat. 1230-1500, 1600-
2200 Sun. Pasta, Mexican
chicken, salads, steaks.

★ **REGGIE'S SEAFOOD
   RESTAURANT** ⌷
145 Strand Rd. ☎ 262050.
1200-1430, 1730-2200 Mon-
Thur & 1700-2230 Fri, 1700-
2230 Sat. Cockles & mussels
in lemon sauce, seafood
chowder. M£, E££.

Rhubarb & Custard
22 Custom House St.
☎ 377977. 0800-1800 Mon-
Sat. Lasagne, vegetable pasta,
baked potatoes, soup.

Richmond Centre
Louis's, Shipquay St.
☎ 264661. 0900-1730 Sat &
1000-1730 Sun. Grills,
chicken, fries. Café in
shopping centre.

Ritz Bar ⌷
27 Fountain Hill. ☎ 342421.
1230-1430 Mon-Sun. Prawn
salad, chicken wings, plaice &
chips.

River Inn ⌷
36/38 Shipquay St. ☎ 371965.
1230-1430 Mon-Sat, 1700-
2100 Wed-Fri & 1200-1930
Sat. Steak, salmon, salads,
sandwiches & snacks.

★ **THE SANDWICH
   COMPANY**
61 Strand Rd. ☎ 266771.
0800-1730 Mon-Tues & 0800-
1630 Wed-Sat. Sandwiches,
rolls, salads.

★ **THE SANDWICH
   COMPANY**
The Diamond. ☎ 372500.
0830-1700 Mon-Thur, until
1730 Fri-Sat. Sandwiches,
rolls, salads.

Schooner's Wine Bar ⌷
59 Victoria Rd. ☎ 311500.
1730-2200 Mon-Fri, until
2230 Sat, 1300-2130 Sun.

Spice of India ⌷
31 Spencer Rd. ☎ 312912.
1700-2300 Mon-Thur, until
2330 Fri-Sun. Indian &
European. E££.

Strand Bar ⌷
31 Strand Rd. ☎ 260494.
1200-1500 & 1700-2230
Mon-Sun. E££. Pasta, salads,
steaks.

Superbites
44a Waterloo St. ☎ 370841.
1100-0230 Mon-Sat, 1800-
0030 Sun. Fast food.

Terminus Restaurant
Foyle St. ☎ 268042. 0800-
1900 Mon-Sat. 1000-1600 Sun
summer only. Breakfast. Steak
casserole, fish & chips, scones,
pastries.

Thran Maggie's ⚲
Craft Village, Shipquay St. ☎
264267. 1130-2200 Mon-Sat,
1230-1430 & 1900-2200 Sun.
Steaks, à la carte. E£.

Townsman Bars ⚲
33 Shipquay St. ☎ 260820.
1130-1700 Mon-Sat. Fresh
soup, sandwiches, grills,
salads.

Tracy's Bar ⚲
1 William St. ☎ 269700.
1200-1500 Mon-Sat, 1230-
1430 Sun. Soups, pies.

Trinity Hotel ⚲
Nolan's Bistro: 24 Strand Rd.
☎ 271271. 1800-2230 Mon-
Thur, until 2300 Fri-Sat, 2100
Sun. Fillet of beef, duck,
seafood. E£.

Villa's Inn ♀
77 Victoria Rd. ☎ 311589.
1200-2300 Mon-Sat. Grills,
steaks.

★ WATERFOOT HOTEL ♀
Caw Roundabout, 14 Clooney
Rd. ☎ 345500. 1215-1415 &
1700-2130 Mon-Sat, 1230-
1400 & 1700-2130 Sun.
Steaks, seafood, salads.

Waterloo Bar ♀
3 Strand Rd. ☎ 266067. 1200-
1500 Mon-Sat. Bar food.

Wheeler's
30 Shipquay St. ☎ 363337.
1130-0200 Mon-Thur, until
0230 Fri-Sat, 1645-0130 Sun.
Grills.

Wheeler's
155 Strand Rd. ☎ 266065.
1130-2400 Mon-Sat, from
1300 Sun. Grills.

White Horse Hotel ♀
68 Clooney Rd, Campsie. ☎
860606. 0700-2130 Mon-Sun.
Fish, steaks. A la carte. E££.

Woodburn ♀
Blackburn Crescent,
Waterside. ☎ 41438. 0830-
2000 Mon-Tues, 0830-2100
Wed-Fri & 0830-1800 Sat. Set
lunch. Grills. Self-service
snacks.

MAGHERA
(STD 01648)

Classic Coffee Shop
6 Hall St. ☎ 45004. Home-
baked bread, pies, pastries.
Café in home bakery.

Crawford's Coffee Lounge
187 Main St. ☎ 43877. 0900-
1730 Mon-Sat. Rolls, pies,
pastries, coffee.

Four Seasons Restaurant
Mid-Ulster Garden Centre,
Station Rd. ☎ 45550. 0830-
1730 Mon-Sat, 1400-1700
Sun. Light lunches, scones,
sandwiches.

★ ARDTARA HOUSE ♀
8 Gorteade Rd, Upperlands.
☎ 44490. 1230-1400 Mon-Sun
& 1700-2100 Mon-Sat. Roast
rack of Sperrin lamb, mussels
in saffron butter sauce. E£££.

Rab's Bistro
6 Coleraine Rd. ☎ 44180.
0900-1800 Mon-Sat, 1130-
1830 Sun. Chicken, quiche,
rolls, cakes.

MAGHERAFELT
(STD 01648)

Alexander's
Market Square. ☎ 31422.
1200-2400 Mon-Sat, 1700-
2400 Sun. Ulster fry, southern
fried chicken, fish.

Bay Leaf
Meadowlane Shopping Centre.
☎ 34299. 0900-1730 Mon-
Wed & Sat, 0900-2100 Thur-
Fri. Pork chops, steaks, lamb
cutlets, egg mayonnaise.

The Depot ⊻
2 Union Rd. ☎ 31244. 1200-
1430 Mon-Sat. Club
sandwiches, casseroles.

Diamond Expresso ⊘
Diamond Centre. ☎ 32223.
0900-1730 Mon-Sat, until
2000 Thur-Fri. Scones, rolls,
baked potatoes, daily specials.

★ **DITTY'S BAKERY** ⊘
33 Rainey St. ☎ 33944. 0830-
1730 Mon-Sat. Breakfast,
lunch. Home-baking.

Dorman's Bar & Cosy Inn ⊻
17 Queen St. ☎ 31194. 1130-
2200 Mon-Sun. Soups,
sandwiches, scampi, lunchtime carvery, a la carte E£.

★ **FIOLTA'S BISTRO** ⊻ ⊘
4 Union Arcade. ☎ 33522.
0930-2100 Mon-Wed, until
2130 Thur-Sat & 1200-2100
Sun. Garlic mushrooms,
lasagne, steak Bushmills. ££.

Golden Gate ⊻
11 Broad St. ☎ 32936. 1700-
2400 Mon-Thur & 1700-2400
Fri-Sat. Chinese & European.
E££.

Imperial Palace ⊻
15 Queen St. ☎ 31709. 1200-
1400 & 1700-2400 Mon-Thur,
until 2430 Fri & Sat & 1700-
2400 Sun. Chinese &
European. £.

Korner Kafe
51 Rainey St. 1100-2330 Mon-
Sat. Ulster fry, burgers,
chicken.

★ **MARY'S BAR
& LOUNGE** ⊻
10 Market St. ☎ 31997. 1200-
1430 Mon-Sat. Pub grub.

McErlains
26 Church St. ☎ 32465. 0800-
1730 Mon-Sat. Sandwiches,
home baking.

No 7
7 Meeting St. ☎ 31293. 0900-
1730 Mon-Sat. Home-made
soup, cakes, rolls. Set lunch,
roasts, chicken.

Sizzlers ⊻
23 Market Square. ☎ 31300.
1000-2000 Tues-Sun.
Breakfast, soups, fish, steak.

Snack Box
76 Rainey St. ☎ 33710. 1200-
2300 Mon-Sat. Burgers, fish,
lunchtime special.

Taste Buds
18 Rainey St. ☎ 32484. 0900-
1730 Mon-Sat. Soups,
sandwiches, set lunches.

Town & Country Inn ⚲
28 Union Rd. ☎ 32473. 1200-
1500 Mon-Sat. Chicken,
curries.

Trompets ⚲
25 Church St. ☎ 32257. 1230-
1500 & 1700-2220 Wed-Sat,
1700-2200 Tues, 1230-1430 &
1700-2130 Sun. Smoked eel,
fillet of beef with oysters,
lamb. E££.

Viva Café
Meadowvale Shopping Centre.
☎ 301008. 0900-1700 Mon-
Wed & Sat, until 2100 Thur-
Fri. Breakfast. Sandwiches,
vegetarian.

MAGILLIGAN
(STD 015047)

Angler's Rest ⚲
Seacoast Rd. ☎ 50265. 1200-
2200 Mon-Sat, 1230-1500 &
1900-2200 Sun. Pub grub.

Mallard Bar ⚲
401 Seacoast Rd. ☎ 50288.
1200-1430 & 1800-2100
Mon-Sat. Pub grub.
A la carte. E£.

Point Bar ⚲
107 Point Rd. ☎ 50440. 1230-
1430 & 1700-2130 Mon-Sat.
Pub grub.

MONEYMORE
(STD 016487)

Bier Keller ⚲
18 Stonard St. ☎ 48282. 1230-
1430 & 1700-2100 Mon-Sat.
Pub grub.

Springhill House
☎ 48215. July-Aug: 1400-1900
Mon-Sun ex Tues. Coffee shop
in National Trust house.

PORTSTEWART
(STD 01265)

The Anchorage ⚲
87 The Promenade. ☎ 832003.
1230-2130 Mon-Sat. Pub grub.

Ashiana Tandoori Restaurant
12A The Diamond. ☎ 834455.
1700 -2200, Indian.

Cromore Halt ⚲
158 Station Rd. ☎ 832218.
1230-1430 & 1700-2115 Mon-
Sun. Local seafood.

Edgewater Hotel ⚲
88 Strand Rd. ☎ 833314.
Last orders 2130, Sun 2000.
Chicken à la king, wild Irish
salmon, tournedos Bushmills.
E££.

Good Food & Company ⊘
44 The Promenade. ☎ 836386.
0900-1730 Mon-Sat, until
2200 July-Aug. Home baking.

★ MORELLI'S/NINO'S
57 The Promenade. ☎ 832150.
1000-2300 Mon-Sun, until
1800 in winter. Pasta, pizza,
ice cream, cappuccino coffee.

Heathron Diner
29 The Promenade. ☎ 834569.
0900-2300 Mon-Sat, from
1200 Sun. Shorter hours
autumn-spring. Steaks, salads.

Hoi Yun Chinese Restaurant
1 Church Pass. ☎ 833370.
1700-2400 Mon-Sun. Chinese.

Montagu Arms ⚲
68 The Promenade. ☎ 834146.
1200-2300 Mon-Sun.
Pub grub.

Morelli's
53 The Promenade. ☎ 832150.
0930-2230 Mon-Sun, until
1800 in winter (2030 Sun).
Fast food.

Piaf's
66 The Promenade. ☎ 833377.
0900-2200 Mon-Fri, until
2400 Sat-Sun (2230 in winter).
Soup, stew, lasagne, curries,
toasties.

Prom Fast Food
The Promenade. ☎ 832586.
1200-1400 & 1700-0200
Mon-Sun. Grills.

Shenanigans ⚲
78 The Promenade. ☎ 836000.
1230-1430 Mon-Sun, 1730-
2100 Mon-Sat, from 1900 Sun.
Steaks, lasagne, salads.

Squires
18 The Promenade. ☎ 834103.
0900-2200 Mon-Sun.
Breakfast. Grills.

Windsor Hotel ⚲
8 The Promenade. ☎ 832523.
Last orders 2000. Local
salmon, set meals. £.

York Bar ⚲
2 Station Rd. ☎ 833594. 1230-
1430 & 1730-2030 Mon-Sat,
1230-1415 Sun. Seafood,
steaks, chicken, pasta.

TOBERMORE
(STD 01648)

Faerie Thorn ⚲
14 Main St. ☎ 44385. 1130-
2200 Mon-Sat &1900-2200
Sun. Steak & Guinness pie,
fisherman's medley, salad bar.
Two beer gardens.

McNally's Inn ⚲
62a Hillhead Rd. ☎ 50095.
0800-2130 Mon-Sat, 1200-
2130 Sun. Breakfast, steaks,
fish, omelettes, sweets.

ARDBOE
(STD 016487)

The Tilley Lamp
11 Mullinahoe Rd. ☎ 37673.
1000-2200 Mon-Sat, until
2100 Sun. Grill menu,
vegetarian.

AUGHER
(STD 016625)

★ ROSAMUND'S
   COFFEE SHOP
Station House. ☎ 48601.
0900-1700 Mon-Sat. Set
lunch. Wheaten bread, bacon
baps, Clogher Valley cheese.
Irish crafts in restored former
railway station.

Queen Anya Steak House
42 Main St. ☎ 48615. 0900-
1930 Mon-Sat. Steaks, set
lunch.

AUGHNACLOY
(STD 016625)

Oriental Palace
57a Moore St. ☎ 57918. 1700-
2330 Mon-Sun. Chinese.
Aughnacloy

Salley's Restaurant ☖
86 Moore St. ☎ 57979. 1000-
2200 Mon-Sat, from 1200 Sun.
Swordfish, steak Rossini,
home-made sweets. Sunday
lunch.

BALLYGAWLEY
(STD 016625)

Ardbeg Lodge
32 Dungannon Rd. ☎ 68517.
0900-1800 Mon-Sun. Home
cooking in craft shop.

Cent Percent ☖
232 Omagh Rd. ☎ 67271.
1800-2200 Mon, Wed-Sun,
1230-1430 Sun. Stuffed quail,
saddle of rabbit with wild
mushrooms, venison.

Kelly's Inn ☖
Garvaghey House, 232
Omagh Rd. ☎ 68339. 1130-
2200 Mon-Sat, 1230-1430 &
1900-2200 Sun. Pub grub.
Braised duckling with
redcurrant sauce, poached
salmon, chicken cacciatore.
££.

★ SUITOR GALLERY
17 Grange Rd. ☎ 68653.
1000-1730 Mon-Sat. Soup,
scones, tray bakes.

BENBURB
(STD 01861)

Cornmill Tea Room
Benburb Valley Heritage
Centre, 89 Milltown Rd.
☎ 549752. 1000-1700 Tues-
Sun. Mon-Fri Oct-Easter.
Teashop in heritage centre.

BERAGH
(STD 016627)

Carrick-Keel ⚲
134 Ballygawley Rd.
☎ (016625) 67156. 113 0-
2330 Mon-Sat, from 1700 Sun.
Pub grub.

Corner House ⚲
29 Main St. ☎ 58155. 1130-
2130 Mon-Sat. Pub grub.

CALEDON
(STD 01861)

Caledon Arms ⚲
44 Main St. ☎ 568161. 1730-
2300 Mon-Sun. Set lunch,
grills. A la carte. E£.

Corner House ⚲
1 Castle Park. ☎ 568688.
1230-1430 Mon-Fri.
Hamburgers, pub grub.

CASTLECAULFIELD
(STD 01868)

Quinn's Corner
175 Ballygawley Rd.
☎ 767529. 1230-2200 Mon-
Sat, 1230-1430 & 1900-2200
Sun. Grills.

CASTLEDERG
(STD 016626)

Allstar Café
13 Ferguson Crescent.
☎ 70488. 1600-2400 Mon-
Thur, until 0200 Fri-Sat. Grills.

Castle Inn ⚲
48 Main St. ☎ 71501. 1130-
2330 Mon-Sun. Pub grub.

Crescent Inn ⚲
1 Ferguson Crescent. ☎ 71161.
1230-1430 & 1900-2200
Mon-Sun. Pub grub, live
music.

Derg Arms ⚲
43 Main St. ☎ 71644. 1200-
1430 Mon-Fri, 1000-2100 Sat-
Sun. Salmon, steak, lamb
cutlets, gammon, roast stuffed
duck. E£.

Derg Valley ⚲
34 William St. ☎ 70860. 1030-
2300 Mon-Sat. Pub grub. E£.

Forge Inn ⚲
13 Ferguson Crescent.
☎ 70488. 1730-2300 Mon-
Sun. Pub grub.

Market Bar ♎
59 Main St. ☎ 79036. 1230-
1500 Mon-Sun. Breakfast.
Tossed salads, fisherman's pie,
baked potato. E£.

Punter's Inn ♎
38 Main St. ☎ 71339. 1200-
2400 Mon-Sat. Pub grub.

Vienna Coffee Shop
75 Main St. ☎ 71379. 0900-
1730 Mon-Sat, closed Wed.
Stews, soup, salads, rolls,
sandwiches.

Village Inn ♎
1 Main St, Killen. ☎ 71490.
1700-2300 Mon-Sat. Pub grub.

CLOGHER
(STD 016625)

Corick House ♎
20 Corick Rd. ☎ 48216. 1730-
2130 Tues-Sun. Pan-fried
Barbary duck, salmon.

McKenna's
5 Main St. ☎ 48183. 1130-
2300 Mon-Sat, from 1500 Sun.
Fish, chips, burgers,
sandwiches.

McSorley's Tavern ♎
39 Main St. ☎ 48673. 1130-
2300 Mon-Sat, Soup, toasties.

Rathmore Bar ♎
127 Main St. ☎ 48240. 1130-
2300 Mon-Sat, 1230-1430 &
1900-2200 Sun.

Trident Inn ♎
97 Main St. ☎ 48924. 1130-
2100 Mon-Sat. Pub grub.,
Breaded scampi, steak,
chicken. A la carte from 1900.
E£.

COAGH
(STD 016487)

Battery Bar ♎
201 Battery Rd. ☎ 36367.
1800-2300 Fri-Sun. Pub grub.

Hanover House ♎
24 Hanover Square. ☎ 37530.
1200-2200 Tues-Sat, 1200-
1500 & 1700-2100 Sun.
Steaks, game, fish. E£.

COALISLAND
(STD 01868)

Golden Grill
Main St. ☎ 740533. 1030-
2300 Mon-Sat, 1030-1330
Wed. Grills.

Landi's Café
The Square, 3 Dungannon Rd.
☎ 740211. 1030-0030 Mon-
Sat, closed Thur. Grills.

Mill Court ♎
40 Main St. ☎ 747830. 1000-
1600 Mon-Wed, until 2000
Thur, 2200 Fri -Sat. 1230-1430
& 1730-2130 Sun. Grills, pub
grub.

Pyramid Centre ⚐
11 Mountjoy Rd. ☎ 748881.
1230-1430 & 1730-2200
Mon-Sat, 1900-2200 Sun.
Steak, fish, chicken.

The Venue ⚐
26b The Square. ☎ 740633.
1000-1600 Mon-Thur, until
1900 Fri -Sat, 1200-1500 Sun.
Steak, peppered chicken.

COOKSTOWN
(STD 016487)

Braeside Bar ⚐
221 Orritor Rd. ☎ 62664.
1400-2300 Mon-Thur, 1130-
2300 Fri-Sat. Pub grub.

Brewery Grill Bar
58 William St. ☎ 65934. 0900-
2430 Mon-Thur, later Fri-Sat,
1600-0200 Sun. Soup, burgers,
stew.

The Café
4 Burn Rd. ☎ 64456. 1100-
1800 Mon-Sat. Snacks.

Cartwheel ⚐
25 James St. ☎ 63672. 1700-
2200 Thur-Sun. Pub grub.

Century 21
Cookstown Enterprise Centre,
Sandholes Rd, Derryloarn
Estate. ☎ 69360. 0800-1600
Mon-Fri. Breakfasts. Hot
dishes, salads, soups.

Chequers ⚐
12 Oldtown St. ☎ 65122. 1130-
1430 & 1700-2200 Mon-Thur,
until 2200 Fri-Sat. Pub grub.
Seafood, steak. E££.

Clubland & Black Horse ⚐
21 Molesworth St. ☎ 64946.
1230-1430 Mon-Sat. Carvery.

Coffee Room
40 William St. ☎ 63438. 0900-
1700 Mon-Sat. Set lunch,
sandwiches, salads.

★ **COURTYARD** ⊘
56 William St. ☎ 65070. 0800-
1715 Mon-Sat, until 1500 Wed.
Breakfast. Chicken curry,
broccoli bake, vegetarian,
soup, scones, sweets.

D's Burger Bar
58 James St. ☎ 66891. 1100-
2400 Mon-Tues, until 0330
Wed-Sat, 1600-2400 Sun.
Fast food.

Dempsey's Food Depot ⚐
Central Arcade, James St.
☎ 63035. 0900-1730 Mon,
until 2130 Tues-Thur, 2230 Fri-
Sat, 1500-2200 Sun. Pizzas,
grills, salads. E£.

Dragon Palace ⚐
44 Loy St. ☎ 63311. 1200-1400
& 1700-2400 Mon-Thur, until
0100 Fri, 1600-0100 Sat, 1600-
0030 Sun. Cantonese &
European. E£.

Dunleath Bar ⚐
58 Church St. ☎ 63344. 1130-
2330 Mon-Sat, until 2230 Sun.
Pub grub, pies, hot dogs.

Farmhouse Restaurant
95 Cookstown Rd. ☎ 747125.
0900-1900 Mon-Wed, until
2130 Thur-Sun. Grills, snacks.

Gaslight ⬚
40 Loy St. ☎ 69299. 1215-
1430 Mon-Fri, 1300-1500 Sat.
Pub grub.

Glenavon House Hotel ⬚
52 Drum Rd. ☎ 64949. Last
orders 2145 Mon-Sun. Hot &
cold carvery. Salmon, prawn
steak. £££.

Greenvale Hotel ⬚ ◈
57 Drum Rd. ☎ 62243. 0800-
2200 Mon-Sun. Set lunch,
chicken kiev, steak Bushmills.
£££.

Halfway House ⬚
81 Pomeroy Rd. ☎ 66372.
1600-2300 Mon-Thur, 1230-
1430 & 1900-2200 Sun. Pub
grub. A la carte. £.

Jack's Café
10 James St. ☎ 61411. 0900-
1730 Mon-Sat. Set lunch,
grills, salads.

Jesters
19 William St. ☎ 63388. 0900-
1700 Mon-Sat, 1900-2130 Fri-
Sat. Home cooking. Snacks.

Joe Mac's
32 Molesworth St. ☎ 63371.
1100-2330 Mon-Thur, until
0100 Fri, 0200 Sat, 1700-2330
Sun. Grills.

Mill Wheel Bar ⬚
60 Dunamore Rd. ☎ 51280.
1200-1700 Mon-Sat. 1230-
1400 Sun. Grills.

Mistletoe
13 Old Town St. ☎ 63476.
0900-1730 Mon-Sat, until
1400 Wed. Café behind
confectionery shop.

Otter Lodge ⬚
26 Dungannon Rd. ☎ 65427.
1200-1400 Mon-Sun, 1730-
2130 Mon-Sat (closes 2100
Fri-Sat). A la carte restaurant
from 1900 Thur-Sat. Tandoori
chicken, honeyed garlic
prawns. Riverbank setting. M£.
£££.

Prairie ⬚
9 Corvanaghan Rd. ☎ 51226.
1230-1430 Sun, 1800-2200
Fri-Mon, (From 1900 Sun).
Grills, salads. A la carte. £.

Red Rose Café ⬚
86 Chapel St. ☎ 62278. 1730-
2230 Mon-Sat, 1230-1430 &
1700-2130 Sun. Chicken,
steaks, salads.

Royal Hotel ⬚
64 Coagh St. ☎ 62224. Last
orders 2145. Steaks, chicken,
salmon. £££.
Cookstown

Sinley ⬚
92 Church St. ☎ 64572. 1700-
0130 Mon-Thur, until 0200 Fri-
Sun. Chinese & European. £.

Sperrin Room (Menary's)
39 William St. ☎ 63364. 0900-1700 Mon-Sat. Chicken pie, lasagne.

Taj-Mahal
8 Orritor St. ☎ 65922. 1700-2400 Tues-Sun. Indian & European. ££.

Thatch Lounge ⚲
19 Molesworth St. ☎ 63787. 1200-2100 Mon-Sat. Pub grub.

★ **TULLYLAGAN COUNTRY HOUSE** ⚲
40B Tullylagan Rd. ☎ 65100. 1200-1400 Mon-Sun ex Sat, 1900-2115 Mon-Sat, 1700-2000 Sun. Scampi souchet, lemon posset. ££££.

White Pheasant ⊗
3a Burn Rd. ☎ 64249. 0900-1700 Mon-Sat, until 1730 Fri. Grills.

DROMORE
(STD 01662)

Salt & Pepper
30 Main St. 1200-2400 Mon-Thur, 1130-0130 Fri-Sat, 1730-0130 Sun. Grills, fish & chips.

DRUMQUIN
(STD 01662)

Eddie O'Kane's ⚲
22 Main St. ☎ 831233. 2000-2300 Thur-Sun. Pub grub.

Post Inn ♉
2 Main St. ☎ 831329. 1900-
2100 Thur-Sat. Pub grub.

DUNGANNON
(STD 01868)

Cohannon Inn Autolodge ♉
212 Ballynakelly Rd,
Tamnamore. ☎ 724488. Last
orders 2130. Grills, burgers,
steaks, chef's special. E£.

The Cottage
37 Scotch St. 0900-1730 Mon-
Sat. Grills.

Edwin's Place ♉
20 Coagh Rd. ☎ 740430.
1230-1430 Wed-Fri, 1800-
2130 Fri-Sun. Smoked salmon,
steak, baked potatoes.

Fort ♉
30 Scotch St. ☎ 722620. 1200-
1430 Mon-Sat. Pub grub.

Gables ♉
40 Cookstown Rd. ☎ 761580.
1230-1430 & 1900-2130 Sun.
A la carte. E£.

Glengannon Hotel ♉
Drumgormal, Ballygawley Rd.
☎ 727311. 1230-1430 &
1730-2200 Mon-Sun. Carvery
lunch & à la carte evenings.
Salmon with raspberry sauce,
steak Diane, chicken
Glengannon. E££.

Inn on the Park Hotel ♉
Moy Rd. ☎ 725151. Last
orders 2130, Fri-Sat 2200.
Steak, lobster bisque, rainbow
trout, lemon pancakes. ££.

Jasmine House
59 Scotch St. ☎ 726556. 1700-
0030 Mon-Sun. Chinese &
European.

Killymaddy Tourist Centre 🍶
Ballygawley Rd. ☎ 767323.
0830-2100 Mon-Sun. Winter:
0900-1800 Mon-Thur, until
2000 Fri-Sun. Breakfast, grills,
snacks.

Landis Café
7 Irish St. ☎ 740211. 0930-
1900 Mon-Sat, until 1430
Wed. Fish & chips, grills,
sandwiches.

Liz's Diner
64 Scotch Street. ☎ 753222.
0900-1700 Mon-Sat. Breakfast,
quiche, fish.

Lough Neagh Lodge ♉
Maghery. ☎ (01762) 851901.
1200-2100 Mon-Sat. Steaks,
wildfowl, pan-fried eels. ££.

Mill Wheel
3 Thomas St. ☎ 753577. 0930-
1730 Mon-Sat. Quiche, stew,
soup. Coffee shop in bakery.

Motorway Restaurant
Drumgormal, Ballygawley Rd.
☎ 723504. 0800-2200 Mon-
Sun. Breakfast. Home-made
soup, toasties, mixed grills, fish
in batter.

Northland Arms ♉
1 Georges St. ☎ 723693.
1200-2100 Mon-Sat. Hot &
cold carvery. Pub grub.

★ **NUMBER 15**
Murray Richardson's
Bookshop. 15 Church St.
☎ 753048. 0830-1730 Mon-
Sat. Pies, pastries, vegetarian.
Café in bookshop.

Oaks Bistro
Oaks Centre. ☎ 753022. 0900-
1700 Mon-Wed, until 2030
Thur-Fri, 0900-1700 Sat.
Breakfast, pies, sweets. Café in
shopping centre.

The Square ♀
35 Market Square. ☎ 753315.
1200-1500 Mon-Sat. Pub grub.

Tally's Bar ♀
Galbally. ☎ 758231. 1230-
1430 Mon-Sun. 1900-2200
Thur-Sun. Pub grub. A la carte.
E£.

Top Bar ♀
73 Castlecaulfield Rd.
☎ 761349. 1800-2200 Wed-
Sat, (from 1900 Sun), 1230-
1430 Sun. Bistro, set meals,
à la carte.

Tree Tops
15 Northland Place.
☎ 723508. 0900-1830 Mon-
Sat (2230 Fri). Grills. £.

Tyrone Crystal Tea Shop
KIllybrackey, Coalisland Rd.
☎ 725335. 0900-1700 Mon-
Sat. Snacks, lasagne. In factory
visitor centre.

Upper Krust ⊗
16 Market Square. ☎ 722812.
0900-1700 Mon-Sat. Pies,
soups, stews, scones.

★ **VISCOUNTS GREAT
    FOOD HALL** ♀
10 Northland Row. ☎ 753800.
1100-2130 Mon-Sat, from
1200 Sun. Brunch, carvery
lunch, à la carte. Chef's
entrecôte, chicken boursin,
rack of lamb, stuffed peppers,
exotic kebabs. In converted
church hall. £.

Weavers ♀
Market Square. ☎ 723144.
1200-2130 Mon-Thur, 1500-
2230 Fri & Sat, 1700-2100
Sun. Grill bar menu. A la carte
in restaurant. Steak, trout and
salad. E££.

FINTONA
(STD 01662)

Charlie's Grill
53 Main St. ☎ 841266. 1130-
1500 Mon-Sat, 1730-2400.
Grills.

Eccles Arms ♀
128 Main St. ☎ 841220. 1230-
1530 daily. Pub grub.

Kitty's Kitchen
☎ 841746. 0900-1800 Mon-
Fri, until 1930 Sat. Home
baking, lunches, lasagne.

FIVEMILETOWN
(STD 013655)

Chestnut Bar 🍷
133 Main St. ☎ 21398. 1200-2300 Mon-Sat. Pub grub.

Fourways Hotel 🍷
41 Main St. ☎ 21260. Last orders 2300. Grills. E£.

Howards 🍷
100 Main St. ☎ 21830. 1200-1900 Wed-Sat. Sunday lunch 1230-1430. A la carte from 1930 Wed-Sun. £.

Valley Hotel 🍷
60 Main St. ☎ 21505. Last orders 2200, Sun 2130. Avocado with prawns, pork & apple sauce. E££.

GORTIN
(STD 016626)

Badoney Tavern 🍷
16 Main St. ☎ 48157. 1800-2100 Mon-Sat. Pub grub.

Sperrin Heritage Centre
Cranagh. ☎ 48142. 1100-1800 Mon-Fri, from 1130 Sat, 1400-1900 Sun. Sandwiches, scones, pastries. 9 miles east of Plumbridge, on B47.

MOY
(STD 018687)

Argory Tea Rooms
The Argory. ☎ 84753. 1400-1800 Sat-Sun April-June & Sept. 1400-1800 Fri-Mon June. 1400-1800 Mon-Sun July-Aug. Garden tea rooms open by arrangement (National Trust).

Auction Rooms 🍷
24 The Square. ☎ 784891. 1230-1530 Mon-Sat. Pub grub.

Sly Fox 🍷
3 Killyman St. ☎ 784296. 1200-1600 Mon-Sat. Pub grub.

Stables 🍷
The Square. ☎ 84629. 1200-1500 & 1800-2200 Mon-Sun. Set lunch. A la carte. E£.

Welcome Inn 🍷
Dungannon St. ☎ 84223. 1800-2200 Mon-Sat. Pub grub.

MOYGASHEL
(STD 01868)

Normandy
40 Main St. ☎ 722397. 0800-2200 Mon-Fri, 1200-1900 Sat. Fish & chips.

NEWTOWNSTEWART
(STD 016626)

Aunt Jane's
Grange Court Complex,
21 Moyle Rd. ☎ 62224. 0900-
1700 Mon-Sun. Breakfast.
bacon rolls, currys,
sandwiches, scones, salads.
Vegetarian.

Castle Bar ♀
1 Castle Brae. ☎ 61039. 1300-
1400 Mon-Sat. Pub grub.

Coffee Pot
24a Main St. ☎ 61565. 0900-
1800 Mon-Sat. Soup, stew,
scones.

Corner Bar ♀
2 Carnkenny Rd, Ardstraw.
☎ 61257. 1800-2130 Sat,
1830-2100 Sun.

Country Chef
78 Strabane Rd. ☎ 61561.
0800-2000 Mon-Sat, from
0900 Sun. Grills, Ulster fry.

County Inn ♀
43 Main St. ☎ 62105. 1130-
2000 Mon-Sun. Steaks, fish.

Harry Avery Lounge ♀
19 Dublin St. ☎ 61431. 1800-
2200 Thur-Sun, from 11.30
Fri-Sat. Steak, chicken, mixed
grills.

Hunting Lodge Hotel ⌷
Letterbin, Baronscourt. ☎
61679. Last orders 2130. Fish,
poultry, steak, lamb, salads.
E££.

Milltown Café
Newtownstewart Rd, Milltown.
☎ 61609. 0900-2400 Mon-Sat,
from 1100 Sun. Soup, grills,
salads.

Olde Mill ⌷
7 Millbrook Rd, Milltown.
☎ 62048. 1030-2130 Mon-
Sun. Steaks, chicken chasseur,
vegetarian. E££.

OMAGH
(STD 01662)

An Creagán Visitor Centre
Creggan. ☎ 61112. 1130-1730
Mon-Sun, 1800-2200 Fri-Sat,
until 2130 Sun. Snacks, bistro
evening menu. E££.

Arches Bistro
23 Bankmore Rd. ☎ 255988
1000-1700 Mon-Wed, later
Thur-Sat. Morning coffee,
lunches. In garden shop.

Bridge Restaurant
32 Bridge St. 0830-1800 Mon-
Sat, until 1400 Wed. Salads,
soup, sandwiches.

Bridge Tavern ⌷
Eskra. ☎ 841521. 1230-1430
Mon-Sun. Pub grub.

Caesar's ⌷
26 Bridge St. ☎ 251133. 1200-
1400 Mon-Sat, 1700-2400
Mon-Sun. Pizza, lasagne,
salads.

Campsie Bake Shop
80 Market St. ☎ 244038.
0830-1730 Mon-Sat. Lasagne,
quiche, Ulster fry.

Carlton Coffee Lounge
31 High St. ☎ 247046. 0900-
1730 Mon-Sat. Home-baked
scones. Lasagne, quiche,
Ulster fry.

Classic Choice
7 Prospect Court. ☎ 252405.
0900-1730 Mon-Sat. Sandwich
bar in shopping arcade.

The Clock ⌷
Old Market Place. ☎ 247355.
1200-1430 Mon-Sat. Pub
grub. River view.

Coach Inn ⌷
1 Railway Terrace. ☎ 243330.
1200-1400 Mon-Sun & 1500-
2200 Mon-Sat, (from 1900
Sun).

Dragon Castle ⌷
2 High St. ☎ 245208. 1200-
1400 & 1700-2400 Mon-Thur,
1600-2400 Sun. Chinese &
European. £.

Eddie's Crossroads Bar ⌷
Greencastle. ☎ (016626)
48266. 1230-1430 & 1800-
2030 Mon-Sat. Pub grub.

El Paso 🍷
62 Market St. ☎ 243125.
1230-1430 Mon-Sat. Pub grub.

Expressway Restaurant
1 Mountjoy Rd. ☎ 243637.
0830-1800 Mon-Sat.
Breakfast, carvery lunch,
salads, scones, sandwiches.

Giovanni's
9 John St. ☎ 252025. 1200-
1400 Mon-Thur, 1700-0300
Fri-Sat. (2400 Sun). Italian.

Grant's of Omagh 🍷
29 George's St. ☎ 250900.
1200-2200 Mon-Sat, 1300-
1500 & 1700-2200 Sun.
A la carte menu, snacks in
wine bar.

★ GREENMOUNT LODGE
58 Greenmount Rd,
Gortaclare. ☎ 841325. 1900-
2130 Fri & Sat. Dinner.
Booking essential. £.

Halfway House 🍷
Tattyreagh. ☎ 243720. 1130-
2300 Mon-Sat, 1900-2200
Sun. Pub grub.

Hawthorn House
72 Old Mountfield Rd.
☎ 252005. 1230-1500 Fri
&Sun, 1900-2200 Wed-Sun.
Pan-fried crab cakes, chicken
liver parfait on crostini, pear &
strawberry shortcake.

Joe's Sandwich Bar
18 Bridge St. ☎ 244890. 0830-
1830. Mon-Sat. Sandwiches.

McElroy's 🍷
30 Castle St. ☎ 244441. 1200-
1430 Mon-Fri, until 1800 Sat.
Pub grub.

McGirr's of Gortnagarn 🍷
Mountjoy East. ☎ 242462.
1230-1430 & 1830-2130
Mon-Sat. Grills. A la carte
Fri-Sat.

**★ MELLON
COUNTRY INN** 🍷 ⊗
134 Beltany Rd. ☎ 661224.
1030-2130 Mon-Sat. Bar
snacks 1730-2130 Mon-Fri,
(2200 Sat). A la carte 1800-
2130 Mon-Sat. Sole bonne
femme, home-baked gammon,
pasta. £££.

**MELLON
COUNTRY
M
INN**

The No. 1 🛑 *on the North West Passage
for Good Food and Courteous Service!*

One mile from The Ulster-American Folk Park,
half way between Omagh and Newtownstewart.

**134 Beltany Road Omagh BT78 5RA
Tel: (016626) 61224**

Mill ⬭
212 Gorticashel Rd.
☎ 248451. 1200-1500 Mon-Sat. Pub grub.

Molly Sweeney's ⬭
28 Gortin Rd. ☎ 251038.
1200-1430 & 1800-2200
Mon-Sat. Sole, red snapper,
beef, home-made desserts.
M£. E££.

Nite Bite
55 Derry Rd. ☎ 252770. 0930-2330 Mon-Fri, 1100-0500 Sat,
1700-2400 Sun. Grills.

Old McDonald's
6 Bridge St. ☎ 247666. 0800-1800 Mon-Fri & until 1730
Sat. Breakfast. Salads,
sandwiches.

Omagh Leisure Centre ⊘
Old Mountfield Rd. ☎ 246711.
1000-1430 & 1530-2100
Mon-Fri, 1000-1700 Sat,
1400-1700 Sun. Snacks.

Omanni ⬥
2 Derry Rd. ☎ 247500. 1700-2400 Tues-Thur, 1600-0100
Fri-Sat, until 2330 Sun. Asian
& European.

Pink Elephant
19 High St. ☎ 249805. 0900-1800 Mon-Sat, 1200-1500
Sun. Snacks.

Pizzarama
28 Campsie Rd. ☎ 244799.
1200-1400 & 1700-2400
Mon-Sun (ex Sun a.m). Pizzas,
salads, baked potatoes.

Sally O'Brien's ⬭
35 John St. ☎ 242521. 1200-1430 & 1900-2100 Thur-Sat.
Grills.

Shoppers' Rest
38 High St. ☎ 243545. 0800-1730 Mon-Sat. Breakfasts,
toasties, salads.

Silverbirch Hotel ⬭
5 Gortin Rd. ☎ 242520. Last
orders 2100. Bar snacks.
Lemon sole in parsley butter,
steaks, vegetarian. E££.

Sperrin Restaurant ⬭
86 Beltany Rd. ☎ 243775.
0900-2100 Mon-Sat, 1230-2100
Sun. Home-made soups, steaks,
stuffed turkey.

The Stockman ⬭
New Aquarium Complex,
Drumquin Rd. ☎ 243311. 0830-1830 Mon-Tues, until 1700 Wed
& Fri. Cabbage & champ, bread
& butter pudding.

Taste of India ⬥
8 Campsie Rd. ☎ 248342.
1630-0030 Mon-Sun. Indian.

Timepiece
Dunnes Stores, 2 Irishtown Rd.
☎ 252705. 0900-1800 Mon,
Tues & Sat, until 2100 Wed-Fri,
1400-1730 Sun. Breakfast.
Lunches, cakes. Restaurant in
store.

Ulster History Park ⊘
Cullion, Lislap. ☎ 48188. 1030-1815 Mon-Sat, & 1130-1845
Sun in summer. Salads, snacks.
B48 north of Omagh.

Ulster-American Folk Park
Mellon Rd, Castletown.
☎ 243292. 1030-1830 Easter-
September & 1030-1700 Oct-
Easter. Sandwiches, grills.

Village Inn ⚰
Killyclogher. ☎ 243865. 1200-
1500 Mon-Sat. Pub grub.

PLUMBRIDGE
(STD 016626)

Pinkertons Café
25 Main St. ☎ 48327. 1100-
2200 Mon-Sat, 1400-2100
Sun. Steak, chicken, curries.

SION MILLS
(STD 016626)

Marjorie's Diner
9 Alexander Place. ☎ 59886.
0900-1730 Mon-Thur, until
1830 Fri-Sat. Breakfast. Lunch,
desserts, scones.

Marshall's ⚰
125 Melmount Rd. ☎ 58638.
1200-1700 Mon-Thur, until
2130 Fri-Sun. Breakfast, lunch,
evening meal. Pub grub.

STEWARTSTOWN
(STD 01868)

Drumcairn Inn ⚰
32 The Square. ☎ 738216.
1200-1430 Mon-Sat, 1800-
2230 Fri-Sat. Pub grub, grills.

Hoff's ⚰
36 The Square. ☎ 738402.
2000-2400 Thur-Sun.
A la carte £.

STRABANE
(STD 01504)

Abercorn Sandwiches
39 Abercorn Square.
☎ 382288. 0900-1730 Mon-
Sat. Sandwiches, lasagne,
toasties pies.

Blue Parrot ⚰
19 Castle St. ☎ 382687. 1200-
1500 Mon-Sat. Pub grub.
Evenings if booked.

Bonne Tasse
49a Abercorn Square.
☎ 383422. 0900-1700 Mon-
Sat. Snacks, sandwiches,
salads.

Country Kitchen
78 Lower Main St. ☎ 382621.
0900-1730 Mon-Sat. Breakfast,
afternoon tea.

Country Kitchen
78 Lower Main St. ☎ 382621.
0900-1730 Mon-Sat. Breakfast.
Fish, chicken and ham pie,
scones, pastries.

Dempsey's
74 Lower Main St. ☎ 886446.
0900-1730 Mon-Wed, until
1900 Thur-Sat, 1100-2000
Sun. Beef hoggie, spicy
chicken on pitta bread,
seafood, sandwiches.

Dicey Riley's ☒
30 Market St. ☎ 383580.
1200-1500 Mon-Sat. Set
meals. Pub grub. A la carte.
E£.

Fir Trees Hotel ☒
Melmount Rd. ☎ 382382.
1200-1730 Mon-Sat, until
2130 Sun. Shark with prawns
& capers, duck in sweet &
sour sauce. E££.

Flann O'Brien ☒
3 Derry Rd. ☎ 884427. 1230-
1430 Mon-Sat. Set lunch,
grills.

Floyd's ☒
421 Victoria Rd. Ballymagorry.
☎ 382905. 1230-1430 &
1730-2145 Mon-Fri, until
2200 Sat, 2100 Sun. A la carte,
carvery. E£.

Home Cuisine
55 Main St. ☎ 382002. 0830-
1700 Mon-Sat. Snacks, grills.

Kelly's Bar ☒
Abercorn Square. ☎ 883551.
1130-2300 Mon-Sat. Pub grub.

King Restaurant ☒
17 Abercorn Square.
☎ 383361. 1100-2400 Mon-
Sat, from 1230 Sun. Chinese &
European.

Kurly Wurly's ☒
9 Bowling Green. ☎ 383353.
1100-2300 Mon-Sat, 1200-
1500 & 1700-2200 Sun. Soup,
sandwiches, pies.

Mill House ☒
37 Patrick St. ☎ 382690. 1230-
1600, 1830-2220 Mon-Sun.
Lemon sole, red snapper, rack
of lamb, mussels. Bistro menu.

Piccolo
Abercorn Square. ☎ 382784.
0900-1800 Mon-Sat. Grills,
sandwiches.

Railway Restaurant
68 Railway St. ☎ 383443.
0800-1700 Mon-Sat (until 1500
Thur).

Teashop
29 Abercorn Square. 0800-
1730 Mon-Sat. Grills.

Traveller's Rest
19 Lifford Rd, ☎ 383139. 0800-
2400 Mon-Sat, from 0900 Sun.
Breakfast. Salads, chicken &
ham pie. £.

Welcome Inn ☒
38 Patrick St. ☎ 382528. 1130-
2300 Mon-Sat, 1230-1430 &
1900-2200 Sun. Pub grub.

Wembley Café
10 Castle Place. ☎ 382307.
0900-1730 Mon-Sat. Breakfast,
grills, salads, fast food.

TRILLICK
(STD 01365)

Bridge Inn ☒ ⊙
2 Kilskeery Rd. ☎ 61201. 1230-
1430 & 1800-2200. Pub grub.

Northern Ireland
Tourist Board

We're here to help!

The tourist information centre, in the heart of Belfast, offers an extensive range of services, including a bureau de change and many locally produced gifts and souvenirs.

An advanced computerised information and reservations system makes accommodation bookings easier and faster.

The centre has a wealth of leaflets and brochures packed with holiday ideas, and the friendly professional staff will be delighted to help you with suggestions and bookings.

Tourist Information Centre
59 North Street, Belfast BT1 1NB
☎ (01232) 246609
Minicom (01232) 233228

Index to towns and villages

Index to towns and villages

Index to towns and villages

Please note

This book is intended only as a convenient reference guide to eating out in Northern Ireland. Care has been taken to ensure entries are up to date. However, information has been gathered from a wide range of sources and the Northern Ireland Tourist Board does not accept responsibility for errors and omissions. In addition, changes will inevitably occur after the book goes to press, so it is advisable to make your own enquiries.

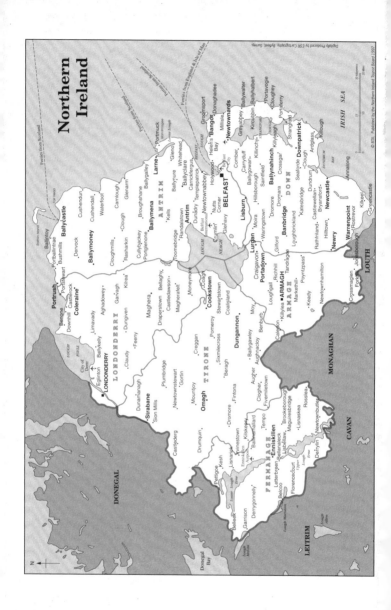

Northern Ireland